access to history

Britain 1900–57

MICHAEL LYNCH

SECOND EDITION

HODDER
EDUCATION
AN HACHETTE UK COMPANY

For Peerson Lynch, born 2002

The Publishers would like to thank Nicholas Fellows and David Ferriby for their contribution to the Study Guide.

The Publishers would like to thank the following for permission to reproduce copyright material:

Photo credits: p16 LSE Library's collections, COLL MISC 0519/81; **p17** Printed and published by the Daily News, Ltd/National Archives/Solo Syndication; **p18** Political Cartoon Society; **p22** Library of Congress, LC-DIG-ggbain-03487; **p41** Topham Picturepoint; **p60** Library of Congress, LC-DIG-ggbain-23315; **p76** TopFoto.co.uk; **p93** Library of Congress, LC-USZ62-133019; **p101** Punch Cartoon Library; **p111** Roger-Viollet/TopFoto; **p156** Library of Congress, LC-USZ62-111781; **p159** British Cartoon Archive, University of Kent/ Solo Syndication/Associated Newspapers; **p161** Mirrorpix; **p167***tl*, *tr*, *bl* Lordprice Collection/Alamy, ***br*** John Robertson/Alamy; **p179** Cartoon by George Whitelaw published in the Daily Herald on the 2nd December 1942, British Cartoon Archive, University of Kent/Mirrorpix; **p193** Fotograaf Onbekend/Anefo/Nationaal Archief/ShareAlike 3.0 Unported (CC BY-SA 3.0) (detail of Attlee); **p199** Punch Cartoon Library.

The Publishers would like to thank the following for permission to reproduce material in this book: 'The General' on page 51, copyright Siegfried Sassoon by kind permission of the Estate of George Sassoon.

Acknowledgements: are listed on page 276.

Although every effort has been made to ensure that website addresses are correct at time of going to press, Hodder Education cannot be held responsible for the content of any website mentioned in this book. It is sometimes possible to find a relocated web page by typing in the address of the home page for a website in the URL window of your browser.

Hachette UK's policy is to use papers that are natural, renewable and recyclable products and made from wood grown in sustainable forests. The logging and manufacturing processes are expected to conform to the environmental regulations of the country of origin.

Orders: please contact Bookpoint Ltd, 130 Milton Park, Abingdon, Oxon OX14 4SB.
Telephone: +44 (0)1235 827720. Fax: +44 (0)1235 400454. Lines are open 9.00a.m.–5.00p.m., Monday to Saturday, with a 24-hour message answering service. Visit our website at www.hoddereducation.co.uk

First published in 2008 by
Hodder Education
An Hachette UK Company
Carmelite House, 50 Victoria Embankment
London EC4Y 0DZ

Impression number   10 9 8 7 6 5 4 3 2
Year   2019 2018 2017 2016

Cover photo © Mary Evans Picture Library
Produced, illustrated and typeset in Palatino LT Std by Gray Publishing, Tunbridge Wells
Printed and bound by CPI Group (UK) Ltd, Croydon CR0 4YY

A catalogue record for this title is available from the British Library

ISBN 978 1471838699

Contents

Dedication

Keith Randell (1943–2002)

The *Access to History* series was conceived and developed by Keith, who created a series to 'cater for students as they are, not as we might wish them to be'. He leaves a living legacy of a series that for over 20 years has provided a trusted, stimulating and well-loved accompaniment to post-16 study. Our aim with these new editions is to continue to offer students the best possible support for their studies.

CHAPTER 1

Britain 1900–11

In 1900 there were two major parties competing for power in Britain: the Conservatives and the Liberals. There were also two smaller parties – Labour and the Irish Nationalists – which were to have an important influence on affairs. This chapter examines the progress and fortunes of these parties as they attempted to respond to the major problems facing Britain at the beginning of the twentieth century. The analysis is developed under the following headings:

★ Britain in 1900

★ The Conservative Party

★ The Liberal Party

★ The Labour Party

Key dates

1899–1902	The Anglo-Boer War	1903	Lib–Lab pact formed
1900	Khaki election victory for Salisbury's Conservatives	1905	Liberals in office under Campbell-Bannerman
	Labour Representation Committee formed	1906	Liberal landslide electoral victory
1902–5	Balfour led the Conservative government	1908–11	Asquith led the Liberal Reform programme

 ## Britain in 1900

▶ *What were the major problems and questions facing Britain in 1900?*

Problems

Britain in the late **Victorian** and **Edwardian** years faced great economic, social and **constitutional** difficulties. These may be listed and examined as:

- the problem of poverty
- Britain's economy
- problems in industrial relations
- Britain's role as an empire
- the franchise question
- the position of the House of Lords
- the Ulster question.

 KEY TERMS

Victorian Relating to the years of Queen Victoria's reign (1837–1901).

Edwardian Refers to the reign of Edward VII (1901–10), but is often extended to include the early years of George V's reign (1910–14).

Constitutional Issues relating to the conventions and methods by which Britain was governed.

Governments of the late Victorian and Edwardian eras

- 1895–1902: Conservatives under Lord Salisbury.
- 1902–5: Conservatives under Arthur Balfour.
- 1905–8: Liberals under Henry Campbell-Bannerman.
- 1908–14: Liberals under Herbert Asquith.

The problem of poverty

By the early twentieth century, Britain had experienced a remarkable increase in the size and the concentration of its population (see Table 1.1). This was largely a consequence of **industrialisation** and was strikingly evident in the growth of towns and the formation of the great **conurbations**.

In the 40 years after 1871, the population in those areas very nearly doubled, which greatly increased the demand for such vital resources as water supply and sanitation. In most areas, however, the means of providing these were either rudimentary or non-existent. The result was the intensifying of such social ills as:

- overcrowding
- malnutrition
- ill-health.

It is true that central and local government in the Victorian age had begun to take measures to alleviate the worst of the conditions, but their efforts fell far short of the needs. Such welfare and relief schemes as there were in the towns and cities were wholly insufficient. It was also the case that, although wage rates had risen, they were not yet at a level where the majority of workers had sufficient surplus cash to improve their living conditions. Poverty was widespread.

The only major scheme for dealing with poverty was the **Poor Law**, introduced in an earlier age when it was believed that poverty could be contained by dealing with it on a local basis, parish by parish. However, the enormous increase in population made this system of parish relief inadequate to deal with the problem.

The grim conditions that shaped the lives of the mass of the people who lived in the towns and cities were graphically revealed in a series of carefully researched

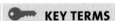

KEY TERMS

Industrialisation
The spread of manufacturing, accompanied by the movement of workers from the land into the towns and cities.

Conurbations
Concentrated urban areas of high population density.

Poor Law As amended in 1834, a scheme for providing relief by taking the destitute into workhouses where the conditions were made deliberately harsh so as to deter all but the most needy from entering them.

Table 1.1 The growth of population in the conurbations

Year	Greater London	South-east Lancashire	West Midlands	West Yorkshire	Merseyside
1871	3,890,000	1,386,000	969,000	1,064,000	690,000
1901	6,856,000	2,117,000	1,483,000	1,524,000	1,030,000
1911	7,256,000	2,328,000	1,634,000	1,590,000	1,157,000

public reports. Outstanding pioneering studies were produced by Charles Booth and Seebohm Rowntree; their meticulously detailed analysis of social conditions in London and Yorkshire, respectively, gave evidence of appalling squalor and deprivation.

SOURCE A

From Seebohm Rowntree, *Poverty: A Study of Town Life*, Macmillan, 1902, p. 133.

The wages paid for unskilled work in York are insufficient to provide food, shelter, and clothing to maintain a family of moderate size in a state of merely physical efficiency. And let us clearly understand what 'merely physical efficiency' means. A family living on the scale allowed for in this estimate must never go into the country unless they walk … They must write no letters to absent children for they cannot afford the postage … They cannot save, nor can they join sick club or Trade union, because they cannot pay the necessary subscriptions. The children must have no pocket money … The father must smoke no tobacco, and must drink no beer. The mother must never buy any pretty clothes for herself or her children … If any of these conditions are broken, the extra expenditure involved can only be met by limiting the diet; or in other words, by sacrificing physical efficiency. In this land of abounding wealth, during a time of perhaps unexampled prosperity, probably more than one-fourth of the population are living in poverty.

> What picture of poverty in Britain emerges from Source A?

National efficiency

The sheer extent of the poverty in Britain revealed by such stark details convinced all but a few that something had to be done. All the parties agreed that government and Parliament had a duty to tackle the deprivation that afflicted so many in the nation. This was not merely for humanitarian reasons. In 1902, it was officially reported by the army high command that nearly two-thirds of those who had volunteered to join the services at the time of the Anglo-Boer War of 1899–1902 (see page 10) had failed to pass their basic medical test.

Such revelations strengthened a widespread conviction current in the Edwardian period that Britain had to re-create 'national efficiency'. This was a term often used at the time to denote the level of well-being and health that it was felt the British people needed to achieve if their nation was to sustain its strength industrially and militarily. The notion of national efficiency was closely linked to **eugenics**, a science that attracted many adherents, particularly among **left-wing intellectuals**. A prominent voice among these was **George Bernard Shaw**, who spoke in favour of 'selective breeding', by which he meant that only couples of a high level of physical and mental health should have children.

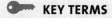

KEY TERMS

Eugenics The science of improving the quality of the human stock by breeding out inherited weaknesses and deficiencies.

Left-wing intellectuals Writers and thinkers who believed in radical social and economic change.

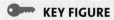

KEY FIGURE

George Bernard Shaw (1856–1950)

Celebrated playwright and social commentator.

Charles Masterman, an influential Liberal writer, represented the basic concern of the national efficiency campaigners in Britain when he described the unhealthy conditions in which the mass of the people who had migrated from the countryside to the industrial towns now lived. He wrote of their cramped living conditions and their long hours of work, and warned that it was on this unhealthy population that 'the future progress of the Anglo-Saxon race' would have to depend.

In 1904, a specially appointed Interdepartmental Committee on Physical Deterioration delivered a formal report to Parliament. Among its recommendations were:

- the appointment of full-time medical officers of health and health visitors in urban areas
- local authorities to lay down standards of purity for all food and drinks
- regular medical examination of all school children
- urban overcrowding to be studied and addressed
- laws against smoke pollution to be introduced
- basic hygiene to be taught in schools
- local authorities to provide meals for school children.

Not all these proposals were implemented immediately, but they helped to define and clarify the problems. One particularly interesting response to the need for national efficiency was the creation of a youth movement: the Boy Scouts. Its founder, Lord **Baden Powell**, who expressed his ideas in *Scouting for Boys* (1908), left no doubt as to his purpose: 'Remember, whether rich or poor, from castle or from slum, you are all Britons first, and you've got to keep Britain up against outside enemies, you have to stand shoulder to shoulder to do it.' By 1914, the movement he had started had spread nationwide, and by 1920 worldwide.

While there was general agreement in Britain that the nation had to address its severe social and economic problems, there were deep disputes between the parties and also between different factions within individual parties as to how these should be tackled. The disagreements over this were to be a prominent feature of pre-1914 Britain.

Britain's economy

Between 1870 and 1914 Britain's trade and industry appeared to be shrinking, relative to other countries, such as Germany and the USA (see the graph on page 5). The decline was most evident in the **staple industries**. The British industrial growth rate of 2.3 per cent was only half that of the USA. By the turn of the century, Germany and the USA had overtaken Britain in the volume of their iron and steel production. By 1910, British industrial exports made up only ten per cent of the world trade compared with figures of 20 per cent for German goods and 40 per cent for American.

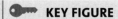

KEY FIGURE

Robert Baden Powell (1857–1941)

A military hero of the Boer War, he became a popular figure in Britain.

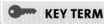

KEY TERM

Staple industries Those enterprises on which Britain's industrial strength had traditionally been based, for example, textiles, coal mining, iron and steel production, and shipbuilding.

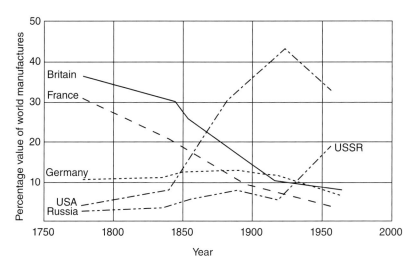

Figure 1.1 Graph showing world trade 1800–1955.

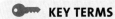
Modern **revisionist historians** have argued that the decline was exaggerated by contemporaries who were unnecessarily frightened by the growth of Germany and the USA. They suggest that in fact British industry was still growing healthily and was more **cost effective** than American and German industry, even though total output of those two countries was higher. Revisionists further argue that it was the First World War which caused Britain's twentieth-century industrial decline by shattering the international economy in which Britain had held such a predominant place (see page 78). While noting the revisionists' argument, it has to be emphasised that late Victorian and Edwardian industrialists truly believed that the trade figures showed that they were losing out to their American and German rivals in the open market.

New industries

The decline in the staple industries was somewhat offset by the growth in the 'new industries'. This was the term for those growing concerns and businesses which began to develop in such areas as the following:

- transport and communication
- distributive trades
- hotels and catering
- financial services
- health provision
- education
- public administration.

Already by 1910, as Table 1.2 (see page 6) indicates, these activities accounted for 44 per cent of the workforce, but, as yet, the profitability of the new industries did not make up for the losses in the staple industries. However, as the century wore on **invisible earnings** were to become increasingly important to the British economy. It was the profits from the sale of Britain's financial and insurance services and the tax revenue that came from them that helped to keep Britain solvent at critical times.

Table 1.2 Distribution of the workforce in the UK (according to the 1911 census)

Sector	Percentage
Mining	6.3%
Agriculture	11.8%
Manufacturing	32.1%
Chemicals	0.9%
Metal manufacture	4.1%
Engineering	6.7%
Textiles and clothing	12.4%
Food, drink and tobacco	2.8%
Other manufacturing	5.3%
Construction	5.1%
Gas, electricity and water	0.6%
Services	44.1%
Transport and communications	7.9%
Distribution	12.2%
Financial services	1.1%
Hotel and Catering	3.0%
Education	1.5%
Health	0.7%
Public administration	4.1%
Miscellaneous	13.6%

KEY TERMS

'Old' unions Established organisations representing skilled workers.

'New' unions Representing large groups of workers, such as dockers, transport workers and miners.

Problems in industrial relations

For much of the nineteenth century, the trade union movement had been dominated by the **'old' unions**. But the last quarter of the nineteenth century witnessed a rapid growth in the number of mass-membership trade unions, composed largely of unskilled or semi-skilled workers. These **'new' unions** were eager to use their collective strength in a campaign for better wages and conditions. By 1890, they had already won some major victories; the gas workers had successfully struck for an eight-hour day, and the 'dockers' tanner' (sixpence a day basic pay rate) had been reluctantly granted by the port authorities.

The employers had attempted to counter what they saw as a major threat to their interests by forming federations, aimed specifically at resisting the strength of organised labour. The scene was set for major conflict on the industrial front. So strong was the threat of industrial disruption that it raised the issue of whether it was the role of government or Parliament to intervene in worker–employer relations. This was to prove a critical question in the pre-1914 years.

Agriculture

As can be seen from Table 1.2, only eleven per cent of the workforce in 1911 were agricultural workers. This compared with 22 per cent in 1841 and seventeen per cent in 1861. This decline is largely attributable to a serious agricultural recession that set in in the 1870s. In that decade foreign cheap corn came into Britain in large quantities from newly developed farm land in North America, Argentina and Australia. British farmers, who could not produce crops as cheaply as they could be imported, were also hit by a series of harvest failures.

The result was that only the largest farmers made reasonable profits. Many smaller farmers left the land or had a much reduced standard of living. In many cases rural poverty was worse than urban poverty (see page 2).

Despite the establishment of a Board of Agriculture in 1889, the situation improved little over the next four decades. It was not until the coming of the war in 1914, which, by greatly reducing imports, increased demand for home-grown food, that British farming began to recover.

Britain's role as an empire

In the last 30 years of the nineteenth century Britain had rapidly increased the size of its existing empire. This was largely the result of its participation in the European **scramble for Africa**, which had begun in the 1870s. The Conservatives had been particularly associated with the development of this new phase of **imperialism**. Although there were also some Liberals, known as liberal-imperialists, who supported overseas expansion, the Liberal Party itself strongly opposed it.

By the end of the century, there was considerable dispute between and within the parties as to whether Britain should continue to pursue expansionist policies or whether the view, espoused earlier by such great Liberal figures as **W.E. Gladstone**, that imperialism was both immoral and a threat to international peace, should prevail. The two opposed viewpoints were to be bitterly and violently expressed at the time of the Anglo-Boer War, fought between 1899 and 1902 (see page 10).

The franchise question

At the beginning of the twentieth century, Britain was not yet a democracy. Nevertheless, significant steps had been taken since 1832 to extend the **franchise**. By 1900, some 60 per cent of adult males had the vote. The question now arose as to whether the nation should become wholly democratic. This would involve, not only the granting of full adult male **suffrage**, but also, far more controversially, the enfranchising of women. All the parties were worried over the political implications of extending the vote to the female population. For which party would women actually vote? It was a leap into the unknown. The battle over this issue became a dramatic feature of pre-1914 politics (see page 40).

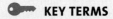

KEY TERMS

Scramble for Africa Between the 1870s and 1914, the major European colonial powers, France, Germany, Belgium, Portugal and Britain, separately took over large areas of the African continent.

Imperialism The acquiring of colonies principally for the purposes of prestige and economic exploitation.

Franchise The right to vote in parliamentary elections.

Suffrage Essentially the same meaning as franchise, the right to vote.

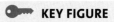

KEY FIGURE

W.E. Gladstone (1809–98)

British statesman who dominated the Liberal Party from the 1860s until his death in 1898.

Two-chamber structure
The elected House of Commons and the unelected House of Lords, made up of hereditary peers; to become law, a Bill has to be passed by both Houses.

Home rule A measure granting a colony or dependent region control over its own affairs.

Bill A legislative proposal that has to go through separate stages in the Commons, before going to the Lords for a similar process. When this is completed the Bill receives royal assent and becomes a binding Act.

The position of the House of Lords

The issue of democracy lay at the heart of another of the major controversies of the time. The **two-chamber structure** of the British Parliament meant that the House of Lords (the Upper House) was constitutionally able to block the legislation sent up to it by the House of Commons (the Lower House). In practice, it was only measures presented by Liberal governments that the Lords chose to reject. This was because Conservative peers were in an overwhelming majority in the Upper House, which enabled the Conservative Party to reject Liberal measures of which it disapproved. The most striking example of this had occurred in 1894 when Gladstone's Irish **Home Rule Bill**, having passed through the Commons, was then thrown out by the Lords. As Britain moved towards democracy, the question was how much longer the anomaly of an unelected assembly having an absolute veto over the elected chamber would be tolerated.

The Ulster question

In the nineteenth century there had been a strong movement for home rule among Irish nationalists, who wanted, as a first step to independence, the creation of a separate government in Dublin, responsible for Irish affairs. However, the demand for independence foundered on the position of Ulster whose largely Protestant population were not prepared to accept an Irish settlement that gave southern Catholic Ireland a controlling hand over them (see page 45). Gladstone, the Liberal leader, had introduced Home Rule Bills in 1886 and 1893 but both had failed to pass through Parliament. His attempts had split his party and had hardened the resolve of the Unionists to reject home rule on the grounds that it undermined the unity of the United Kingdom and betrayed Ulster.

The issues and problems which have been introduced in the preceding sections may be expressed as a series of demanding questions confronting the government, Parliament and the political parties in the period between the beginning of the century and the outbreak of the Great War in 1914:

- How could poverty be tackled?
- How far should the government be responsible for running the economy?
- What were the best means of Britain's earning its living?
- How much power should the State have over ordinary people's lives?
- Should wealth be redistributed by the government's taking it from the wealthy in taxes to give to the poor?
- How far should the government be involved in industrial disputes?
- What was Britain's relationship to Ulster?
- How far should the right to vote be extended?
- Was the House of Lords in need of radical reform?
- What was the position and status of Ulster?

It is interesting to note how modern these questions seem. They were the issues which were to continue to demand attention throughout the twentieth century and into the twenty-first.

Summary diagram: Britain in 1900

Problems for Britain in 1900
- Poverty
- A declining economy
- Crisis in industrial relations
- The disputed role of empire
- The franchise
- The anomalous position of the House of Lords

The Conservative Party

▶ *What was the character of the Conservative and Unionist Party at the start of the twentieth century?*

Nineteenth-century Britain had seen the rise of a powerful middle class, which had grown wealthy on the profits of commerce and industry. Much less wealthy but no less important politically were the industrial workers who had grown in number as industry expanded. The majority of the men in both these classes had gained the vote. They now had an electoral importance no party could afford to disregard.

Here it is important to stress that the term 'class' does not have a fixed meaning. As Arthur Marwick, one of Britain's most esteemed social historians, points out, classes do not belong in 'the same category as the facts of geography, demography and economics.' 'Classes', Marwick says, 'evolve and change as circumstances change.' This does not prevent our using the word in a descriptive sense; class can be helpfully applied to broad groups which experience common social and economic change. Most people in early twentieth-century Britain would have accepted that there were three major social groups or classes:

- upper classes, drawn from the traditional landed aristocracy
- middle classes who worked in trade or the professions
- people who worked for wages in industry or on the land.

These were not exact definitions, of course; there were grades within each class, particularly the middle class. It also became increasingly possible in the course of the twentieth century to move from one class to another.

The response of the Conservatives

The **Conservative and Unionist Party**, which had traditionally been the party of the **landed** classes, had skilfully modified itself in the nineteenth century in order to appeal to both middle-class and working-class voters. Its influential leader, **Benjamin Disraeli**, had accepted that if the party was to survive as a political force it had to adapt itself to the changes that industrialisation had brought. Disraeli's recognition of this was made clear in a series of important social reforms that his Conservative government introduced.

By 1900 the Conservatives had been in power under their leader **Lord Salisbury** for all but three of the previous fourteen years. It has been said that under him Conservatism became 'an organised rearguard action' to prevent the growing democracy of the times from becoming too disruptive. Yet this view needs to be balanced against the fact that Salisbury came to accept the wisdom of Disraeli's belief that it was possible to win over the enfranchised working classes to the Conservative side. That is why Salisbury put great stress on party organisation. It was under him that Conservatism, with its emphasis on recruitment of supporters in the constituencies, began to take its modern shape. His success in this was shown in Conservative victories in the general elections of 1886, 1895 and 1900.

The Anglo-Boer War 1899–1902

The dominant issue preoccupying Salisbury's government when the century opened was not a domestic but an imperial one: the Anglo-Boer War. The war arose from a dispute between the British and the Dutch **Boer** settlers as to who controlled southern Africa. In 1884 Britain had agreed to a division which gave it Cape Province and Natal and granted the Boers the Transvaal and the Orange Free State. However, although Britain formally recognised Boer rights of self-government in the Transvaal, it continued illogically to claim that it had authority over the region.

There is now little doubt that Britain deliberately provoked the war that broke out in 1899. For Joseph Chamberlain (see page 22), the colonial secretary, British supremacy in southern Africa was essential in order to maintain Britain's imperial strength. He held that unless Britain was a powerful empire it could not be a powerful nation. So he plotted with the aggressive British high commissioner in the Cape to make such unreasonable demands on the Boers that they would have no choice but to fight.

From the beginning there was a significant group in Britain who were deeply unhappy with the war. Referred to as 'pro-Boers', they questioned the morality of Britain's position as the aggressor who had started the war. Initially, however, the war was widely popular in Britain, and Salisbury sought to exploit this by calling an election in 1900. The Conservatives deliberately played on the

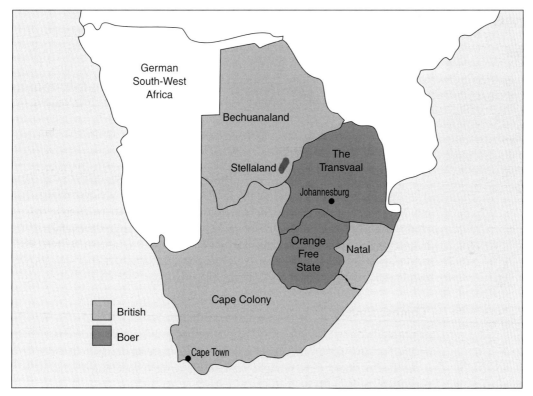

Figure 1.2 Southern Africa on the eve of the Anglo-Boer War, 1899–1902.

patriotism of the electorate in what became known as the **Khaki** election. Salisbury's government was returned with a very comfortable majority over the Liberals (see Table 1.3).

However, from that point on things went badly for the government. Although the war was eventually won, with the surrender of the Boers in 1902, the Conservatives' handling of it proved dismal. The pro-Boers drew constant attention to the failure of British forces to win the conflict quickly. Still more unsettling for the government were the reports of the extreme measures which the British forces employed to break Boer resistance. The most notorious of these was the internment of civilians in 'concentration' camps, where the cramped and unhygienic conditions frequently led to the spread of fatal diseases. This had not been the intention, but it was the deadly outcome.

 **KEY TERM**

Khaki British forces adopted this as the colour of their standard uniform during the Boer War.

Table 1.3 The 1900 general election result

Party	Votes	Seats	Percentage of vote
Conservatives	1,797,444	402	51.1
Liberals	1,568,141	184	44.6
Labour (Labour Representation Committee)	63,304	2	1.8
Irish Nationalists	124,586	82	2.5

Henry Campbell-Bannerman (1836–1908)

Led the Liberals 1899–1908, prime minister 1905–8 and was the first British premier to be officially entitled 'prime minister'.

Arthur Balfour (1848–1930)

MP 1874–1922, secretary for Ireland 1887–91, prime minister 1902–5, leader of the Conservative Party 1905–11, foreign secretary 1916–19.

The Liberal leader since 1899, **Henry Campbell-Bannerman**, accused Salisbury's government of employing 'the methods of barbarism', while David Lloyd George (see page 93), a dynamic young Liberal, declared: 'we have now taken to killing babies'. Britain's inhumane strategy against Boer civilians, added to the fact that it took the might of the British imperial army three long years to overcome an outnumbered and outgunned group of farmers, caused embarrassment at home and aroused ridicule abroad.

Conservative problems

When **Arthur Balfour** succeeded Salisbury as prime minister in 1902 he inherited the poor reputation that the Conservatives had gained over their embarrassing Boer-war record. But his troubles did not end there. Despite the credit his party had earned since the mid-1880s for their progressive reforms in which he had played a prominent part, Balfour's years in office from 1902 to 1905 were overshadowed by a set of problems that would lead to the defeat of his party in a crushing Liberal victory in the 1906 election.

'Chinese slavery'

Africa again came to haunt the Conservatives. Balfour's government was accused of having permitted large numbers of Chinese labourers, referred to as 'coolies' or slaves, to be brought from Asia to work in appalling conditions for pitiful wages in the gold and diamond mines of southern Africa. It was widely felt that the government's claim that this was a matter for British officials in Africa to deal with on the spot was an inadequate response. Opponents suggested Balfour's government was simply passing the buck and that its moral authority was compromised.

The Taff Vale decision 1901

The significant part industrial relations now played in British politics was evident in this landmark case. In June 1900, the employees of the Taff Vale Railway Company in South Wales went on strike with the full backing of their union, the Associated Society of Railway Servants (ASRS). The company tried to break the strike by bringing in non-union labour and by taking the ASRS to court for illegal **picketing**. The tactics worked and the strikers reluctantly returned to work with nothing gained. Boosted by its victory, the company again took the union to court, this time claiming damages for the financial losses caused by the strike.

The first court hearing went in favour of the company but, on appeal by the ASRS, a higher court reversed this decision in November 1900. The company was not prepared to give up. It presented its case to the House of Lords, the highest legal authority in the land. The Lords overruled the appeal court decision and found for the company. The Lords' ruling, delivered in July 1901, came at the end of many months of legal wrangling. The time span meant that

Picketing Strikers stationing themselves at the gates of the factory or workplace so as to deter other workers from entering.

the issue excited the widest interest; both the unions and the employers knew that it was a test case in industrial relations. Source B contains the key part of the Lords' decision:

SOURCE B

From the Taff Vale ruling delivered by the senior judge, Lord MacNaughten, in 1901.

Has the Legislature authorized the creation of numerous bodies of men capable of owning great wealth and of acting by agents with absolutely no responsibility for the wrongs they may do to other persons by the use of that wealth and the employment of those agents? In my opinion, Parliament has done nothing of the kind. I cannot find anything to warrant or suggest such a notion. It was intended by the strongest advocates of trade unionism that persons should be liable for concerted as well as for individual action; and for this purpose it seems to me that it cannot matter in the least whether the persons acting in concert be combined together in a trade union, or collected and united under any other form of association. I have no doubt whatever that a trade union, whether registered or unregistered, may be sued in a representative action if the persons selected as defendants be persons who, from their position, may be taken fairly to represent the body.

In Source B, on what grounds does Lord MacNaughten give his ruling against the ASRS?

The ruling was accompanied by the awarding of damages and costs against the ASRS amounting to £42,000 (equivalent to over £3 million in 2015). It was now clear that the unions' right to strike and to picket had been effectively destroyed by the Lords' decision. Only an Act of Parliament could alter this. But, when Balfour declared in 1902 that his government had no intention of formally reversing the Taff Vale decision against the trade unions, it reinforced the conviction among the workers that Conservatism was wholly unsympathetic to their interests.

Balfour's Education Act 1902

The measure, which bears Balfour's name, since he was largely responsible for its drafting, is now regarded as an important and progressive step. It:

- raised the school-leaving age to twelve
- granted subsidies to church schools from local **rates**
- abolished the locally elected school boards, and passed the authority over schools to the county or borough councils.

However, at the time, the credit Balfour might justifiably have expected was largely lost because of the furious row that broke out among religious rivals over the nature of the schooling to be provided. Ever since educational reforms had been attempted in earlier decades there had been a stand-off between the **Anglican Church** and the **Nonconformists**.

🔑 KEY TERMS

Rates Taxes levied on householders to pay for local government services.

Anglican Church The established English Protestant Church, the nation's official religion.

Nonconformists Members of the various Protestant Churches who refused to accept the doctrines and authority of the Anglican Church. Nonconformists had become an influential moral force in Victorian Britain.

Historically, most of the schools in England and Wales had been set up and run by the Anglican Church. When the nineteenth-century reformers sought to extend State education to all, they had necessarily to use the existing Anglican schools, otherwise schooling simply could not have been provided on the necessary scale. It followed that schools teaching the Anglican faith now received State funding. It was this that offended the Nonconformists, who complained bitterly of **heresy** being taught on the rates. For their part, Anglicans were unhappy at the thought that as State education was extended they would lose their traditional hold over it. These anxieties and resentments were intensified by Balfour's 1902 measure.

The Licensing Act 1904

It was angry Nonconformists who were also the most vociferous in attacking the government's Licensing Act introduced in 1904 to regulate the sale and consumption of liquor. The aim of the new controls was to protect children and to prevent the adulteration of alcoholic drinks. However, the Nonconformists were unimpressed by this. They chose instead to condemn the clauses in the Act which provided generous compensation to the brewers and the landlords who stood to lose their licences under the new liquor regulations. Why, the Nonconformists asked, should the Treasury use its funds to reward vice? Their objections were not simply killjoy puritanism. All the prominent movements dealing with social distress, such as the **Salvation Army**, testified that drink was a major factor in deepening the poverty from which so many families suffered.

The Irish Land Act 1902

Another Conservative measure which was well intended but which brought the government more scorn than praise was the 1902 Irish Land Act, often referred to as **Wyndham's Act** after George Wyndham, the Irish secretary 1900–5. The reform is now seen as a very enlightened step which went a long way towards finally solving the land problem in Ireland. It made £100 million available to tenants to buy out their English landlords and thus become owners of the land which they farmed, something for which the Irish peasantry had yearned for centuries.

However, Ireland's sense of grievance, recently intensified by the English Parliament's rejection of home rule, was too deep-rooted for one measure, no matter how enlightened, to end Anglo-Irish bitterness. The Act received only grudging thanks from the Irish Nationalists, who regarded it as a belated recognition of their long-withheld rights, while the Irish Unionists dismissed the measure as a craven submission to nationalist pressure. It is notable that although Balfour, as Irish secretary, had often taken a very progressive attitude towards Ireland, as in his support for land reform, he had combined this with tough measures to control disorder. For this, the Nationalists had given him the title 'bloody Balfour'.

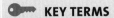

KEY TERMS

Heresy False religious doctrine; all faiths are heretical to each other.

Salvation Army Founded in 1878 by William Booth to put Christian values into practical form by directly helping the unfortunates of society, such as the destitute, the homeless and the victims of alcohol abuse.

Tariff reform

Damaging as the problems listed above were, it was the question of tariff reform that most seriously weakened the Conservatives. In a misguided attempt to outmanoeuvre the Liberals on economic matters, Balfour's government adopted **imperial preference** as its official economic programme in 1903. It was a policy most closely associated with Joseph Chamberlain, who wanted the establishment of an imperial economic federation, based on the principle of free trade between its member states and protection against non-members; a modern parallel is the European Union. These member states would receive preferential treatment; their goods would enter free of duty. British exports would be granted a corresponding preference in the colonies. The idea behind this was to develop the British Empire as a worldwide protectionist trading bloc.

Chamberlain's motives

There was a deeper intention behind Chamberlain's thinking. He was not seeking to maintain Britain's prosperity simply for its own sake. He believed that so great was the poverty and destitution blighting the nation that unless these were remedied the grievances of the dispossessed would lead to widespread social violence. National efficiency had to be restored. Money had to be found and distributed to raise people from the squalor in which so many lived. But how was the money to be raised? One simple answer was through taxation.

For Chamberlain, this answer was unacceptable; he feared that the taxing of one group in society for the benefit of another would encourage **revolutionary socialism** and class war. His proposed answer was imperial preference. If the empire was developed through protection into a worldwide trading association it would bring Britain the wealth it needed to cure its social ills. And all this would be achieved without recourse to unjust and disruptive taxation. This was why Chamberlain was such an ardent imperialist. His belief in the maintenance and extension of the empire came together with his belief in the need for social reform.

The battle over protection

Chamberlain's dream of empire was never to become a reality, but he argued his case with such persuasive force that he was largely responsible for making tariff reform a national issue. It is certainly the case that few issues in any age have excited so much interest in the British people as tariff reform did in the Edwardian era. Although to later generations it may seem a rather dry topic, in its time it was regarded as vitally important. Ordinary people saw it in terms of whether they could afford to feed themselves and their families. Manufacturers and industrialists saw it as a question of whether they could survive in a competitive trading world. Workers felt somehow that their jobs and wages depended on it. While few of the electorate had the knowledge of economic theory to enable them to follow the tariff-reform debate in detail, they were well

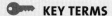

KEY TERMS

Imperial preference
An alternative term for tariff reform, a system for protecting home-produced food and manufactured goods by placing restrictive duties on imports unless they came from the British dominions and colonies.

Revolutionary socialism
The wish to overthrow the existing state and replace it with a worker-led government.

able to grasp that it was about the choice between dear food and cheap food, between having a job and being out of work.

Despite their adoption of it as party policy, few Conservatives were genuinely happy with the tariff-reform programme. They accepted it because it seemed to offer a means of raising revenue without resorting to taxation. A notable feature of Conservatism was that it was not, as its critics often tried to make out, against social reform in principle. Indeed, from Disraeli onwards, Conservative governments had introduced many significant reforms in this area (see page 20). The problem for most Conservatives was that they were unwilling to increase taxes to pay for reform, their argument being that heavy taxation imposed an unfair burden on those who were efficient and successful.

SOURCE C

? What message are the tariff reformers endeavouring to put across in the poster in Source C regarding the results of free trade?

A pro-tariff reform poster produced for the Liberal Unionist Council depicting John Bull (UK), Uncle Sam (USA) and Kaiser Bill (Germany).

SOURCE D

'Which Will You Have?' A free trade poster from 1905.

What basic message is the 'big loaf, little loaf' illustration in Source D attempting to put across?

The 1906 election

Conscious that matters were not going well for his government and party, Balfour resigned as prime minister in December 1905 and advised King Edward VII to dissolve Parliament, knowing that this would oblige the Liberals, led now by Henry Campbell-Bannerman, to form an interim government before an election was held. Balfour's intention was to play on the divisions among the Liberals over Irish home rule. He hoped that the Liberals would either be unable to form a government at all or be so divided when in government that this would hand the initiative back to the Conservatives, who would then doubtless win the ensuing election.

It is also likely that Balfour was engaging in what would now be called a damage-limitation exercise. By forcing an election earlier than was necessary, he hoped his party might suffer less badly at the polls than if he waited until 1907 when, under the **seven-year rule**, an election would have to be held.

Balfour's manoeuvring let him down. The Liberals were far from being as disunited as he had believed. Campbell-Bannerman accepted office enthusiastically and had no problems in forming a loyal cabinet. Having established his government, he then confidently called an immediate general election. In the impassioned campaign that followed, the dominant issue was free trade. The results showed that the electorate judged that the protectionists had lost the argument. Apart from Joseph Chamberlain himself, there were few advocates of imperial preference who were able to put over a convincing case or conduct a successful campaign. Sceptical observers said it was clear that the

 **KEY TERM**

Seven-year rule At this time, the law required that a general election be held at least once every seven years.

SOURCE E

Which of the problems has the cartoonist chosen to include and which to omit in Source E?

STEPPING STONES TO OFFICE.

'Stepping stones to office'. A cartoon illustrating the problems confronting the Conservatives between 1900 and 1906.

Conservatives did not understand, let alone believe in, the tariff-reform policy with which Chamberlain had saddled them. As one contemporary put it: 'the Conservatives went into the polling-booths with the albatross of tariff reform about their necks'.

The result of all this was a sweeping victory for the Liberals in the election held in January and February 1906. Henry Campbell-Bannerman now headed a Liberal ministry with a majority of 243 over the Conservatives.

Table 1.4 The 1906 general election result

Party	Votes	Seats	Percentage of vote
Conservatives	2,451,584	157	43.6
Liberals	2,757,883	400	49.0
Labour Representation Committee (Labour in 1906)	329,748	30	5.9
Irish Nationalists	35,031	83	0.6

Electoral problems for the Conservatives

In 1906, it was not so much the attraction of the Liberals that won them the day as the dissatisfaction felt by the electorate towards the Conservatives. However, a note of caution should be sounded here. When dealing with the results of elections, it is tempting to talk of sweeping victories and landslides. Yet, such dramatic terms tend to distort the real picture. The truth is that the result of an election is invariably the consequence of a slight shift in public attitude. The characteristic of the British electoral system is that parliamentary seats are awarded not in proportion to the number of votes a party receives overall, but according to how many individual constituencies it wins. Since each elected MP gains his or her seat simply by being **'first past the post'**, he or she could win by a very large majority or a very small one. So whether a party wins or loses is not a matter of how many votes it gets nationally but how those votes are distributed.

This can be seen by comparing the figures in Tables 1.3 and 1.4 (page 11 and above). Across the two elections the Liberals more than doubled their number of seats while the Conservatives saw their number more than halved. However, in terms of overall votes, the returns were nowhere near as dramatic; there had been a marginal shift in the popular vote, not a landslide. This is not to argue that the Conservatives had not lost support or that the Liberals had not gained it. Between 1900 and 1906 there certainly had been a major movement from the Conservatives to the Liberals. The former had improved their vote by only 654,140, while the Liberals had picked up an extra 1,189,742. Yet the Liberals' popular-vote majority over the Conservatives was only 306,299, hardly sufficient in proportional terms to justify a majority of 243 in the House of Commons. To put it as a ratio: in 1906, it required 15,615 votes to return a Conservative, but only 6894 to return a Liberal.

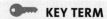

KEY TERM

First past the post
The electoral process by which the candidate with more votes than his or her nearest rival wins the seat, irrespective of whether he or she has an overall majority of the votes cast.

This imbalance would not always work in the Liberals' favour. It is one of the ironies discussed later in the book (see page 91) that although the Liberals gained from the oddity of the British electoral system in 1906, they were to become its victims after 1918 when they consistently failed to turn their popular vote into parliamentary seats. That development, however, lay in the future. In 1906 their great moment had arrived. They were in power with a massive majority which gave them the freedom to turn their political ideas into practical policies.

The Conservative record

Six years after winning a handsome victory in the 'khaki election' the Conservatives had squandered that supremacy and suffered a crushing electoral defeat at the hands of the Liberals that was to keep them out of office until 1922. It appeared to the electorate in 1906 that the Conservatives had been unsuccessful in tackling the great questions facing Britain. It was now the turn of the Liberals to test whether their ideas and programmes were better fitted to the times.

However, before turning to consider the Liberals, it is to be noted that it would be unhistorical to regard the Conservatives of this era as reactionaries vainly trying to hold back the forces of progress. The record of the Salisbury and Balfour governments shows a willingness to entertain reform. While this may not represent a systematic programme, it does indicate a readiness by the Conservatives to contemplate progressive legislation in key social areas. When the Liberals came into office in 1905 intent on reform they were working on prepared ground.

Major social reforms of Conservative governments 1886–1905

- Provision made to improve working-class housing.
- Steps taken to prevent cruelty to children.
- Landlords rather than tenants to be responsible for paying tithes.
- Factory Act 1891, improved safety condition in the mines.
- Education Act 1891, established free elementary education.
- Measures to improve the conditions of shop assistants and mill hands.
- Factory acts tightening safety regulations.
- Workmen's Compensation Act 1897, provided payments for injuries sustained at the workplace.
- Factory and Workshop Act 1901, improved working conditions.
- Education Act 1902, extended compulsory education for all into the secondary area.
- Wyndham's Land Act 1902, settled the landlord–tenant problem in Ireland.

```
Summary diagram: The Conservative Party

┌─────────────────────────────────────────────────┐
│  The character of the Conservative and Unionist Party  │
└─────────────────────────────────────────────────┘

┌─────────────────────────────────────────────────┐
│          Conservative difficulties 1902–5        │
│   • The Anglo-Boer War, 1899–1902                │
│   • 'Chinese slavery'                            │
│   • The Taff Vale decision, 1901                 │
│   • Balfour's Education Act, 1902                │
│   • Irish Land Act, 1902                         │
│   • Licensing Act, 1904                          │
│   • Tariff reform                                │
└─────────────────────────────────────────────────┘

┌─────────────────────────────────────────────────┐
│                  1906 election                   │
│   • Balfour's miscalculation                     │
│   • Liberals' landslide victory                  │
└─────────────────────────────────────────────────┘

┌─────────────────────────────────────────────────┐
│            The Conservative record               │
│   • Electoral problems                           │
└─────────────────────────────────────────────────┘
```

 # The Liberal Party

▶ *In what sense were these years the age of 'New Liberalism'?*

'New Liberalism'

The electoral landslide of 1906 was not simply a victory for the Liberal Party after a decade in the wilderness; it was a victory for **'New Liberalism'**, the movement among progressive Liberals who wanted their party to commit itself fully to social reform. In the last part of the nineteenth century, the Liberal Party had faced a crisis of identity. Its traditional character was Gladstonian; that is to say, it had developed into a major party in accordance with the ideas and attitudes of its leader, William Ewart Gladstone, the towering figure of late Victorian politics. The policies and principles that the Liberal Party had come to represent under him were succinctly captured in Gladstone's own slogan, 'Peace, Retrenchment and Reform'. By 'peace', he meant the settling of international disputes by negotiation; by 'retrenchment', the cutting of wasteful central government expenditure and by 'reform', the acceptance of essential change provided it did not encroach on the freedom of the individual.

A prominent feature of these policies was that, while they included the principle of necessary change, they excluded the idea of the State's undertaking a comprehensive programme of social and economic reform. This was because traditional Liberalism championed the cause of the individual. It was very reluctant to allow the State to intrude on the economic and social liberties of

 **KEY TERM**

'New Liberalism'
The movement within the Liberal Party that pressed for the adoption of social reform as the principal party policy.

Joseph Chamberlain

1836	Born
1880–5	Liberal president of the **Board of Trade**
1885	Presented 'Unauthorised programme'
1886	Joined Conservatives
1895–1903	Colonial secretary
1899	Pushed Britain into Anglo-Boer War
1902	Advocated tariff reform
1914	Died

Having made an impression as a young radical, Chamberlain was appointed president of the Board of Trade in Gladstone's Liberal government of 1880–5. However, in 1885 his alternative 'Unauthorised programme', advocating an extensive scheme of social reform, was a sign of his dissatisfaction with Gladstonian Liberalism, and in 1886 he resigned.

Chamberlain's decision was motivated in part by his anger at Gladstone's attempt to grant home rule to Ireland, but he was equally concerned to press his schemes for dealing with national poverty. Chamberlain feared that if the plight of the industrial masses was left untouched they would turn to socialism. He explained his attitude in these terms: 'Politics is the science of human happiness, and the business of politicians is to find out how they can raise the general condition of the people.' Having left the Liberals, Chamberlain gravitated towards the Conservatives whom he joined as a Liberal Unionist. As colonial secretary he showed his passionate belief in the need to preserve and expand the British Empire by making claims in South Africa that led to the Anglo-Boer War.

Chamberlain's last major contribution to British politics was to persuade the Conservatives to adopt tariff reform as a basic part of its policy. For him, empire, tariff reform and relief of poverty were inextricably linked. His conviction was that tariff reform with its system of imperial preference would provide the revenue to pay for economic reform, thereby depriving socialism of the chance to exploit social unrest.

Chamberlain split the Liberals in 1886 and then saddled the Conservatives with a tariff-reform programme that pushed them out of office for decades. Yet, notwithstanding his destructive tendencies, he more than any other politician of his day had made social reform the pervading issue of the age. Although he left the Liberals, his legacy to them was New Liberalism, the ideology of the liberal reforms that were soon to follow.

 **KEY TERM**

Board of Trade
A government department concerned with promoting British manufacturing and exports.

the people. That was why it supported free trade (see page 17). By the 1890s, however, such an approach was too restrictive for the progressive, radical Liberals who began to chaff against the limitations that Gladstone's pervading presence imposed upon their party. Despite retiring on a number of occasions, Gladstone continued to dominate the Liberal Party until his death in 1898. His longevity had prevented the younger members from pushing their ideas on to the party agenda.

The major victim of this was Joseph Chamberlain, who was unable to persuade the Liberal Party to accept his radical ideas (see page 15). Dismayed by the unwillingness of a party led by Gladstone to adapt itself to adopt modern policies, Chamberlain took the dramatic step in the late 1880s of abandoning the Liberals and joining the Unionists.

The outstanding representative of this new force in the Liberal party was David Lloyd George, who regarded Chamberlain as his political hero. Sharing Chamberlain's dislike of socialism, Lloyd George also wished to prevent its rise and believed this could best be done by the Liberal Party's widening its political appeal by a commitment to the relief of poverty. He expressed this view powerfully in 1906, when, as president of the Board of Trade (1905–8), he explained why the Liberals had to embrace social reform as their major objective (Source F).

SOURCE F

From a speech by Lloyd George in Cardiff, October 1906, quoted in *Better Times: Speeches by the Right Hon. D. Lloyd George*, University of Michigan Library, 1910, p. 36.

If at the end of an average term of office it were found that a Liberal Parliament had done nothing to cope seriously with the social condition of the people, to remove the national degradation of slums and widespread poverty and destitution in a land glittering with wealth; that they had shrunk from attacking boldly the main causes of this wretchedness; that they had not arrested the waste of our national resources in armaments, nor provided an honourable sustenance for deserving old age; that they had tamely allowed the House of Lords to extract all the virtue out of their Bills; then would a real cry arise in this land for a new party. But if a Liberal Government tackle the landlords and the peers and try to deliver the nation from this pernicious control then the Labour Party will call in vain upon the working men of Britain to desert Liberalism that is so gallantly fighting to rid the land of the wrongs that have oppressed those who labour in it.

What illustration of Lloyd George's political motives does Source F provide?

Lloyd George's great Liberal ally in this period was Winston Churchill, destined to be among the greatest statesmen of the twentieth century (see page 157). In 1906, Churchill gave a precise definition of the practical need for New Liberalism: 'No view of society can be complete which does not comprise within its scope both collective organisation and individual incentive. The ever growing complications of civilisation create for us new services which have to be undertaken by the State.'

'The sovereignty of social welfare'

There were Liberals who saw New Liberalism not as a break with the party's past but as a continuation of it. They argued that the progressive elements in traditional, Gladstonian Liberalism could be expanded to embrace the demands of the times. An important voice in the formulation of such thinking was J.A. Hobson, a prominent Liberal intellectual. Writing in 1909, he summed up the essential change in attitude.

SOURCE G

From J.A. Hobson, *The Crisis of Liberalism*, 1909, Forgotten Books, 2012, p. 49.

Liberalism is now formally committed to a task which certainly involves a new conception of the State in its relation to the individual life and to private enterprise. From the standpoint which best presents its continuity with earlier Liberalism, it appears as a fuller appreciation and realisation of individual

According to Source G, what adjustment did Liberalism have to make as a political ideology?

liberty contained in the provision of equal opportunities for self-development. But to this individual stand-point must be joined a just apprehension of the social, viz., the insistence that these claims or rights of self-development must be adjusted to the sovereignty of social welfare.

What Hobson meant by 'the sovereignty of social welfare' was that New Liberalism had accepted social reform as its paramount policy. Personal liberty and freedom of enterprise remained valid objectives, but the rights of the individual must not be pursued at the expense of the general social good. Equal opportunity through social reform ought now to be the goal of Liberal policies. Writing in 1909, Hobson had the luxury of knowing that in the three years since their victory in the 1906 election Liberalism had clearly committed itself to 'the sovereignty of social welfare'.

The social reforms of the Liberals, 1906–11

It was Campbell-Bannerman, prime minister from 1905 to 1908, who set the Liberals on the path to reform by claiming that the 1906 election had given the party a mandate to pursue the radical policies for which the New Liberals had pressed. The pace of reform quickened in 1908 when Campbell Bannerman retired and was replaced by Herbert Asquith, who was to remain prime minister for the next eight years. What proved to be one of the new leader's shrewdest moves was the appointment of the radical Lloyd George as chancellor of the exchequer. Lloyd George brought an infectious energy to the government's programme. He and the equally dynamic Winston Churchill, who took over from him at the Board of Trade, were largely responsible for the reputation that the pre-1914 Liberal government gained as a great reforming ministry. Inspiring much of the legislation introduced in this period was the Royal Commission on Poverty which sat between 1905 and 1909. It was this body that collected and presented to Parliament the evidence on which the reforms were based.

In the box on page 25 there are three particular measures that most directly illustrate the character of the Liberals' approach to social welfare: old age pensions, 'the people's budget' and National Insurance.

Old Age Pensions Act 1908

- Granted 5s. (25p) a week to people over 70 years of age who had incomes of less than £31.10s. (£31.50) a year and who had not previously received help from the Poor Law.
- The pension was non-contributory; that is, it was funded entirely from government revenues.

Pensions for the elderly was not a new idea. Other countries, Germany and New Zealand, for example, had already adopted them, and they had been considered by all the parties, including the Conservatives, during the previous twenty years. It could be argued, therefore, that the introduction of pensions was a long

The main Liberal social reforms 1906–11

- 1906: Trade Disputes Act reversed the Taff Vale decision by protecting union funds from claims for damages arising from strikes.
- 1906: Education Act empowered local education authorities (LEAs) to provide school meals for 'needy' children. Yet, since the measure was not compulsory, only a third of LEAs were providing meals by 1911.
- 1907: Education Act introduced compulsory medical examinations – children had to be examined at least three times during their school years.
- 1907–12: a set of measures improved conditions in prisons, created the probation service and ended imprisonment for debt.
- 1908: Children's Act created special provisions for young offenders by setting up juvenile courts and remand homes. This measure became known as the 'Children's Charter' since it helped to establish the principle that the needs of children were to be separately treated. The belief was that it was by improving the conditions of the young and treating their offences in a specially understanding way that 'national efficiency' was to be achieved.
- 1908: Old Age Pensions Act (see page 24)
- 1909: 'the people's budget' (see below)
- 1909: Trade Boards Act laid down minimum wages in the notorious '**sweated**' industries.
- 1909: Labour Exchanges Act provided easily accessible centres where employers could advertise jobs and workers could go to be advised on what positions were available. The aim was to take away the uncertainty and hit-and-miss nature of the job market.
- 1909: Development Commission created to organise the funding of State welfare.
- 1911: National Insurance Act (see page 26).
- 1911: Shops Act established the legal right of shop workers to a weekly half-day holiday.

 **KEY TERM**

Sweated Unhealthy, overcrowded premises, such as clothing workshops, where unscrupulous employers exploited cheap, often immigrant, labour.

overdue measure and that what made them so contentious in 1908 was not the principle behind them but the method of paying for them. To meet the necessary revenue, Lloyd George planned to increase taxes on the propertied classes. This was the purpose of his 1909 budget, which became known as 'the people's budget'.

'The people's budget' 1909

The main terms of the budget were as follows:

- The standard rate of income tax to be raised from 9*d*. (4p) to 1*s*. 3*d*. (7p) in the pound on incomes up to £3000 a year.
- A new 'super tax' of 6*d*. (2.5p) in the pound on incomes over £5000 a year.
- Death duties to be paid on estates valued at over £5000.
- A twenty per cent levy on the unearned increase in land values.
- Increased taxation on the sale of alcohol, tobacco and motorcars.

It was the proposal to impose death duties and to tax increases on land values that aroused the bitter opposition of the propertied classes. The Conservatives attacked the budget by asserting that in taxing the landowners so heavily Lloyd George was deliberately waging class war. He retaliated by claiming that it was indeed a war budget but not of the kind described by the Conservatives. 'This is a war budget. It is for raising money to wage implacable warfare against poverty and squalidness.'

Lloyd George's incensed opponents claimed that there was hypocrisy behind his words. They had a case; only a portion of the proposed revenue from the budget was earmarked for pensions. The greater part of the £16 million that Lloyd George was hoping to raise was to go towards the costs of the new warships that were being built for the navy. What sharpened the battle between the parties was the free trade versus protection argument, which was still the dominating economic issue of the day. To maintain themselves as a free-trade party it was essential for the Liberals to be able to pay for their welfare programme without resorting to trade tariffs.

For their part, the Conservatives realised that they would lose the protectionist argument if the Liberal government were to succeed in raising the necessary revenue through domestic taxation. The Conservatives organised a Budget Protest League in the country, while in the Commons they delayed the budget in a long ten-week debate. Even though the government eventually pushed it through, the Conservatives were far from broken-spirited. They took comfort from knowing that their Conservative colleagues in the House of Lords would use their majority to throw the budget out when it reached them there.

National Insurance Act 1911

The principal terms of this Act were as follows:

- The Act covered workers aged between 16 and 60 who earned less than £160 a year against sickness and unemployment.
- It did not apply to all industries, but only to building, engineering and shipbuilding covering 3 million workers.
- Sickness benefit of 10s. (50p) for men and 7s. 6d. (35p) for women, paid for a period of 26 weeks.
- A maternity grant of 3s. (15p).
- The scheme was to be funded by compulsory weekly contributions: 4d. (2p) from the employer, 3d. (1.5p) from the employee and 2d. (1p) from the State.
- Contributions were to be paid by buying adhesive stamps which were then affixed to a card.

Interestingly, National Insurance met strong initial resistance from the very people it was intended to benefit. Its compulsory character was particularly disturbing to the five and half million people, many of them working class, who already paid privately into schemes run by insurance companies, **friendly societies** and trade unions. The workers doubted that they were going to gain more from an imposed State plan than from their own private insurance. The popular press attacked the compulsory contributions as theft from the workers' pay packets.

Lloyd George showed remarkable skill in meeting the objections to National Insurance. He pointed out that the workers were 'getting 9d. for 4d.' and quietened the protests from the insurance companies, who feared losing out to the State scheme, by making them an integral part of the operation of the new plans. He was also able to overcome the complaints of the Labour Party, which had wanted National Insurance to be funded wholly from taxation of the wealthy. He pacified Labour by promising to introduce payment for MPs, a commitment which he honoured in 1911 (see page 37).

The resistance of the workers and the Labour Party to measures, which were supposedly in their interest shows that attitudes to welfare reform in the Edwardian period were often complex. It is notable that Churchill's Trade Boards Act of 1909, which aimed at providing minimum wages in the 'sweated' industries, was also initially opposed by the unions because they feared that the enforcement of a minimum wage would lead to job cuts by the employers. The minimum wage was also seen as undermining the customary right of unions to negotiate **differentials**. It was also dislike of the State's interfering between employer and worker that led the unions to look suspiciously at the labour exchanges introduced by Churchill in 1909.

The suspicious reaction of working-class people was understandable. They had a well-founded distrust of State intervention, which they saw as patronising and disruptive. Their practical experience of officialdom in the nineteenth century in such developments as the workhouse, compulsory education and vaccination had seldom been a happy one. They felt that too often they were being pushed around by State-employed snoopers. Workers suspected that State welfare was primarily intended to keep them in their place and make them conform. R.H. Tawney, one of the outstanding social historians of his day and a strong Labour Party supporter, explained the workers' reasoning (Source H).

SOURCE H

From R.H. Tawney, writing in 1912, quoted in J.M. Winter and D.M. Joslin, editors, *R.H. Tawney's Commonplace Book*, Cambridge University Press, 2006, p. 6.

The middle and upper-class view in social reform is that it should regulate the workers' life in order that he may work better. The working-class view of economic reform is that it should regulate his work, in order that he may have a change of living. Hence to working people licensing reform, insurance acts, etc. seems beginning at the wrong end.

KEY TERMS

Friendly societies
Non-profit-making bodies which pooled contributions from members and paid out when members were in need.

Differentials Separate rates of pay for different levels of skill.

In Source H, how does Tawney explain the resistance among the workers to government-led social reform?

The Liberals' achievement

The Liberal social-reform programme has come to be seen as a key stage on the path to the modern **Welfare State**. Introduced in the face of strong opposition, the reforms may not have been as radical as some New Liberals had wanted. Nevertheless, collectively they were a considerable achievement; they had established that it was the responsibility of government to provide for people who could not provide for themselves. The Liberals' social reforms did not create a full welfare state; the resources simply did not exist for that. But the measures were significant steps towards what has been termed 'the social service state', a centrally organised administration capable of improving the living and working conditions of large portions of the British population.

However, intention should not be confused with achievement. It would take time for the measures to have a discernible effect. Historians point out that, despite the good will and energy which the Liberals put into their reform programme, little real improvement had occurred by 1914 in the actual conditions of the nation's underprivileged. By 1914, the cost of living was fourteen per cent higher than in 1906 and unemployment had risen sharply during the same period. Despite the Liberal welfare measures, the gap between rich and poor was widening. An illustration of this was that **pawnbroking**, one of customary ways by which the poor struggled to make ends meets, had reached a peak by 1914.

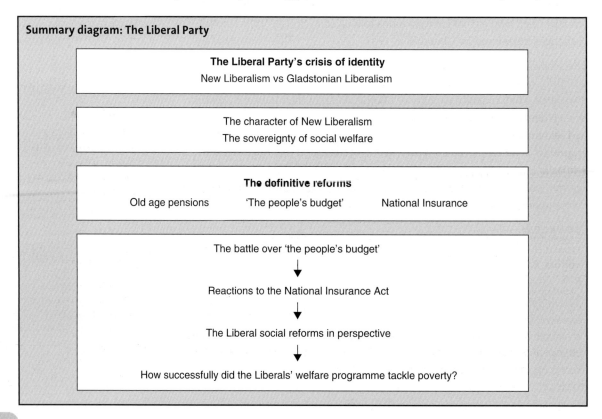

Summary diagram: The Liberal Party

The Liberal Party's crisis of identity
New Liberalism vs Gladstonian Liberalism

The character of New Liberalism
The sovereignty of social welfare

The definitive reforms

Old age pensions   'The people's budget'   National Insurance

The battle over 'the people's budget'
↓
Reactions to the National Insurance Act
↓
The Liberal social reforms in perspective
↓
How successfully did the Liberals' welfare programme tackle poverty?

The Labour Party

▶ *What were the main features of the Labour Party in 1900?*

In the second half of the nineteenth century, parliamentary reform had extended the vote to a growing number of working men. The Liberals had hoped that these new voters would support them as the only party able to represent the workers. Initially, this tended to happen. However, by 1900 a view had developed among working-class organisations that the Liberals, as an essentially middle-class party, did not really understand the problems faced by ordinary working people. What was needed, therefore, was a completely separate political party devoted solely to representing and defending the working class.

The Labour Representation Committee (LRC)

The result of such thinking was the coming together in 1900 of a variety of reforming and radical groups to form the Labour Representation Committee (LRC). Judging that it was too small to have a realistic chance of getting into government on its own, the LRC calculated that its best chance of gaining political influence was by co-operating with the Liberals. One outcome of this was the **Lib–Lab pact** of 1903. Some Labour supporters were not very impressed with this compromise and felt that the party had condemned itself to being a weak pressure group.

The Labour Party 1906–14

In 1906, the groups which had made up LRC formally merged as the Labour Party. The principal organisations were:

- The trade unions, which wanted a distinct political party to represent them.
- The Social Democratic Federation (SDF), led by **H.M. Hyndman**, which wanted class war against the ruling establishment.
- The Socialist League, similar to the SDF in its revolutionary aim.
- The Fabians (intellectuals such as George Bernard Shaw), who wanted to spread socialism not by revolution but through propaganda and education.
- The Independent Labour Party (ILP), founded by **James Keir Hardie** in 1893, and strongly influenced by Christian values in its desire to change Britain into a fair and moral society.
- The co-operative societies, formed in the nineteenth century to run shops and stores as non-profit-making ventures providing workers with food at affordable prices. Any dividends were shared among the customers.

Of the groups that made up the Labour Party, the trade unions were the most significant. It was they who provided the bulk of the funds and the members. Without trade union backing there would not have been a viable Labour Party. It was the formal resolution of the **TUC**, in 1899, to work for the organisation of a specifically workers' parliamentary party that enabled the Labour Party to become a reality in 1906.

 KEY TERMS

Lib–Lab pact An agreement between the LRC and the Liberal Party that their constituency candidates would not stand against each other in parliamentary elections.

TUC Trades Union Congress. The body created in 1868 to represent the unions collectively.

KEY FIGURES

H.M. Hyndman (1842–1921)

A strong advocate of the ideas of the German revolutionary, Karl Marx, who believed the workers should unite to overthrow the capitalist system.

James Keir Hardie (1856–1915)

Legendary pioneering figure in the Labour movement; elected MP in 1892, he believed that politics should be about the creation of social justice; he was the first chairman of the Labour Party 1906–8.

Not all the unions had accepted the move; some doubted the wisdom of following the parliamentary path. However, the anti-union Taff Vale decision (see page 12) appeared to be a dramatic vindication of the TUC's decision; it greatly strengthened the argument for a new political party to plead the unions' cause. By 1903, 127 unions had affiliated to the LRC. The Taff Vale decision had stifled the doubts regarding the wisdom of unions engaging in political as opposed to industrial action and had forged the historic link between the trade union movement and the Labour Party. Some historians suggest that this marks the beginning of 'class' politics in Britain, the suggestion being that the awareness of the working class of its own potential became the most significant factor in electoral politics.

Tables 1.5 and 1.6 clearly show how dependent the Labour Party was on the trade unions for sustaining its membership. Another interesting indicator is that, pre-1914, it was very much a minority of trade unionists who had joined the party. The Labour Party was in the odd position of being heavily reliant on the trade unions and yet unable to win the majority of them over to its side.

Table 1.5 LRC and Labour Party membership 1900–14

Year	Number of members through trade union affiliation	Number of individual members	Total
1900	353,000	23,000	376,000
1901	455,000	14,000	469,000
1902	847,000	14,000	861,000
1903	956,000	14,000	970,000
1904	885,000	15,000	900,000
1905	904,000	17,000	921,000
1906	975,000	23,000	998,000
1907	1,050,000	22,000	1,072,000
1908	1,127,000	32,000	1,159,000
1909	1,451,000	35,000	1,486,000
1910	1,394,000	35,000	1,431,000
1911	1,502,000	37,000	1,539,000
1912	1,858,000	37,000	1,895,000
1913	–	–	*
1914	1,572,000	40,000	1,612,000

* The Osborne judgment (see page 33) made figures unavailable for 1913.

Table 1.6 Number of workers in trade unions

Year	Number of workers
1900	1,911,000
1905	1,967,000
1910	2,477,000
1911	2,565,000
1912	3,139,000
1913	3,416,000
1914	4,135,000

Nevertheless, despite the pessimism this induced in some supporters, the Labour Party had made progress. By 1910 it had 42 MPs in the House of Commons compared with 30 in 1906. The party seemed to be more than holding its own. In the period before 1914, the number of trade unions affiliating themselves to the party continued to grow. This meant an increase both in the number of party members and in the party's funds. Since the unions which joined included the powerful Miners' Federation, there were firm grounds for claiming that the party was becoming increasingly representative of the workers.

Labour also appeared to benefit from the political situation created by the 1910 election results, which had ended the Liberal government's parliamentary majority (see the tables on page 38). Asquith's Liberals now had to stay on working terms with Labour and the Irish Nationalists in case they needed their support in a Commons' vote. This did not give Labour an overwhelming influence and it did not mean that it was in any sense a party of government, but it did mean that the Liberals had a radical rival in the country.

Labour's difficulties

Yet there was a sense in which Labour suffered from the **hung parliament** produced by the 1910 elections. The Liberal government certainly wanted the support of the Labour MPs but it was not dependent on it. It was the Irish Nationalists, whose 82 MPs outnumbered Labour's by two to one, whom Asquith's government were most concerned to placate (see page 86). How strong the rival Labour Party would become nobody could foretell at this stage. In the years 1910–14 the omens were not particularly favourable. In the second election of 1910 the Labour vote slumped and it failed to win a single by-election in the following four years, its failures reducing its number of parliamentary seats by four to 38. There were fears that the party would remain merely a fringe movement or wither away altogether.

Part of the problem was that, small though it was, the Labour Party was an amalgam of interests, not a party with one clearly defined aim. Its Marxist members were angered by the party's willingness to support the Liberal government's measures and its reluctance to adopt a revolutionary stance in Parliament. However, the moderates found the left's talk of revolution unrealistic; as they saw it, the actual situation demanded that Labour first establish its credibility as a parliamentary party with the electorate. This could not be achieved by pretending that the party would be swept to power by the electors in a wave of revolutionary fervour. Of course, principles were important, but to turn these into realisable goals a mixture of patience and political opportunism was necessary.

For their part, the trade unionists, predominantly working-class men, were often exasperated by the revolutionary socialists in the party who were strong on ideas but who were invariably middle-class intellectuals who had little experience of real work. The great majority of trade unionists wanted a Labour Party that

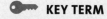 **KEY TERM**

Hung parliament
A situation in which no single party has an overall majority in the House of Commons.

would make its main task the increase of workers' pay and the improvement of conditions. They were concerned not with political theory but with immediate material gains. As one worker put it: 'Party's task is not t' natter on but to put food int' ours bellies and clothes ont' ours backs.'

The gap between the workers and the intellectuals and the dispute between the moderate centre and the revolutionary left over the aims and methods to be followed were to prove defining characteristics of the Labour Party over the next 100 years.

Labour's attitude towards the Liberal reforms

It is reasonable to assume that Labour had an influence on the Liberals' social and economic reforms in the pre-war period. However, the evidence does not suggest that any of the measures were introduced primarily because of Labour Party pressure or that the government needed Labour's support to get the legislation through Parliament. So strong was the commitment of the Liberals to social reform at this time that the measures would have doubtless been adopted even had there been no Labour MPs in the Commons.

Moreover, there were occasions when Labour showed a deep suspicion of the reforms (see page 26). For example, **Beatrice Webb**, a leading Fabian, opposed the National Insurance Act of 1911 on the grounds that working-class voters were 'too dull witted to understand' and that 'millions of public money will be wastefully collected and wastefully spent [on the] wholesale demoralisation of character through the fraudulent withholding or the fraudulent getting of benefits'.

The most that can be claimed is that the presence in the Commons of a group of Labour MPs indicated the temper of the times. It was in that sense that the Labour Party might be said to have had an influence, not as a promoter of any particular reform but as a reminder that Britain was moving into the age of welfare, with the needs of the deprived classes becoming an issue that no party could afford to ignore. Lloyd George had put this very clearly in 1904 before the Liberals came to power: 'We have a great Labour Party sprung up. Unless we [Liberals] can prove that there is no necessity for a separate party in order to press forward the legitimate claims of labour, then you will find that the Liberal Party will be practically wiped out.'

Labour's record before 1914

In the light of the subsequent replacement of the Liberals by Labour, Lloyd George's warning seems prophetic. But in 1914, contemporaries had no reason for regarding the Labour Party as having been especially successful. It may have returned MPs to Parliament but these had achieved little. Its membership may have grown but this was largely a result of trade union affiliation, not because the party had become popular in the country at large.

KEY FIGURE

Beatrice Webb (1858–1943)

Writer and dedicated, if patronising, social reformer who worked with her husband, Sidney Webb, to advance a range of socialist causes.

Significantly, it had played little part in the industrial disputes that troubled Britain between 1911 and 1914 (see page 43). This was not so much a lack of will as a failure of confidence. The Labour Party felt hamstrung by the **Osborne Judgment**, which like the earlier Taff Vale decision, indicated the anti-worker bias that then prevailed in English law. It is true that Asquith's government in 1913 introduced an Act reversing the judgment. However, Labour could claim little direct credit for this even though it benefited from the measure, which entitled the party to resume receiving funds from the unions with the proviso that individual union members could contract out from paying the **political levy**.

The inglorious performance of the Labour Party in this period, when it too often appeared a mere bystander in the dramatic conflict between bosses and workers, led a significant number of trade unionists to murmur that, since Labour was so ineffectual, the better option was for the workers to fight for their rights not through parliamentary representation but by direct action on the streets and in the factories.

Yet, in spite of its poor pre-1914 performance, historians sympathetic to the Labour Party have tended to regard its rise as logical and natural, if not inevitable. This is an interesting but controversial viewpoint since it largely relies on hindsight and tends to ignore the way people at the time viewed matters. The Labour Party's record in its short history up to 1914 was not impressive. Beatrice Webb commented in 1913: 'The parliamentary Labour Party is in a bad way and has not justified its existence either by character or intelligence, and it is doubtful whether it will hold the Trade Unions.' A year later she added: 'if we are honest, we have to admit that the party has failed'. She was referring to Labour's failure to establish itself as a distinct and separate alternative to the Liberals as representative of working-class interests.

In 1914, there were no clear reasons for thinking that the Labour Party was destined for political power. Nobody could foresee the great shift in British politics that would be brought about by the 1914–18 war. It was to be the war that would make it possible for the Labour Party to displace the Liberals as the major radical force in Britain.

KEY TERMS

Osborne Judgment
A 1909 appeal court ruling that it was illegal for a trade union to use its funds to support a political party or to pay candidates or MPs.

Political levy The portion of a member's trade union subscription that went to the Labour Party.

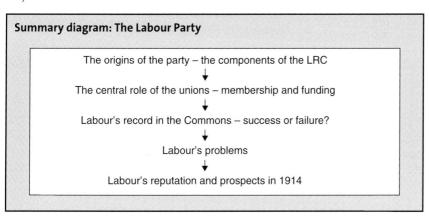

Summary diagram: The Labour Party

The origins of the party – the components of the LRC
↓
The central role of the unions – membership and funding
↓
Labour's record in the Commons – success or failure?
↓
Labour's problems
↓
Labour's reputation and prospects in 1914

Chapter summary

Britain in 1900 faced a range of social, economic and military problems that included poverty, economic decline, poor industrial relations, war in South Africa, tension in Ireland and divisive constitutional questions. The Conservative government, whose conduct of the Boer War (1899–1902) had damaged its reputation, was eventually overwhelmed by these problems and lost power in 1905. Confirmed in office by an overwhelming election victory in 1906, the Liberals embarked on a programme of welfare reform in which the introduction of old age pensions and National Insurance figured prominently. Welfare was part of New Liberalism, a movement to transform the Liberal Party into a progressive political force. The perception that the Liberals were too restricted in outlook to become a truly modern party had led to the creation in 1906 of the Labour Party, committed to representing working-class interests. Although Labour achieved little before 1914, its existence was evidence that class had entered as a significant factor in British politics. The Liberals' narrow majority after the 1910 elections left it dependent on support from Irish Nationalist MPs in order to stay in office.

 Refresher questions

Use these questions to remind yourself of the key material covered in this chapter.

1 Why was poverty so widespread in Britain by 1900?

2 Why had the extension of the vote become such a controversial matter?

3 How did Britain become involved in the Anglo-Boer war?

4 Why was opinion deeply divided in Britain over the Boer War?

5 Why did problems mount for the Conservatives between 1900 and 1906?

6 Why was tariff reform such a controversial issue?

7 Why did Balfour's Education Act, 1902, cause anger among religious groups in Britain?

8 What strategic mistakes did Balfour make in preparing for the 1906 election?

9 How successful had the Conservatives been in their period of office?

10 What was New Liberalism?

11 What accounts for the Liberals' overwhelming victory in the 1906 election?

12 In what ways were the Liberal reforms of 1906–11 the implementation of New Liberalism?

13 Why did the 1909 budget cause fierce controversy?

14 Why did the intended recipients of National Insurance initially oppose it?

15 Why had the Labour Party been formed in 1906?

Question practice

ESSAY QUESTIONS

1 Assess the reasons why the Conservatives lost so heavily in the general election of 1906.

2 'Lloyd George's people's budget of 1909 was an act of class warfare.' Explain why you agree or disagree with this view.

3 How important politically was the formation of the Labour Party in 1906?

4 'The Liberal reforms of 1906–11 were an example of New Liberalism in action.' How far do you agree?

SOURCE ANALYSIS QUESTIONS

1 With reference to Sources A (page 3) and B (page 13) and your understanding of the historical context, which of these two sources is more valuable in explaining why New Liberalism developed within the Liberal Party?

2 With reference to Sources A (page 3), B (page 13) and F (page 23), and your understanding of the historical context, assess the value of these sources to a historian studying the problems facing the Liberals in the first decade of the twentieth century.

3 Study the three Sources A (page 3), F (page 23) and G (page 23), and then answer both questions. a) Using your knowledge of living conditions in Britain at the start of the twentieth century, assess how useful Source A is as evidence for the poverty that existed in some areas. b) Using these three sources in their historical context, assess how far they support the view that the Liberals were ill-equipped to deal with the problem of poverty in Britain.

4 Study the four Sources A (page 3), F (page 23), G (page 23) and H (page 27), and then answer the following question. Using these four sources in their historical context, assess how far they support the view that the Liberal Party was struggling to adapt itself to the problem of poverty and welfare.

CHAPTER 2

Britain in crisis and war 1911–18

From 1911 to 1914, Asquith's government struggled to contain four acute crises which threatened to subvert the traditional political order: the Lords–Commons conflict, the combative suffragette protest movement, militant trade unionism and a warring Ireland. From August 1914 to November 1918, Britain was at war with Germany and its allies, an experience that proved highly formative, politically, socially and economically. In this chapter the pre-war crises and the impact and the consequences of the 1914–18 war are studied in five main sections:

★ The pre-war domestic crises 1911–14
★ Britain's attitude to the 1914–18 war
★ The politics of war 1914–18
★ The political parties in wartime
★ The Home Front 1914–18

Key dates

1911–14		Domestic crises
1914	**Aug.**	Britain declared war on Germany
		Parties agreed to a political truce
1915–16		Unsuccessful Gallipoli campaign
1915	**March**	Treasury agreement
	May	Coalition government formed under Asquith
1916	**Jan.**	Conscription introduced
	July–Nov.	Battle of the Somme
	Dec.	Conservatives withdrew support from Asquith

1916		Lloyd George became prime minister and formed a new coalition government
		War cabinet formed
1917	**April**	U-boat menace threatened Britain's lifeline
1918	**Feb.**	Representation of the People Act
		Adoption of the Labour Party constitution
	May	Lloyd George survived the Maurice debate
	Nov.	Armistice on the Western Front
	Dec.	Lloyd George won the 'coupon election'

1 The pre-war domestic crises 1911–14

▶ *Why did Liberal Britain experience a series of major crises in the pre-war period?*

The Liberals' reforming energy was sustained until 1914, but from 1911 onwards Asquith's government had to contend with a serious set of problems which tended to overshadow its achievements in social welfare provision. A notable feature of government policy from 1911 was its concern with the constitutional and industrial-relations issues that dominated the political scene.

Four major crises occupied the Liberals in the period from 1911 to 1914:

- the conflict between the Lords and Commons
- the votes for women campaign
- industrial strife
- the threat of civil war in Ulster.

These proved so disruptive that they threatened the social and political order itself. The severity of the crises has been interpreted by some observers as evidence of the failure of the Liberals to deal with the problems of their time.

Chief political and constitutional reforms 1911–14

- 1911: introduction of payment for MPs (initially, £400 a year). This allowed those without a private income to consider standing for Parliament.
- 1911: Parliament Act removed the power of the House of Lords to veto Acts passed by the House of Commons.
- 1912: Act granting home rule for Ireland.
- 1913: Trade Union Act allowed union funds to be used for political purposes.
- 1914: Act disestablishing the Welsh Church.

The conflict between the Lords and Commons 1910–11

Arguably, a major struggle between the House of Commons and the House of Lords became unavoidable once the Liberals had won their crushing victory in 1906. Unable to outvote the government in the Commons, the Conservative **Opposition** had reverted to using its in-built majority in the Lords to block measures to which it objected. Matters came to a head in the controversy over the 'people's budget' of 1909, in which Lloyd George had proposed special taxes on rich landowners to pay for old age pensions (see page 24).

The Conservatives decided to resist the budget on the grounds that it was an unprecedented attack upon the rights of property. They argued that this entitled

 **KEY TERM**

Opposition The official title given to the main party opposing the government. In recognition of its place in the constitutional system, it is referred to as His/Her Majesty's Loyal Opposition.

them to ignore the long-standing convention that the Lords did not interfere with finance bills. Lloyd George, the chancellor of the exchequer and a strong opponent of aristocratic privilege, thought the whole affair could be turned to the Liberals' advantage. He led the Liberals in denouncing the peers' attempt to maintain their privileges at the expense of the old and the poor of the nation. In a memorable turn of phrase he mocked the Lords for being not, as the peers claimed, 'the watchdog of the constitution' but 'Mr Balfour's poodle'.

In a brilliant speech in 1909, which established the government's line of approach over the next two years, Lloyd George had savaged the peers for opposing the will of the British people.

SOURCE A

? What is Lloyd George's essential argument in Source A?

From a speech by Lloyd George in Newcastle, October 1909, quoted in Herbert du Parq, editor, *Life of David Lloyd George*, Caxton Publishing, 1912, p. 696.

Who made ten thousand people owners of the soil, and the rest of us trespassers in the land of our birth? Who is it who is responsible for the scheme of things whereby one man is engaged through life in grinding labour to win a bare and precarious subsistence for himself, and when, at the end of his days, he claims at the hands of the community he served a poor pension of eight pence a day, he can only get it through a revolution, and another man who does not toil receives every hour of the day, every hour of the night, whilst he slumbers, more than his poor neighbour receives in a whole year of toil?

Victory for the government

The Lords lost the battle that followed. In 1910, two general elections wiped out the Liberals' overall majority, leaving them exactly equal with the Conservatives in number of seats. However, knowing that they could rely on the support of Labour and Irish Nationalist members in the Commons, the Liberals remained in government, determined to persevere with Lloyd George's budget.

Table 2.1 The 1910 general election result

January/February			
Party	Votes	Seats	Percentage of vote
Conservatives	3,127,887	273	46.9
Liberals	2,880,581	275	43.2
Labour	505,657	40	7.6
Irish Nationalists	124,586	82	1.9
December			
Party	Votes	Seats	Percentage of vote
Conservatives	2,420,566	272	46.3
Liberals	2,295,888	272	43.9
Labour	371,772	42	7.1
Irish Nationalists	131,375	84	2.5

The Lords had earlier agreed that if, after two elections, Asquith's government was still in office, they would allow the budget to pass through the Upper House. Having reluctantly kept their word, the peers were promptly presented with a Parliament Bill, which set out to limit their powers.

For well over a year the Lords resisted the Parliament Bill, arguing that the 1910 elections had failed to give Asquith's government a clear mandate for such radical constitutional change. Added tension was created by the awareness on both sides that were the Lords' veto to be removed there would be nothing to prevent the Liberals from forcing Irish home rule through Parliament.

Eventually, in August 1911, in the middle of a heat wave that melted the peers' starched collars, the Lords gave in. What finally pushed them was the threat of being swamped by 500 new Liberal peers whom Asquith had persuaded the new monarch, King George V, to create should the Lords continue with their resistance. Even then, the narrow majority of seventeen was achieved only by the decision of 37 Conservative peers to vote for the Bill rather than suffer the 'pollution' of their House.

Main terms of the Parliament Act 1911

- The delaying power of the Lords to be restricted to two years.
- A Bill sent up by the Commons in three consecutive sessions to become law even though it might be rejected by the Lords.
- General elections to be held at least once in every five years instead of once in every seven.

The Lords' argument

For the sake of balance, the argument of the peers who resisted needs to be understood in its historical setting. The use of the Lords' veto to block the budget was not simply blind reaction on the part of the Conservatives. They asserted that the only way the free-trade Liberals could pay for their ambitious schemes was by resorting to punitive taxation of the landed class. A government, which in two elections had failed to win an overall majority in the Commons, was attempting to bypass the legitimate constitutional rights of the class under attack by improper use of the budget. What the Liberals had done was tantamount to a declaration of class war. Far from defending privilege, the Lords believed they were speaking for the legal and constitutional freedoms of the nation. Such an argument may sound unconvincing to the modern ear, but in its time it was sincerely held by its proponents. The **'ditchers'**, as they were called, may have been one of history's losing sides, but their argument still commands the historian's attention.

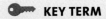 **KEY TERM**

'Ditchers' Those peers who were prepared to defend their power of absolute veto to the 'last ditch'.

The votes for women campaign

The right of women to vote might be thought to have been a cause that the Liberals would eagerly support. John Stuart Mill (1806–73), the great Liberal philosopher, had regarded it as an essential freedom in a civilised society. However, the fine balance between the two main parties after the elections of 1910 made many Liberals hesitate. Asquith, in particular, dragged his feet because he feared the political and electoral consequences of what would be a large and irreversible extension of the franchise.

The slowness of Parliament to deal with the matter had led to the development of a **suffragist** and a **suffragette** movement. Both groups campaigned for votes for women, but whereas the suffragists, led by **Millicent Garrett Fawcett**, were opposed to violent methods, the suffragettes believed that it was only by being prepared to break the law that women could force a male-dominated Parliament to respond to their demands.

The major suffragette organisation was the **WSPU**, led by the dynamic **Emmeline Pankhurst**, aided by her daughters Sylvia and Christabel. The WSPU undertook a campaign of disruption, which became increasingly violent as the Liberals persisted in their refusal to provide parliamentary time to debate the question. Between 1911 and 1914, a series of violent suffragette actions, including arson and physical assault, showed the degree of WSPU frustration. One of the most famous incidents occurred when a suffragette, Emily Davison, threw herself in front of Anmer, a horse owned by the king, during the running of the Derby at Epsom racecourse in 1913. The horse and jockey survived, but Emily died from her injuries four days later.

However, the violence tended to alienate moderate female and male supporters. It also provided an excuse for the government to impose heavy prison sentences on convicted suffragettes. In 1913 Parliament passed the Prisoners (Temporary Discharge for Ill Health) Act 1913. Better known as the Cat and Mouse Act, this measure allowed the authorities, without having to resort to the previous fearsome practice of force-feeding, to overcome the resistance of the imprisoned suffragettes who went on hunger strike. When the women's health deteriorated, they were released on licence, but as soon as they had recovered they were brought back to prison.

A question of prejudice?

'Votes for women' is now viewed as part of the broader campaign for female emancipation that developed in the twentieth century. It is seen as a major step in the overcoming of prejudice. There was certainly prejudice aplenty. Gladstone's wife, Catherine, had suggested that the only way women should be involved in politics was 'to help our husbands'. Marie Corelli, a popular novelist, later supported this view, asking rhetorically 'Shall we sacrifice our Womanhood to Politics?' Far better, she thought, for women to stay in the background,

SOURCE B

THE CAT AND MOUSE ACT

PASSED BY THE LIBERAL GOVERNMENT

THE LIBERAL CAT
ELECTORS VOTE AGAINST HIM!
KEEP THE LIBERAL OUT!

BUY AND READ 'THE SUFFRAGETTE' PRICE 1ᴅ

How effectively does the poster in Source B make its point?

The Cat and Mouse Act poster of 1913, showing the bitterness with which the Act was regarded by the suffragettes.

supporting men in their 'victorious accomplishment of noble purpose'. Lord Salisbury thought politics was too difficult for women 'to worry their pretty little heads about', while a male doctor wrote to *The Times* newspaper in 1912 claiming that the votes for women campaign was a plot by embittered spinsters, 'strangers to joy', to get their own back on the men who would not marry them.

Yet while there were undoubtedly Edwardian MPs who would now be termed male chauvinists, the majority of MPs were not primarily concerned with the rights or wrongs of women's suffrage as a principle. Their worries were party political. For them a female electorate was an unknown quantity. They feared that it would have a harmful impact on their parliamentary strength. This worry applied to all the parties, Conservative, Liberal and Labour. They simply did not know how women would vote. For the Labour Party, whose leader before 1908, Keir Hardie, was an enthusiastic campaigner for women's suffrage, there was a particular concern. It feared that, if, as some Labour members had proposed, female franchise were to be phased in by granting it to selected groups of women, this would weaken the case for complete male suffrage, which was the party's first priority, since 40 per cent of men were still without the vote in 1914.

It was also the case that the suffragettes were not always clear in their objectives and there were many disputes within the movement. Even the Pankhursts fell out. Sylvia and Christabel split the WSPU by taking opposed views over suffragette militancy and whether the movement should throw in its lot with the Labour Party. In 1910, their mother, Emmeline, appeared to have compromised her own position when she accepted a **Conciliation Bill**. This was doubtless a tactical move on her part, but it did illustrate how unclear the votes for women issue could be.

Lloyd George is an interesting individual example of Liberal Party difficulties. As an MP, he supported the moderate suffragists and consistently voted in favour of the private members' bills promoting women's right to vote. But, as a minister, his reactions were governed by political considerations. His worry was that if the extension of the vote was to be made, as with men, on the principle of some form of property qualification, then only middle-class women would be eligible. This he feared would chiefly benefit the Conservatives electorally. As was his way, he negotiated with the various interested groups with a view to reaching a compromise. His motives were not always trusted, however, and he suffered for his pains; in 1912, he was physically assaulted by a group of suffragettes and his house in Surrey was bombed.

Although Lloyd George tried to find a satisfactory settlement, his leader, Asquith, refused for too long to give ground to the central principle of female suffrage. There is little doubt that the Liberals were damaged by the suffragette issue. They claimed that it was 'a constitutional not a moral question'. But for a party that claimed to be 'the party of principle' their apparent reluctance to treat female suffrage as a matter of fundamental rights weakened their moral standing. In political terms, their failure to resolve the issue proved a major embarrassment.

The issue of votes for women was no nearer to being settled when the war intervened in 1914. Emmeline Pankhurst immediately called off her campaign and dedicated herself and her followers to the war effort (see Source C).

🔑 **KEY TERM**

Conciliation Bill A 1910 cross-party compromise which proposed dropping the idea of votes for working-class women in return for Parliament's granting it to women who owned property. It came to nothing since Asquith's government declined to support it.

SOURCE C

From a speech by Emmeline Pankhurst in Plymouth, November 1914, as reported in *The Western Evening Herald*, 17 November 1914, p. 10.

We have now suspended our work for women's suffrage, and are taking part in a national effort to prepare to resist the reign of militarism as an ideal in Europe. It is perfectly true that until the war broke out we were engaged in a civil war the purpose of which was to win from a reluctant government the citizenship of the women of this land. But never throughout the whole of that fight did we relax one jot of our patriotism, it was because we love our country so much that we could not bear to be the serf sex in that country. When war broke out the situation was changed. We said to ourselves it is true we have an inter-family quarrel with those who govern the country but the country is ours as much as theirs. And when the country is in danger and it is their duty to prepare for the defence of the country them it is our duty to help them do it.

> What insight into the character of the suffragette movement is offered by Emmeline Pankhurst's statement in Source C, 'we could not bear to be the serf sex'? **?**

Industrial unrest

Despite the gains made by the Trade Disputes Act of 1906 (see page 25), the years preceding the First World War were a particularly troubled period for the trade unions. The presence of Labour Party MPs in the Commons did not appear to have brought any clear benefits to the workers. Faced with these failures, many trade unionists began to doubt whether the existing political structure could ever be made to respond to working-class needs. The belief that the legal and parliamentary systems were fundamentally opposed to their interests encouraged a number of unions to consider direct action.

Their views were reinforced by legal decisions such as the Osborne Judgment in 1909 (see page 33), which in denying the unions the right to use their funds for political purposes, proved that the governing system had an inbuilt hostility to them. The increase in trade union membership from 1.9 million in 1900 to 4.1 million in 1914 was a measure of the growing frustration of the industrial workers. Few British workers were drawn to **syndicalism** but in the excited atmosphere of pre-war Britain direct action became increasingly attractive to the more militant unions.

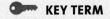 **KEY TERM**

Syndicalism A revolutionary movement calling on workers to smash the industrial–capitalist system by violent action.

The miners' strike 1910–11

The miners, traditionally the most combative of the unions, had already in 1908 won the legal recognition of a maximum eight-hour working day. They now struck for the right to a minimum wage. The strike was particularly serious in South Wales, where syndicalist influences were at their strongest. In 1910, Winston Churchill as home secretary was accused by the miners of ordering the shooting of strikers. The accusation followed an incident at Tonypandy in November, when a violent clash between strikers and the local police led the chief constable to appeal for troop reinforcements to be sent to help control the situation. Churchill did send an army detachment, as he did to other trouble spots, but he did not issue specific orders that soldiers should use their weapons. Critics, however, found this a weak defence, since the very fact that they were armed troops meant there was always a high probability of their using their weapons. Why else would they be armed?

Interestingly, the initial attack on Churchill came from the Conservative newspapers which accused him of being too conciliatory towards the strikers. *The Times* went furthest by suggesting that he had responded too slowly to the chief constable's appeal for troops to be sent. It declared that if any lives were lost, 'the responsibility will lie with the Home Secretary'. In a Commons statement in late November, after the event, Churchill explained why he had been slow to send in the troops. 'It must be an object of public policy to avoid collisions between troops and people engaged in industrial disputes.' The House seemed willing to accept Churchill's defence of his belated response to the Tonypandy troubles. It was at this point that Keir Hardie, the Labour spokesman, put a different twist on the story by referring to the 'impropriety' of dispatching troops in the first place. It was Keir Hardie's contribution that became the basis of all subsequent censures of Churchill's conduct. Martin Gilbert, the major biographer of Churchill, suggested (1991): 'It was this [Keir Hardie's] charge, not the original Conservative criticism of lack of ruthlessness, which created the Labour myth that Churchill had been, not the conciliator withholding troops and offering arbitration, but the belligerent sending troops and seeking confrontation.'

Churchill was involved in another violent episode soon afterwards, when early in January 1911, he oversaw the ending of the **Sidney Street siege**. As home secretary, he insisted on going in person to the siege that followed the shooting of three policemen by anarchists, and giving advice and instruction to the police and troops who were dealing with it. He ordered thirteen-pounder field guns to be brought up. In the event, these were not used since the besieged killed themselves and set ablaze the building they had held.

For Asquith's government, the most disturbing feature of the striking miners was their call for sympathetic action throughout the whole industrial workforce. The threat grew larger in the summer of 1912, when three major unions – the dockers, the railwaymen and the seamen – went on strike. It was calculated that 40 million working days were lost through stoppages in 1912. Lloyd George, the chancellor of the exchequer and the government's chief negotiator, managed, however, to persuade the railway workers to end their strike in return for a wage increase and the recognition of their union rights by the employers.

The 'triple alliance' 1914

In a further move to appease the miners, the government introduced legislation appointing local district wage boards, which were responsible for fixing minimum wages in each region. The strike ended, but the tension remained. By 1914 the miners appeared to be coming together with the dockers and

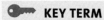

railwaymen, to form a 'triple alliance'. The alliance was unofficial and the three unions did not in fact act in unison. It was this lack of co-ordination among the unions rather than government conciliation that prevented the threat of a general strike materialising before 1914. Moreover, as with the suffragette and Ulster questions, the coming of the war in 1914 brought a temporary halt to the strife.

The challenge to traditional Liberal values

An interesting aspect of the industrial troubles was the willingness of the government to intervene directly in relations between employers and workers. It was another example of the extension of State power. It was a development that would soon be quickened by war and which would challenge the thinking of those remaining Liberals who still believed in minimum government and maximum individual liberty.

The Ulster crisis

In the nineteenth century there had been a strong movement for home rule among Irish nationalists. However, the demand for independence foundered on the position of Ulster, whose largely Protestant population were not prepared to accept an Irish settlement that gave southern Catholic Ireland a controlling hand over them (see page 8). Gladstone, the Liberal leader, had introduced Home Rule Bills in 1886 and 1893 but these had failed to pass through Parliament. His attempts had split his party and had hardened the resolve of the Unionists to reject home rule on the grounds that it undermined the unity of the United Kingdom and betrayed Ulster.

Hard economics also came into it. Ulster was the most industrially advanced region in Ireland. This made nationalists determined that the area should remain part of the nation should Ireland ever be granted independence. Clearly, Ulster Unionism and Irish Nationalism were incompatible.

The period following the failure of Gladstone's Home Bills had been one of relative calm in Ireland, but by 1905 the situation had become dangerous again. In that year a number of radical nationalist groups in Ireland had come together to form **Sinn Féin**, a political party which claimed that Ireland was a free nation temporarily enslaved by the British. It sought the creation of a *Dáil* (Parliament) to rule in the name of the Irish people. According to its chief spokesman, **Arthur Griffith**, Sinn Féin's aim was to break both the political and the economic stranglehold Britain had over Ireland.

Sinn Féin regarded the Irish Nationalist MPs at Westminster as far too moderate in their approach. For Sinn Féiners, home rule did not go far enough since it merely gave Ireland independence in domestic affairs; they wanted complete separation from Britain. This meant that there was constant conflict between the Irish Nationalist party and Sinn Féin. Yet it was the Nationalists who gained a rapid increase in influence in 1910 after the two general elections of that year

KEY TERM

Sinn Féin Gaelic for 'Ourselves Alone', the title adopted by the ultra-nationalist party, formed in 1905 and committed to freeing Ireland from its bondage to Britain.

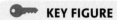

KEY FIGURE

Arthur Griffith (1871–1922)

An ardently anti-British socialist who claimed that there could be no Anglo-Irish peace until Ireland was wholly independent.

which left the Liberal government dependent on them for its parliamentary majority (see page 38). Such were the growing tensions in Ireland that Asquith's Liberal government turned again to home rule as the only solution.

In 1912, in a Commons evenly split between Liberals and Conservatives, the government relied on the 84 Irish Nationalists, led by **John Redmond**, to force through the Third Home Rule Bill. As was expected, the Lords refused to pass the Bill in 1913, but, since their power to veto measures passed by the Commons had been ended by the Parliament Act in 1911, the Bill was delayed by only a year before becoming law in September 1914 (see page 37).

The eventual passing of the Home Rule Bill did not fulfil Asquith's hope that it would ease the situation in Ireland. Quite the reverse; the Ulster Protestants reacted to the delay in its passing by swearing to the Covenant, a document pledging those who signed it to use 'all means which may be found necessary' to resist home rule for Ireland. The Covenanters claimed that the Liberal government had no electoral mandate for home rule. Led by **Edward Carson**, they prepared to fight to prevent what they regarded as the subjection of Protestant Ulster to the Catholic south. In 1913 they formed the **UVF**.

By the summer of 1914 Ireland had split into two armed camps, Carson's UVF confronting the **Irish Volunteers**, both engaged in gun-running to build up their stock of weapons. Civil war seemed imminent, a situation made worse by a remarkable development known as the Curragh Mutiny.

> ## Growing tensions over Ulster
>
> - 1905: Radical Nationalist groups amalgamated to form Sinn Féin.
> - 1910: General elections left Irish MPs holding the balance in Commons. Edward Carson elected chairman of the Ulster Unionist Party.
> - 1911: Parliament Act ended the Lords' absolute veto.
> - 1912: Commons passed the Third Home Rule Bill.
> - 1913: Lords rejected the Home Rule Bill. Ulster Volunteer Force formed by the Unionists. Irish Volunteers formed by the Nationalists.
> - 1914: The Curragh Mutiny. Britain entered First World War. Home rule suspended until the end of the war.

The Curragh Mutiny 1914

In the spring of 1914, 60 British Army officers, stationed at the Curragh army base in southern Ireland, resigned their commissions in order to avoid being sent north against the UVF. Technically this was not a mutiny since their resignations meant they were no longer in the army, but in the tense atmosphere the word was seized on by the press to show how dangerous the Irish crisis had become.

Constitutional conference 1914

Asquith managed to defuse the situation by calling a constitutional conference in June 1914. Reluctantly both sides agreed to consider a form of compromise. Ireland would be partitioned between the Catholic south, which would be granted home rule, and the Protestant north, which would remain part of the United Kingdom.

Conscious of how fragile the compromise was, Asquith persisted in trying to achieve a workable solution. He proposed an Amending Bill which would suspend the operation of home rule in Ulster for six years. This made some headway with the moderate Unionists, but it was the coming of the European war in August that made it acceptable as an interim measure. It was agreed that while the Home Rule Bill would technically become law in September, it would be suspended for the duration of the war. This was a respite, not a permanent settlement; Ireland was destined to undergo still greater turmoil (see page 85). But it allowed the Liberals and Conservatives at Westminster to suspend their differences for the time being.

Summary diagram: The pre-war domestic crises 1911–14

> **LORDS VERSUS COMMONS**
> Issues at stake
>
> • Conservative power monopoly in the Lords
> • Irish home rule

> **VOTES FOR WOMEN**
> Issues at stake
>
> • Liberal values
> • The parties' electoral support
> • Votes for working men

> **INDUSTRIAL STRIFE**
> Issues at stake
>
> • Union rights
> • Syndicalist threat to the State
> • The political levy

> **ULSTER**
> Issues at stake
>
> • Home rule
> • Ulster Volunteers vs Irish Volunteers
> • Character of island of Ireland

2 Britain's attitude to the 1914–18 war

▶ *What was the attitude in Britain towards its entry into the war in 1914?*

British response to the outbreak of war in 1914

When, in July 1914, war broke out between Austria and Germany on one side and Russia and France on the other, the great question facing Britain was whether it had any obligation to become involved. Oddly, Asquith's Liberal government had no precise answer to that question. A remarkable feature of British foreign policy before 1914 was that it had been regarded as the individual concern of the foreign secretary. Cabinet scrutiny was unsystematic and, except at times of crisis, seldom demanding. **Edward Grey** held the position of foreign secretary continuously from 1905. By nature a withdrawn man, he had chosen to act alone and in secret. Reluctant to be drawn into formal commitments, Grey tried to protect British interests by leaving the position deliberately vague. Foreign governments were known to complain that they could rarely be certain where Britain stood on international questions. It is true that Britain had entered into an *entente*, with France in 1904 and with Russia in 1907, but these were not formal alliances and no binding military agreements had been made.

The secrecy of Grey's diplomacy since 1905 and the uncertainty of Britain's diplomatic position resulted in considerable division within the cabinet over the question of entering the war. The Liberal Party, which had strong non-interventionist traditions in foreign policy, did not immediately incline to war. Its prevailing view was that since Britain had no formal commitments to either France or Russia, it would require a specific issue to tilt the balance in favour of war. That issue, Grey maintained, came in the form of Belgian neutrality. It was Germany's violation of that neutrality by sending its armies through Belgium in order to attack France that united the cabinet and the nation after their initial wavering.

Grey stressed that, although there was no 'obligation of treaty', the defence of Belgium gave Britain a great moral purpose which had 'animated the nation'. It is certainly true that it was the announcement of Germany's formal rejection of Britain's demand that Belgian independence be honoured that rallied government and Parliament in favour of war. Grey announced that 'to stand aside would mean the domination of Germany; the subordination of France and Russia; the isolation of Britain and ultimately that Germany would wield the whole power of the Continent.'

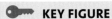

KEY FIGURE

Edward Grey (1862–1933)

MP 1885–1916; one of the longest serving foreign secretaries (1905–16) ever.

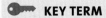

KEY TERM

Entente Not a formal or binding alliance, but an expression of mutual goodwill between states.

The people's attitude

A key factor that predisposed ordinary people to war was the naval race with Germany. Under the Liberals, defence expenditure in the period 1906–14 had risen from £35 million to £91 million. Much of this had been spent on building Dreadnoughts, the great battleships that represented British naval strength. The Admiralty's argument was that Germany's warship programme had to be met by an equivalent expansion of the Royal Navy. The service chiefs were convinced that Germany was intent on outstripping Britain's naval strength as a first step to waging an aggressive war. Their view informed popular attitudes in Britain. Winston Churchill expressed this succinctly when he said Britain's navy was a necessity whereas Germany's was a luxury.

An interesting insight into popular opinion was provided by Churchill's colleague, Lloyd George. After initial uncertainty about going to war, Lloyd George was convinced that the invasion of Belgium provided a 'heaven-sent' justification for taking up arms. He later said that what helped persuade him to support the declaration of war was the urgent clamour for war that he witnessed among the ordinary people as he drove through the crowded streets of London. Whatever may have been the responsibility of Grey and Asquith's government for Britain's entering the war, it cannot be claimed that the British people were dragged into the struggle against their will. This was evident in the huge rush of volunteers to fight once war had been declared; before conscription was introduced in 1916, over 3 million men had voluntarily enlisted.

Nevertheless, from the beginning there was a small but significant number of **conscientious objectors**. They faced social ostracism and condemnation from the majority of the public, and were liable to receive white feathers, sent as symbols of cowardice. Although officially tolerated, conscientious objectors had to go before an inquiry board, to prove they were sincere in their beliefs, and could be required to serve in a non-combative role. Some 16,000 men registered on these grounds.

The experience of the British soldier: the trenches

There was an expression frequently heard during the early days of the war that it would 'all be over by Christmas'. That expectation was to be cruelly shattered. The truth is that Britain was not prepared for war in 1914. That is to say, it was not prepared for the war which actually took place. Nobody foresaw in 1914 what was to come – that the struggle would last for over four years and would be on such a scale and of such an intensity that it would change for ever people's understanding of the nature of war.

In all major respects, the conflict on the Western Front was a simple affair; it was a **war of attrition**, a slogging match. The French and the British, and after 1917 the Americans, on one side, and the Germans on the other, were reduced to a strategy in which each tried to wear the other down. From the North Sea coast

 **KEY TERMS**

Conscientious objectors
Those who opposed war on moral or religious grounds and refused to fight.

War of attrition Wearing the enemy down by sheer persistence and willingness to suffer casualties.

to Switzerland there stretched two long lines of zig-zagging trenches, behind which each side amassed huge numbers of troops and vast amounts of artillery. In the belief that sheer firepower and weight of numbers would crush the enemy, large-scale infantry attacks were launched, preceded by a ferocious artillery bombardment, which was intended to wreck defences and break morale.

Yet, invariably what happened was that the bombardment, far from smashing the enemy defences, simply made the ground impassable. As the invading infantry, whose only armour was a tin helmet, tried to pick its way across the cratered surface of no-man's-land, the machine gunners would emerge from their deep trenches and with interlocking arcs of fire mow down the oncoming ranks. The lucky ones managed to crawl back to their lines. Too many, however, were either killed directly in the hail of machine-gun bullets or died from wounds and exposure in the shell holes into which they had scrambled for refuge. There were countless horrifying incidents of men, too weak to drag themselves out, drowning as water and liquid mud filled the shell holes. Attempts at rescue were seldom made. Early in the war it was soon realised that such efforts simply produced more deaths among the would-be saviours.

The character of the war for the ordinary soldier was graphically captured by a veteran when later recalling his experience.

Size of the British army (to nearest 100,000)

Aug. 1914	734,000
Dec. 1914	1,187,000
Nov. 1918	5,900,000 (amounting to nearly 15% of the UK population)

? What evidence is there in Source D to suggest that this is a description by a sensitive officer?

SOURCE D

From a description of trench life in 1917 by a front-line officer, quoted in Vyvyen Brendon, *The First World War 1914–18*, Hodder & Stoughton, 1985, p. 41.

Imagine a man being in those trenches a week, where he couldn't wash. He got a petrol tin of tea given him, but when you get a hot substance in, you got petrol oozing from the tin. But they had to drink it because it was the only hot drink they had. And that of course gave the men violent diarrhoea. The conditions were terrible. You can imagine the agony of a fellow standing for twenty four hours sometimes to his waist in mud, trying with a couple of bully beef tins to get water out of a shell hole that had been converted to a trench. And he had to stay there all day and all night for about six days.

KEY FIGURES

Wilfred Owen (1893–1918)

Served as second lieutenant in the Manchester Regiment; killed one month before the war's end in 1918; often described as 'the voice of the lost generation'.

Siegfried Sassoon (1886–1967)

Decorated for bravery, 'Mad Jack', as he was known, survived the war to write poems and memoirs which vividly depicted the experience of life in the trenches.

Literary responses

The poetry of the First World War has had a strong and lasting influence on perceptions of war. The works of such gifted poets as **Wilfred Owen** and **Siegfried Sassoon** left a powerful and evocative image of 1914–18. Owen said that his poems were about war and the pity of war – 'the poetry lies in the pity'. A poignantly representative example is his sonnet 'Anthem for Doomed Youth'.

SOURCE E

'Anthem for Doomed Youth' by Wilfred Owen, 1917.

What passing-bells for these who die as cattle?
Only the monstrous anger of the guns.
Only the stuttering rifles' rapid rattle
Can patter out their hasty orisons.
No mockeries for them from prayers or bells,
Nor any voice of mourning save the choirs,—
The shrill, demented choirs of wailing shells;
And bugles calling for them from sad shires.

What candles may be held to speed them all?
Not in the hands of boys, but in their eyes
Shall shine the holy glimmers of good-byes.
The pallor of girls' brows shall be their pall;
Their flowers the tenderness of silent minds,
And each slow dusk a drawing-down of blinds.

One of Sassoon's poems illustrates the bitterness and irony he felt towards those running the war.

SOURCE F

From 'The General' by Siegfried Sassoon, 1918.

'Good morning; good morning!' the General said
When we met him last week on our way to the line.
Now the soldiers he smiled at are most of 'em dead,
And we're cursing his staff for incompetent swine.
'He's a cheery old card', grunted Harry to Jack
As they slogged up to Arras with rifle and pack
But he did for them both with his plan of attack.

> In what ways do the poems in Sources E and F capture the atmosphere of war on the Western Front?

However, modern historians now calculate that the works of such poets as Owen and Sassoon were not typical and that the great majority of war poets and writers took a much more positive approach. A count shows that of the 2225 published poets in the First World War the great majority did not share Owen's bleak vision. The emphasis in their work was on the adventure and excitement of the times and the heroism of the soldiers and the uplifting nature of their sacrifice. Most poets believed Britain was fighting a just cause. This was in accord with the prevailing view of the people. Allowing for the obvious exception of conscientious objectors, Britons in 1914–18, despite their being made only too aware of the tragedies of death and disfigurement, did not regard the war as futile.

A representative example of what has been called the 'patriot poetry' of 1914–18 is **Julien Grenfell's** poem (page 52).

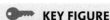 **KEY FIGURE**

Julien Grenfell (1888–1915)

A cavalry officer, fatally wounded at the Battle of Ypres, May 1915.

Why might the verse in Source G be regarded as an example of 'patriot poetry'?

SOURCE G

'Into Battle' by Julien Grenfell, 1915.

The naked earth is warm with spring,
And with green grass and bursting trees
Leans to the sun's gaze glorying,
And quivers in the sunny breeze;
And life is colour and warmth and light,
And a striving evermore for these;
And he is dead who will not fight;
And who dies fighting has increase.

The fighting man shall from the sun
Take warmth, and life from the glowing earth;
Speed with the light-foot winds to run,
And with the trees to newer birth;
And find, when fighting shall be done,
Great rest, and fullness after dearth.

The thundering line of battle stands,
And in the air death moans and sings;
But Day shall clasp him with strong hands,
And Night shall fold him in soft wings.

The reason why Owen's style of poetry came to dominate treatments of the First World War is that his doleful sentiments appealed to later, sceptical, anti-war generations. An example of this was 'Oh, What a Lovely War', a highly successful musical, first staged in 1963, which portrayed the war as a bloody and futile affair and mocked the generals who led it as uncaring dolts. This theme was taken up in *Blackadder Goes Forth*, a BBC television comedy which, in 1989, presented an undeniably amusing but distorted depiction of the officers and men who fought in the First World War. Critics of this line of interpretation suggest that such parodies, which have shaped modern popular perceptions of 1914–18, do a disservice to history since they take too little account of the range of reactions of ordinary soldiers, the bulk of whom did not have the pessimistic view of sensitive intellectuals like Owen and Sassoon.

Attitude of the Labour Party

Although the Labour Party was relatively small in 1914 there were serious divisions within it over the war. The basic question in August 1914 was whether the party should support the war at all. The majority of party members in the Commons and in the country decided to do so out of a genuine sense of patriotic duty. They were also worried on political grounds that if the party went against the tide of public opinion, which was overwhelmingly in favour of war, it might damage itself beyond recovery. This viewpoint was represented by **Arthur Henderson**, the effective leader of the Labour Party at the beginning of the war (although the party at this stage had not formally created the post of leader).

KEY FIGURE

Arthur Henderson (1863–1935)

Chairman of the Labour Party 1914–17; the first Labour Party member to hold a cabinet post, paymaster general 1916.

However, there were also strong pacifists in the party, such as **James Ramsay MacDonald**, who resigned his position as leader of the Labour MPs in the Commons in August 1914 and remained consistently opposed to the war throughout its duration. In addition, there was a vocal Marxist element on the left of the party who condemned the war as a capitalist conspiracy against the workers. It was this section of the party which became involved in such bodies as the **No-Conscription Fellowship** and which attempted regularly throughout the war to organise disruptive strikes in the war industries.

SOURCE H

From a speech by Ramsay MacDonald in the House of Commons, 3 August 1914.

I am convinced that this war is no people's war. It is a war that has been made by men in high places, by diplomatists working in secret, by bureaucrats who are out of touch with the peoples of the world. I want to make an appeal on behalf of the people, who are voiceless except in this House, that there should be a supreme effort made to save this terrible wreckage of human life, that we may not make further sacrifice upon the altar of the terrible bloodstained idol of the balance of power, but should be willing to make great sacrifices of patience in the sacred cause of peace.

Attitude of the Conservatives

From the outset the Conservatives, regarding themselves as the 'patriotic party', were totally supportive of a declaration of war. Indeed, it is arguable that it was the dedication of the Conservatives that pushed the Liberal government into action. There are a number of prominent British historians who argue that the Liberal government's decision to go to war was ultimately taken not for reasons of national honour but out of party-political calculation. Among the most provocative analysts is modern historian Niall Ferguson, who suggests (1999) that Asquith's government declared war for fear that, if it did not, it would be forced from office by the Conservatives, who were wholly committed to war. Ferguson believes that, after the bitter political battles over such issues as the 'people's budget', the House of Lords and Ulster (see page 45), the Liberals were not prepared to allow the Conservatives to outmanoeuvre them by presenting themselves as the patriotic party that truly represented the mood of the nation.

Ferguson claims that throughout the four-day crisis of 31 July to 3 August, during which Asquith's government considered whether it should go to war, 'one thing above all maintained cabinet unity: the fear of letting in the Conservative and Unionist opposition. After years of bellicose [warlike] criticism from the Tory press, this was the one thing calculated to harden Asquith's resolve.' Strength is given to Ferguson's case by a statement of Austen Chamberlain, a leading Conservative. Quoting a comment made in August 1914 by his half-brother, Neville Chamberlain, that the government's lack of decision had brought it 'within a hair's breadth of eternal disgrace', Austen described how confused and uncertain the Liberal government had been over the issue of war.

🔑 KEY FIGURE

James Ramsay MacDonald (1866–1937)
MP 1906–18 and 1922–37, Labour Party chairman 1911–14, Labour Party leader 1922–31, prime minister 1924 and 1929–35, leader of National Labour Party 1931–7.

In Source H, what is Ramsay MacDonald's justification for claiming that 'this war is no people's war'? ?

🔑 KEY TERM

No-Conscription Fellowship A body set up in 1914, devoted to resisting any attempt by the State to introduce measures obliging citizens to fight.

In Source I, what is Austen Chamberlain's complaint against the Liberal government?

SOURCE I

**Austen Chamberlain writing in December 1914, quoted in Niall Ferguson,
The Pity of War, Penguin, 1999, p. 165.**

*There had been nothing beforehand in official speeches or official publications
to make known to our people the danger that we ran to prepare for the
discharge of our responsibilities and for the defence of our interests. Those who
knew most were silent; those who undertook to instruct the mass of the public
were ignorant, and our democracy with its decisive voice on the conduct of
public affairs was left without guidance by those who could have directed it
properly, and was misled by those who constituted themselves its guides.*

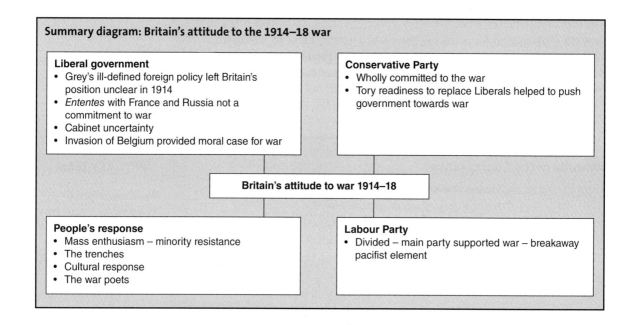

Summary diagram: Britain's attitude to the 1914–18 war

Liberal government
- Grey's ill-defined foreign policy left Britain's position unclear in 1914
- *Ententes* with France and Russia not a commitment to war
- Cabinet uncertainty
- Invasion of Belgium provided moral case for war

Conservative Party
- Wholly committed to the war
- Tory readiness to replace Liberals helped to push government towards war

Britain's attitude to war 1914–18

People's response
- Mass enthusiasm – minority resistance
- The trenches
- Cultural response
- The war poets

Labour Party
- Divided – main party supported war – breakaway pacifist element

3 The politics of war 1914–18

▶ *How did the war influence the development of British politics?*

The 1914–18 war had profound effects on British politics in general and the Liberal Party in particular. So protracted and so draining was the struggle of the **Allies** against the **Central Powers** that it became a **total war**, which necessitated an unprecedented extension of State authority. Notions of individual freedom and limited government meant little in the face of the State's claim to direct the lives of its people in the desperate struggle for survival. The demands of total war created a great challenge to Liberal values. The principles

> ## Wartime governments
>
> Aug. 1914–May 1915: Asquith's Liberal government.
> May 1915–Dec. 1916: Asquith's coalition government.
> Dec. 1916–Nov. 1918: Lloyd George's coalition government.

of personal freedom, peace and retrenchment were impossible to preserve uncompromised in wartime. The economic free-trade, non-interventionist notions which Liberals had held now seemed largely irrelevant.

Once the Liberals had accepted the necessity of going to war, they had to adjust their political values to it. The powerful anti-war feelings expressed at the time of the Boer War (see page 10) now had to give way to the spirit of patriotism necessary to sustain the war effort. Rationing, conscription and the extension of State authority in many areas of the economy were responses to the needs of waging total war. Survival was the prime objective.

The Liberal dilemma was expressed in the very first measure necessitated by the war. In August 1914, Parliament rushed through the Defence of the Realm Act (DORA), which granted the State and its agencies extensive powers over the lives of ordinary citizens. DORA was regularly re-enacted during the war. The following list shows the powers that it granted to the government:

- Control of arms factories.
- Censorship of the press and restriction of freedom of information.
- Controls on imports and exports.
- Control of the rail and coal industries.
- The Ministry of Munitions was set up to direct wartime industrial production.
- Trade unions were granted greater recognition and higher wages in return for their agreement to aid the war effort by not striking.
- Companies were required to accept restrictions on their profits and guarantee minimum wages to workers.
- To lessen social unrest, measures were introduced to improve living standards and control rents.
- Conscription was introduced, obliging males aged between 18 and 42 to serve in the armed forces.
- Food rationing was imposed.
- Restrictions were placed on the opening hours of public houses.
- Passports were required for travel abroad.
- Limitations were placed on freedom of movement within Britain.

The pacifist element among the Liberals had hoped that the chancellor of the exchequer, Lloyd George, who was famous for his vehement denunciation of the Boer War, might lead an anti-war faction in the party or even in the government. He soon disappointed them. It was true that he had entertained doubts about entering the war, but, once Britain was involved, his commitment to it was total.

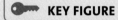
One remarkable feature was that the political truce, which the parties agreed to for the duration of the war, allowed Lloyd George to develop his ideas of **consensus politics**. He was an advocate of inter-party co-operation and from the beginning of the war strongly urged Asquith to consider broadening the basis of the government.

Lloyd George as wartime chancellor

The outbreak of war in August 1914 brought no immediate change in the structure of the government, but, as it became increasingly clear that the war was going to last much longer than originally thought, the pressure for change mounted. Asquith's calm demeanour and refusal to be panicked into rash action, attributes which had proved highly effective during the pre-war domestic crises, now suggested a lack of dynamism.

In contrast, Lloyd George's dynamic style seemed ideally suited to wartime needs. His two wartime budgets in 1914 and 1915 doubled income tax and greatly increased government expenditure. Gone was the restraint he had shown in pre-1914 budgets when he had tried to keep defence expenditure to a minimum. Lloyd George's wartime measures raised income tax from 6*d*. (2.5p) to 6*s*. (30p) in the pound and introduced super-tax on annual incomes over £2500. Alcohol and tobacco were taxed and Lloyd George aroused much unpopularity by his introduction of licensing laws which severely restricted the opening hours of public houses. He sincerely believed that the drinking habits of the British workers lowered production and weakened the war effort. In a characteristic statement, which recalled the Welsh **temperance** background of his youth, he declared: 'This country is facing three enemies – Germany, Austria and drink – and the deadliest of these is drink!'

The Asquith coalition 1915–16

The implicit understanding among the political parties who had agreed to a political truce in 1914 was that Asquith's government would conduct the war in a way that was acceptable to them all. By May 1915, however, serious criticism had begun to be made of Asquith's performance as war leader. The strongest objections came from the Conservatives who, unlike the Labour and Irish parties, had never questioned the rightness of Britain's going to war. The **shell crisis** and the failure of the **Gallipoli campaign** were the main pretexts for the Conservative demand for a government shake-up. Asquith gave way before the pressure and accepted that the seriousness of the war situation necessitated the formation of a coalition government. **Andrew Bonar Law**, Arthur Balfour and Edward Carson were among the leading Conservatives and Unionists who received government posts. The Labour Party was represented by Arthur Henderson at the Board of Education.

From Lloyd George's point of view, the formation of the coalition was welcome in that it provided the opportunity to advance the principle of centrist politics.

From 1914, he had encouraged Asquith to use the truce agreed between the parties as a means of widening the political base of the government. Lloyd George acted as something of a political broker after 1914. It was he rather than Asquith whom Bonar Law approached in 1915 when considering the prospect of coalition. Lloyd George's pre-1914 record helped in this respect. At the time of the impasse over the Lords, he had unofficially discussed with the Conservatives the possibility of a coalition. Although this came to nothing at the time, it did indicate that he took the idea of inter-party dealings seriously.

Benefits for the Conservatives

The prospect of a coalition was especially attractive to Bonar Law, the Conservative leader. It offered his party a return to government office after ten frustratingly powerless years; this without the necessity of a general election which should have occurred in 1915, but which the Conservatives judged they had little hope of winning. In marked contrast to Conservative elation was the depression that the coalition created in many Liberals. They felt the party had compromised its principles by allowing the Conservatives back into office, albeit at first only in minor positions. Moreover, as some Liberals saw it, the coalition was really a face-saving exercise for Asquith, a way of hiding how badly the war effort was going under his uninspiring direction.

Lloyd George at the Ministry of Munitions

In the ministerial reshuffle that accompanied the formation of the coalition (see Table 2.2), Lloyd George moved from the Treasury to head the newly created Ministry of Munitions. He was able to make the ministry a model of what could be achieved when a government department was inspiringly led. His essential aim was to produce more shells, the lack of which was the chief reason for the mounting criticism of Asquith's handling of the war.

Lloyd George, ably served by his departmental officials and by a series of experts he drew from outside politics, had outstanding success in increasing the production of armaments. One particular statistic shows this:

- when the war began, the army possessed 1330 machine guns
- by the time it ended, it had 250,000.

Furthermore, by 1918, the supply of shells had begun to exceed demand. Lloyd George ascribed this success to the fact that the ministry was 'from first to last a business-man organisation'. His use of experts from the areas of industrial production and supply was a step towards his concept of a government of national efficiency, drawing from a pool of the best talents and subordinating party politics to the needs of the nation.

Table 2.2 Party composition of the coalition cabinet, May 1915

Liberals	Conservatives	Labour
27	10	1

Conscription

As 1915 wore on, it became clear the war was to be a long one, requiring vast resources in manpower. This meant that the existing system of voluntary enlistment would not be able to keep the army up to strength. Something approaching a national campaign, led principally by the Conservatives, had developed by the autumn; it demanded that in the hour of the nation's need able-bodied men should be compulsorily called up for military service.

Knowing how unacceptable this would be to many in his party, Asquith tried to avoid the issue by suggesting various alternatives short of conscription. But eventually he bowed to pressure and supported the **Military Service Act**, introduced in January 1916. A group of 50 Liberals voted against the Bill on the grounds that to oblige citizens to engage in warfare was an unprecedented invasion of individual freedom. The majority of Liberals shared this view but, nonetheless, voted for the Bill, believing that circumstances made it necessary. It was this acceptance of the argument from necessity that gravely damaged liberalism as a political philosophy.

Conscription caused dissension in the cabinet. Edward Grey and **Reginald McKenna** were among those who were strongly against it. Lloyd George, however, convinced that the war justified extraordinary measures in mobilising the nation, threatened to resign if it were not introduced. He also objected to the concession written into the Act that allowed exemption from war service for conscientious objectors (see page 49).

How far Lloyd George's authoritarianism stretched was shown later, when, disregarding Bonar Law's plea in 1918 that the Conscription Act should never be used 'as an agent in an industrial dispute', Lloyd George helped Churchill to break a strike among munitions workers in Leeds. Significantly, the strike had begun as a protest by workers at their being transferred against their wishes from one factory to another. Lloyd George had no compunction in threatening to send the strikers straight to the war front.

The success Lloyd George had as minister of munitions did not prevent his becoming increasingly depressed by the slow progress of the war on the Western Front, which had settled by 1915 into a confrontation between two massive sets of entrenched armies, neither being able to inflict a decisive defeat on the other. Lloyd George felt that the wrong strategy was being followed. He wanted diversionary campaigns to be mounted that would end the stalemate. This was why he had backed the Gallipoli campaign in 1915. However, the tragic failure of that venture gave weight to those army chiefs who asserted that the only way to defeat Germany was by the deployment of massive force on the Western Front; hence their demand for ever more manpower and resources.

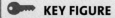

KEY TERM

Military Service Act
Imposed compulsory enlistment on single males between the ages of 18 and 41; by 1918, the age limit had been raised to 50 and the scheme extended to include married men.

KEY FIGURE

Reginald McKenna (1863–1943)
First lord of the admiralty 1908–11, home secretary 1911–15, chancellor of the exchequer 1915–16; a bitter opponent of conscription he left politics in 1918.

Lloyd George as war minister

Lloyd George grew so frustrated with the military leaders that he considered resigning from the government. What stopped him was a turn of fate that dramatically altered his own position and had a profound effect on the eventual outcome of the war. On 5 June 1916, Lord **Kitchener**, the war secretary, was drowned at sea after the ship on which he was travelling to Russia struck a mine off Scapa Flow in the Orkney Isles. The original plan had been for Lloyd George to accompany him on a morale-raising visit to Russia, but he had had to withdraw to attend to the crisis that followed the Easter Rising in Ireland (see page 85). This change of plan both saved Lloyd George's life and led to his taking the post that Kitchener had held.

Lloyd George became war minister only five days after the launching by the British of the **Somme offensive**, the most costly single campaign ever fought by a British Army in any war. When it became evident that the Somme was a deadly strategic miscalculation, Lloyd George turned bitterly against General **Haig**, whom he held principally responsible for the carnage, since he had advocated and planned the offensive. From the autumn of 1916 Lloyd George was at loggerheads with the military. He came to believe that it was the incompetence of the generals that was limiting Britain's success in the war. He could not accept that they were planning adequately or using their resources effectively.

The creation of the Lloyd George coalition 1916

Lloyd George's exasperation with the military soon expanded into the conviction that what was needed was a much more committed political leadership. He proposed, therefore, the setting up of a three-man war council with himself as its chairman. This was not simple arrogance. He considered that his achievements at munitions and as war minister indicated that he, more than any other civilian politician, both understood and represented the expectations of the nation. He claimed that he knew the people and the people knew him. He seems also to have genuinely believed that Asquith's duties as prime minister were so heavy that it was unreasonable to expect him to be able to dedicate himself solely to the task of running the war.

Unsurprisingly, the Conservatives keenly supported Lloyd George's initiative. They had never been fully content with Asquith as war leader, even after the formation of the coalition in May 1915. Bonar Law and Edward Carson let Lloyd George know that they were prepared to back him against Asquith. A series of complicated manoeuvres followed in the autumn of 1916. The key question was whether Asquith would be willing to allow the proposed war council to function without him. In the end, judging that this would be too great an infringement of his authority as prime minister, he insisted that he must be the head of the council. Lloyd George offered his resignation, whereupon the Conservatives informed Asquith that they were not willing to serve in a coalition government if Lloyd George was not a member.

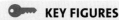

KEY FIGURES

Herbert Kitchener (1850–1916)

Iconic British military leader, he became war secretary in 1914. Foreseeing a protracted war, he used powerful propaganda to raise the largest volunteer army in British history.

Douglas Haig (1861–1928)

Commander-in-chief of the British armies in France 1915–18; a controversial historical figure; critics condemn his mass attack strategy as unimaginative and costly; defenders claimed that it was the only strategy available to him and eventually proved successful.

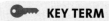

KEY TERM

Somme offensive On the first day of battle, 1 June 1916, Britain suffered 57,000 casualties; by the time the offensive had petered out four months later the figure had risen to 420,000.

What helped to tip the balance was that Lloyd George could count on his side all the major national newspapers. He numbered among his friends at least five of the leading editors or proprietors. This proved of obvious political value to him. In 1916 only the *Daily News* supported Asquith unreservedly. It was an article in *The Times,* asserting that the prime minister was 'unfit to be fully charged with the supreme direction of the war' that appears to have finally broken Asquith's resistance.

Importance of the leadership crisis

The crisis in December 1916 showed that Asquith had no natural allies. The willingness of the Labour Party to support him earlier had reflected a commitment to the war effort generally rather than to Asquith personally, while the Irish MPs had largely lost interest in English domestic politics following the Easter Rising (see page 85).

Herbert Henry Asquith

1852	Born into a middle-class family
1886	Became an MP
1892–5	Home secretary
1905–8	Chancellor of the exchequer
1908–16	Prime minister
1916–26	Leader of the official Liberal Party
1925	Became Earl of Oxford
1928	Died

Born into a comfortable rather than wealthy family, Asquith from an early age showed considerable academic ability, which he used to become a successful and prosperous barrister. He entered politics and quickly rose up the Liberal Party, serving as home secretary and chancellor of the exchequer, in the later role showing himself as a committed free trader.

As prime minister, his first major achievement was to lead a great reforming administration. Between 1908 and 1911, drawing on the particular talents of David Lloyd George and Winston Churchill, his government continued with a ground-breaking programme of social and economic reform. Although overshadowed in terms of personality by those two ministers, there is no doubt that Asquith was a guiding hand. Deprived by the 1910 elections of the large Commons majority the Liberals had enjoyed since 1906, Asquith's government between 1911 and 1914 faced serious industrial unrest and crises over Ireland, votes for women and the House of Lords. These problems were largely shelved after the government declared war on Germany in 1914, a declaration prompted, some said, not by a principled desire to defend Belgium but by a fear of the Conservatives taking over. Asquith proved an uninspiring leader of the wartime coalition he formed and in 1916 was ousted by Lloyd George. This caused a split in the Liberal ranks that in retrospect can be seen to have marked the end of the Liberals as a party of government. Asquith continued as official leader of the Liberal Party, but by the time of his death in 1928 it was in terminal decline.

Whatever the reason, Asquith's stubbornness or Lloyd George's disloyalty, the unhealed split between the two men was a major factor in the decay of Liberalism. Yet, in any balanced judgement of Asquith, his later political failures were more than outmatched by his earlier leadership of a government that laid the basis for the Welfare State.

More significantly for the future of the Liberal Party, 130 of the 272 Liberal MPs declared their readiness to follow Lloyd George. This created a split that would never be fully healed. Although Asquith ceased to be prime minister in 1916, he continued as party leader, refusing to serve in Lloyd George's cabinet; instead, he led the parliamentary opposition. This anomaly meant that in effect the Liberals were divided from 1916 onwards between the Asquithians, who claimed to be the official Liberal Party, and the followers of Lloyd George.

It is possible to view this as marking the final great divide between old-style and New Liberalism. Indeed, some historians have interpreted it as part of the class politics of the time, a challenge by the former outsiders in British politics against the existing political establishment. For example, the historian A.J.P. Taylor, writing in the 1960s, described it as 'a long-delayed revolt of the provinces against London's political and cultural dominance: a revolt on behalf of the factories and workshops where the war was being won'.

Lloyd George's opponents believed that it was a desire for personal power that led him to bring Asquith down. Modern scholarship, however, tends to view this as a myth. The reality was that Lloyd George was never in a strong enough position to plot Asquith's downfall. It was the refusal of the Conservatives to remain loyal to Asquith that made all the difference. By 1916, Lloyd George may well have been dissatisfied with Asquith's leadership, but he could not have removed Asquith simply by his own efforts; it was the Conservatives who were responsible for making it impossible for Asquith to continue. Asquith must also take some of the blame for his own downfall. Throughout the political crisis, he seemed blind to the larger issues involved. He tended to regard the behaviour of those who declined to support him as betrayal rather than a genuine attempt to improve Britain's war effort.

Lloyd George as wartime prime minister 1916–18

After 1918, Lloyd George was frequently referred to as 'the man who won the war'. No one person, of course, can win a modern war singly, but as a reference to the inspiration he brought to bear as prime minister it is not too great an exaggeration. His leadership was extraordinary.

At the time he took over as premier, late in 1916, British morale was at its lowest point in the war. The intense German U-boat (submarine) campaign early in 1917, sinking ships and interrupting supplies of food and raw materials, threatened to stretch Britain's resources beyond the limit. Lloyd George privately confided in April 1917 that if shipping losses continued at their current rate Britain would be starving within months. In some quarters there was talk of a compromise peace, and defeatism was in the air. But Lloyd George's refusal to contemplate anything other than total victory inspired his colleagues, reassured the waverers and put heart into the nation.

Continuing struggle with the military

Given Lloyd George's unrelenting determination, conflict between him and the military could only intensify. The generals objected to an interfering civilian politician deciding war strategy. For his part, Lloyd George would not accept that the generals were entitled to make their demands for huge numbers of men and vast amounts of material without being directly answerable to the government as to how they used them.

At the root of the conflict lay the question of who was ultimately responsible for running the war. This dispute has sometimes been portrayed as a struggle to decide whether Britain in wartime was to be governed by politicians or generals. There are writers who see Lloyd George as having saved Britain from becoming a military dictatorship, but only at the price of its becoming a political one.

This remains controversial. What can be said is that while Lloyd George never wavered in his resolution to carry on the war to complete victory, he was appalled by the scale of the slaughter. He believed that there had to be alternatives to the mass offensives which seemed the only strategy the generals were willing to consider. He spent a great deal of his time as prime minister trying to outwit the generals without, at the same time, weakening the war effort overall.

Part of Lloyd George's technique was to keep the army deliberately under-resourced while maintaining that his government was making every effort to meet the demands of the service chiefs. His hope was that this would force the generals to reconsider their unimaginative strategy of mass attack. His success in persuading the Admiralty in 1917 to adopt the **convoy system** as the main defence against the deadly U-boat attacks on the merchant ships showed what could be achieved militarily when new thinking was given a chance.

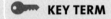

KEY TERM

Convoy system Merchant ships sailing in close groups, protected by a ring of accompanying warships.

Lloyd George's methods as prime minister

In keeping with his idea of consensus politics, one of Lloyd's George's first moves as prime minister was to increase the number of Conservatives in the government. Furthermore, Lloyd George chose to run the war by means of a small inner war cabinet that operated largely without reference to either the full cabinet or Parliament. Remarkably, he was the only Liberal in it.

Table 2.3 Party composition of the coalition government, December 1916

Liberals	Conservatives	Labour
12	44	2

Table 2.4 Party composition of the inner war cabinet, December 1916

Liberals	Conservatives	Labour
1	5	2

The figures in Tables 2.3 and 2.4 suggest a major decline in Liberal influence; Lloyd George had turned his government into a predominantly Conservative affair. This was to have very significant consequences for him and the parties.

Lloyd George's centralising style of government was evident in other prominent ways. To retain central direction and control of the new State agencies, a special cabinet secretariat was set up under **Maurice Hankey**. Still more significant was the adoption by Lloyd George of his own private secretariat, directly responsible to him as head of the war cabinet. Known as the **'Garden Suburb'**, this secretariat was made up of a group of advisers and experts in constant touch with the prime minister. Lloyd George justified its existence by his need to be in immediate day-to-day contact with the constantly changing war situation; it made possible the instant decision-making demanded by the war.

Sceptics detected a more dubious purpose. The workings of the secretariat appeared to them to detach government even further from parliamentary scrutiny. Lloyd George seldom attended Parliament between 1916 and 1918. By relying increasingly on outside experts rather than elected politicians, he appeared to be abandoning the traditional methods of parliamentary government. Critics suggested that he was turning the British premiership into an American-style presidency; some even went so far as to accuse him of adopting the methods of a dictator.

Challenge to Lloyd George 1918

Lloyd George's methods did not go unchallenged. In the summer of 1918, Asquith in a reversal of what had happened to him two years earlier, led an attack on Lloyd George's handling of the war. In May 1918, General Maurice, a former director of military operations, publicly accused Lloyd George of deliberately distorting the figures of troop strength in order to suggest that the British Army in France was stronger than it actually was. Maurice's aim was to prove that it was not the army leaders, but the government who were responsible for Britain's failure to win a decisive breakthrough on the Western Front.

Taking the side of the generals, Asquith used the accusation to justify introducing a Commons **vote of no-confidence** in the coalition government. Lloyd George bluffed his way out of the problem by claiming that the figures he had originally quoted had been provided by Maurice himself. This was a distortion, but Lloyd George defended himself so confidently that it was Asquith who appeared unconvincing. His performance in the debate fell far short of Lloyd George's. Asquith surrendered the initiative and the Commons voted 293 to 106 in favour of Lloyd George. The result left Asquith and his supporters looking like a group of disgruntled troublemakers who had irresponsibly sought to embarrass the government at a time of great national danger.

KEY FIGURE

Maurice Hankey (1877–1963)
Secretary to the Committee of Imperial Defence in 1912–38, secretary of the War Council 1914–16, cabinet secretary 1916–38.

KEY TERMS

'Garden Suburb' So-called because the secretariat was housed in a makeshift building in the gardens of 10 Downing Street, London.

Vote of no-confidence A standard parliamentary method for testing the strength of a government. If a government defeats such a vote, its security is confirmed; if the vote goes against it, its resignation invariably follows.

The importance of the Maurice debate was that it destroyed the chance of Liberal reunification. Asquith's attack on the government's policy may not have been personally motivated but it showed how wide the gap had grown between him and Lloyd George. It deepened the divide between the two factions in the Liberal Party and gave shape to politics for the next four years. Those who opposed Lloyd George in the debate were those who would stand as official Liberal Party candidates against him in the general election held in December 1918.

Representation of the People Act 1918

The divisions over the Maurice debate in May 1918 have tended to overshadow a major piece of legislation that became law a month later. The main terms of the Representation Act were:

- All males over the age of 21 were granted the vote.
- The vote was extended to women over 30.
- Servicemen over the age of nineteen were entitled to vote in the next election.
- Candidates were to deposit £150 in cash, which would be forfeit if they did not gain one-eighth of the total votes cast.
- Constituencies were to be made approximately equal in number of voters (around 70,000).
- The number of seats in the Commons was increased from 670 to 707 to accommodate the enlarged electorate.
- All voting was to take place on a designated single day.
- Conscientious objectors had their right to vote suspended for five years after the war.

Votes for women

To later audiences, one of the most interesting features of the reform was the extension of the vote to women. The clause in the Bill relating to women's voting rights was overwhelmingly accepted by the Commons on **a free vote**. Nearly all the ministers who had opposed it earlier now voted for it. In explaining his own change of heart, Asquith probably spoke for all those who now believed that the vital role women were playing in the war made the demand for 'votes for women' irresistible. 'Some years ago I ventured to use the expression, "Let the women work out their own salvation." Well, Sir, they have worked it out during this war.' In 1919, a Sex Disqualification (Removal) Act allowed women to stand for Parliament, enter most professions including the law, and serve on juries. The first woman to be elected as an MP was **Constance Markiewicz**.

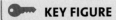

KEY TERM

Free vote Individual MPs allowed to vote without instructions from their party.

KEY FIGURE

Constance Markiewicz (1868–1927)

Daughter of an Irish landowner, and wife of a Polish aristocrat; she became a suffragette and a member of Sinn Féin. Although elected in 1918, she was one of the 73 Sinn Féiners who refused to take up their seats at Westminster.

'Coupon election', December 1918

The war finally came to an end in November 1918 when Germany, with no longer any realistic hope of defeating the Allies on the Western Front and exhausted and starving at home, agreed to an armistice, pending the imposition of Allied peace terms. At the war's end, Lloyd George and Bonar Law, the Conservative leader, agreed to continue their coalition into peacetime. A joint letter carrying both their signatures was sent to all those candidates who were willing to declare themselves supporters of the coalition. This written endorsement became known as 'the coupon', a reference to the ration coupons introduced during the war, and led to the election being known as the 'coupon election'.

Table 2.5 The 1918 general election

Party	Votes	Seats	Percentage of vote
Coalition Conservatives	3,504,198	335	32.6
Coalition Liberal	1,445,640	133	13.5
Coalition Labour	161,521	10	1.5
(Coalition total)	(5,121,259)	(478)	(47.6)
Labour	2,385,472	63	22.2
Asquith Liberals	1,298,808	28	12.1
Conservatives	370,375	23	3.4
Irish Nationalists	238,477	7	2.2
Sinn Féin	486,867	73	4.5

Judged purely as a piece of opportunism, the election was a remarkable success for Lloyd George and the coalitionists. However, in the light of later developments, which saw the Liberal Party decline into impotence, it can be argued that Lloyd George's decision to perpetuate the Liberal split by carrying the coalition into peacetime permanently destroyed any chance the Liberal Party had of reuniting and recovering. A leading modern scholar, Kenneth Morgan, describes the coupon election as 'the greatest of disasters for the Liberal Party and the greatest of tragedies for Lloyd George'. This modern estimation reinforces the view expressed in 1919 by Herbert Gladstone, the former Liberal chief whip, who wrote: 'The result of 1918 broke the party not only in the House of Commons but in the country. Masses of our best men passed away to Labour. Others gravitated to Conservatism or independence.'

Summary diagram: The politics of war 1914–18

Asquith's Liberal government, August 1914–May 1915
↓
Liberal values challenged by needs of war
↓
Defence of the Realm Act
↓
Lloyd George's wartime budgets

Asquith's coalition government, May 1915–December 1916
↓
Conservatives returned to share government
↓
Lloyd George's dynamism as munitions minister and war minister
↓
Conscription issue divided the Liberals
↓
Lloyd George and Conservatives combined to bring down Asquith

---

Lloyd George's coalition government, December 1916–November 1918
↓
The struggle with the military
↓
Lloyd George as inspirational war leader
↓
Lloyd George's centralising methods as prime minister
↓
The Maurice debate
↓
Electoral Reform Act
↓
The 'coupon election'

 # The political parties in wartime

▶ *How did the war change the character of the British political parties?*

By 1918, the war had affected all the parties individually in ways that were unforeseen when the war began.

The Liberal Party

By the end of the war an increase in State power had occurred that would have been unimaginable, let alone acceptable, in peacetime. Among the major extensions of State authority were:

- large areas of British industry brought under central control
- all public transport brought under government control
- military conscription imposed
- food rationing introduced
- controls imposed on profits, wages and working hours.

In 1917 alone, the worst year of the war for Britain, six new ministries came into being with separate responsibilities for:

- blockade
- food
- labour
- national service
- pensions
- shipping.

This growth in government power led to a major extension of State bureaucracy. The civil service, in terms of personnel and premises, underwent a rapid expansion. In the face of these developments, the traditional Liberal suspicion of bureaucracy was swept aside in the rush to adapt Britain's institutions to the needs of war.

Challenge to Liberal values

The measures were justified by reference to the struggle for national survival, but there were Liberals who protested. They saw the growth of State control as a challenge to the principle of individual liberty. They were usually the same protesters who had opposed the declaration of war; their voice, however, sounded faintly against the general clamour for war and for the reorganisation of society that the war effort demanded. Lloyd George declared: 'a perfectly democratic State has the right to commandeer every resource, every power, life, limb, wealth, and everything else for the interest of the State.'

Even those Liberals who had supported the war from the first were unhappy when faced with the fundamental changes that were being brought about by the war effort. Of necessity, British government during the war became illiberal. DORA, restrictions on free trade and the introduction of conscription were outstanding examples of a whole series of measures and regulations which Asquith's and Lloyd George's governments felt obliged to introduce. The Liberal State at war was very different from the Liberal State at peace.

Liberal decline

There is no doubt that the Liberal Party was greatly changed by its experience of war. To put it in negative terms, if the 1914–18 war had not intervened, Asquith might not have resigned, the Liberal social reform programme might have continued with Lloyd George as its main promoter, and the challenge to traditional Liberal values would not have become as demanding as it did.

The Liberals lost irrecoverable political ground because of the war. The existence of the **Union of Democratic Control**, representing the Liberals' anti-war tradition, was a constant reproach to the government. The Irish Nationalists felt betrayed by the government's policy towards Ireland. Asquith was heavily criticised for the British handling of the Easter Rising, as was Lloyd George for his use of irregular paramilitary police (see page 87). The Irish Catholic vote in England switched significantly to Labour, while in Ireland the Nationalists moved into Sinn Féin.

Most of the signs indicate that the Conservatives, still wounded after their defeat over the 'people's budget' and the House of Lords, would not have been able to oust the Liberals in the foreseeable future. Much of this, of course, is speculation. We cannot know what impact the Ulster question would have had on party strength and alignment had the war not led to the shelving of this issue, but it is highly improbable that the traumas and transformations experienced by the Liberals would have occurred without the pressure of the war years.

The impact of Lloyd George's premiership

As prime minister between 1916 and the end of the war, Lloyd George was necessarily preoccupied with ensuring the nation's survival in war. This diverted both him and the Liberals from the progressive policies they had followed before the war. Lloyd George's very success in persuading many of his colleagues to accept increasing State intervention had the effect of diluting his own Liberalism and detaching him from the radical element in his party. Conscious of this, he made a number of important moves towards reconstruction in the last year of the war. His aim was partly political in that he hoped to prevent the radicals from becoming too disgruntled over the slowing down of social reform. It was this that lay behind his 1918 election promise to make Britain 'a land fit for heroes to live in'. The idea took particular shape with the creation of the **Ministry of Reconstruction**. One of the most notable products of this was the Education Act of 1918.

Education Act 1918

The main terms of this measure were:

- raising of the school leaving age to fourteen
- the abolition of fees for elementary education
- the introduction of compulsory medical inspections of secondary school pupils
- authorising of local education authorities to set up nursery schools
- the creation of day-release colleges at which young people in work could continue their formal education one day a week
- restricting of the employment of children of school age.

The Act was largely the work of H.A.L. Fisher, a university vice-chancellor and one of the outside experts that Lloyd George had invited into government. It was a further step in the provision of State education as a universal, compulsory system.

Liberal reaction to the growth of the State

While a particular measure such as Fisher's Education Act could be seen as enlightened and progressive, many Liberals were left with the feeling that, overall, four years of war had undermined their most cherished values. By 1918, the principal causes that had defined pre-war Liberalism had been jettisoned or gravely compromised:

- Britain's entry into the war destroyed the image of the Liberals as a peace party.
- The economic regulation of the State by the wartime governments effectively marked the abandonment of free trade.
- Conscription undermined the concept of the freedom of choice of the individual.

The main problem for the Liberals was that, although the majority of them came to accept that the war was justified and, therefore, had to be fought to the utmost, it was hard to accommodate it easily within the Liberal programme as developed since 1906. After struggling to establish the primacy of welfare issues, the Liberals now found themselves diverted from social reform by the demands of war.

Equally distressing for many Liberals was the thought that, having overcome the reactionary opposition of the Conservatives and Unionists on a whole range of issues before 1914, they now had to witness their leaders sharing government with the Conservatives. All this tended to take the heart out of Liberal Party activists at grass-roots level. Liberal morale sank.

The importance of personality

An issue that commands attention is one of personality. Parties are not only about principles; they are also about people. The roles of Asquith and Lloyd George were critical. Asquith's continuing resentment at what he regarded as Lloyd George's disloyalty in 1916 meant that a genuine ***rapprochement*** between the two was impossible. The fracturing of the Liberal Party left Lloyd George dependent on the support of Bonar Law and the Conservatives. Whether this amounted to his being the 'prisoner of the Conservatives' is another of the lively debates among historians. It has to be said that many Conservatives at the time did not regard Lloyd George as a prisoner; on the contrary, they saw their party being dragged along behind this maverick and dangerous ex-Liberal leader.

The Labour Party in wartime

The reward for mainline Labour's support of the war came with the inclusion of Labour ministers in the coalition governments that were formed under Asquith in 1915 and Lloyd George in 1916 (see page 62).

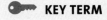 **KEY TERM**

Rapprochement A French expression for the resumption of working relations.

However, a curious incident was to lead to the end of Labour's wartime co-operation with Lloyd George.

Stockholm conference, July 1917

In July 1917, a meeting was called in Stockholm, the capital of neutral Sweden, by the socialist parties of all the countries still fighting the war. The aim of the gathering was to consider ways of bringing about a negotiated peace. The cue for this had come from the new Russian government set up after the **February Revolution**, which had proposed that a peace settlement should be considered on the basis of all sides abandoning the demand for **war indemnities**. For obvious reasons, all this was regarded by the governments of the combatant countries as undermining the war effort.

Lloyd George had first agreed that Arthur Henderson, who had earlier gone to Russia on an official government visit, could attend. However, when the French, who wanted heavy post-war penalties to be imposed on Germany, complained, he backtracked and withdrew his permission. Henderson promptly resigned from the cabinet.

In the event, this worked to Labour's advantage. Now that Henderson was no longer a minister, he was able to put his energies into improving his party's organisation and shaping its proposals for both the peace settlement and the domestic policies that Britain should follow after the war was over. This helped to lessen the differences within the Labour Party and give it a more responsible image in the country at large. This contrasted favourably with the divided Liberals and a Conservative Party that appeared willing for the sake of being in government to subordinate itself to Lloyd George. There was a sense in which the Labour Party came out of the war far less damaged politically than either of its two rivals.

The Labour Party constitution 1918

A critical result of Henderson's efforts at restructuring the party was the adoption in February 1918 of a Labour Party constitution. Before then, it had not put its various principles and aims into a clearly stated programme. The constitution was an attempt to define the party for the twentieth century. It was largely the work of Henderson and Ramsay MacDonald and drew heavily on Fabian ideas (see page 29). Its key features were:

- The party was to be composed of the affiliated trade unions, socialist societies, co-operative societies, trade councils and local Labour parties.
- The party was to be managed by a party executive of 23 members elected at the annual party conference.
- The annual conference would vote on the policies to be followed.
- The means of production, distribution and exchange were to be taken into common ownership, that is nationalised (Clause IV).

KEY TERMS

February Revolution
In February 1917 the Russian tsar, Nicholas II, had abdicated and been replaced by a Provisional Government.

War indemnities
Reparations paid by the losing side for the cost of the war.

- A commitment to the taxing and redistribution of surplus wealth.
- Co-operation with the trade unions in the formation of policy.
- Block voting to be allowed (for example, affiliated trade union delegates would be entitled to cast the total votes of all their members).

Throughout the following decades there would be continued debate and disagreement among party members about the constitution's strengths and limitations, but at the time it helped to give the Labour Party a sense of permanence and stability. It emboldened the Labour members in Lloyd George's coalition to break free of him; as soon as the armistice had been announced in November 1918, all the leading Labour ministers resigned, thus reclaiming their political independence. It was a remarkable move for a parliamentary party little more than a decade old and hinted at the confidence that Labour's brief experience of government had brought it.

The impact of electoral reform

An equally important factor in improving the status of the Labour Party was the electoral reform introduced in the last year of the war. The 1918 Representation of the People Act swelled the number of voters from some 7 million to around 21 million. This trebling of the electorate had momentous political consequences. Not all the newly enfranchised working class voted Labour in the 1918 election; nonetheless, the Labour Party's share of the vote rose proportionally with the increase in the electorate from seven per cent to 22 per cent and its number of MPs increased from 42 to 60. The interwar trend towards the replacement of the Liberal Party by Labour as the second largest single party had been established (see page 97).

Conservative gains from the war period

The coalition governments which Asquith and then Lloyd George formed involved a governmental restructuring that resulted in Conservatives taking key executive posts in the inner cabinet. The Conservatives thus found themselves in positions of authority for the first time since 1905.

In addition to becoming the majority in Lloyd George's coalition, the Conservatives derived a number of other unplanned gains from the war period. The marked increase in the size of the electorate that followed the 1918 parliamentary reform certainly helped the Labour Party, but not exclusively so. Not all working-class voters supported the Labour Party. Indeed, in the 1918 'coupon election', approximately a third of working class voters in practice opted for a party other than Labour. A similar proportion of trade unionists did the same. One reason for this was the Conservatives' wholehearted and consistent support for the war. The Conservative Party was always less compromised by the war than either the Liberals or the Labour Party. It had never had any doubts about the correctness of Britain's entry into the conflict or the need to continue fighting. This won it substantial support among servicemen and their families in the 1918 election.

Electoral changes

There was the further factor that, as the electorate grew in size, constituencies had to be reshaped to accommodate this. How the Conservatives benefited from this is neatly summed up by Stuart Ball, a modern expert on the history of the Conservative Party: 'Conservative seats in the Home Counties with expanding populations were sub-divided to form several new constituencies, whilst many Liberal seats with small electorates in the West, the North and in Scotland disappeared.'

Conservative adaptation

These electoral benefits were in a sense accidents; the luck had fallen to the Conservatives. But there were other advances which they could be said to have earned for themselves. They gained, for example, from their willingness to learn the social lessons that the war had provided. This applied particularly to the Conservative officer class, who by tradition came from a privileged background. Their experience in mixing with the men they led and lived with in the hazardous conditions of war often had the effect of breaking down their prejudices. Certainly, young Conservatives like Harold Macmillan came back from the trenches with a respect for the serving men that easily transformed into a wish to make the world a better place for them and their families in peacetime. Such an attitude was to help modernise the Conservative Party in its thinking and make it adaptable to the democratic politics of the twentieth century.

The new-found confidence among the Conservatives showed itself in the eagerness with which the party went about reorganising itself as an electoral force. In marked contrast to the depression and faintheartedness with which the Liberals approached the 1918 election (see page 65), the Conservatives began to streamline their local constituency branches with a view to getting their supporters out in strength at elections. It was a sign that the Conservatives were coming to the realisation that politics was no longer a matter of relying on their traditional support. Their task now was to win over the new electorate.

Summary diagram: The political parties in wartime

Liberals

Damaged by:

↓

The extension of State power an affront to Liberal values

↓

The impact of Lloyd George's premiership

↓

Effects of electoral reform

↓

Loss of active support at grass-roots level

↓

Personal dispute between leaders

Labour

Initial divisions between pro-war and peace elements in the party

↓

But party gained from inclusion in Asquith and Lloyd George coalitions

↓

Breach with Lloyd George strengthened the party's moral status

↓

Adoption of a constitution added to party's political stability and acceptability

↓

1918 electoral reform helped treble its popular support

Conservatives

Gained from:

↓

Inclusion in Asquith and Lloyd George governments

↓

Consistent support for the war won the patriotic vote

↓

1918 electoral reform benefited the party

↓

War experience of young Conservative candidates broadened the party's understanding of society

↓

Attention paid to party organisation and fund raising

5 The Home Front 1914–18

▶ *What impact did the war have on British society?*

So vital was the part played by the civilian population in the war effort that it is arguable that the outcome of the First World War was decided as much on the domestic front as on the military one.

The civilian role

The efforts of the armies on the Western Front would have counted for little had they not been backed by a working population capable of sustaining the industrial output that the war demanded. This was an aspect of total war; everybody was a participant. There was a particular sense in which ordinary people were directly involved in the struggle. The huge number of volunteers and conscripts who entered the armed forces meant there was hardly a family in Britain not directly affected by the war. Deaths and casualties at the front brought bereavement and grief into all but a few British homes.

Table 2.6 UK troop casualty figures 1914–18

Total number of troops	Killed	Wounded
5,700,000	702,000	1,670,000

To this figure could be added the number of civilian deaths. Zeppelin airships and aircraft raids on Britain during the course of the war accounted for over 1500 civilian fatalities. When the results of the war are examined it is natural that the death and casualty lists overshadow all other considerations. One in every eight soldiers died and one in four was injured. Yet there were certain aspects which historians now see as positive. When the war first broke out in 1914, there was fear that the disruption it would bring would cause severe distress to the mass of the working population. Yet, as it happened, the war brought a number of advantages to some of the working-class population. This was largely because the war created a huge demand for extra industrial workers. The trade unions gained greatly from this since it increased their bargaining power; so essential were industrial workers to the war effort that their co-operation was vital. The most striking example of this was the Treasury Agreement of 1915.

Treasury Agreement, March 1915

Lloyd George, as chancellor of the exchequer, used his negotiating skills to thrash out with the TUC what proved to be one of the most important social contracts of the war. This was a settlement that enlisted the trade unions as an essential component in the war effort. In return for accepting non-strike agreements and **'dilution'**, the unions were guaranteed improved wages and conditions. The real significance of the Treasury Agreement lay not in its details but in its recognition of the trade unions as essential partners in the war effort. They were now participants in the running of the State; they could no longer be regarded as outsiders. Lloyd George aptly referred to the Treasury Agreement as 'the great charter for labour'.

Conscription

One of the unexpected consequences of the introduction of conscription in 1916 (see page 58) was the boost in status it gave to many industrial workers. There had been estimates that some 650,000 'slackers' would be netted by conscription.

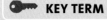

KEY TERM

'Dilution' The employment of unskilled workers in jobs previously restricted to skilled workers.

But in fact the imposition of compulsory military service saw an initial drop in the number of men enlisted. This was because of the need to exempt workers in reserved occupations. Men working in jobs that were considered vital to the war effort, mining and munitions being key examples, were not to be called up. The result was that 748,587 exemptions were added to the million and a half already **starred workers**. In the early months following the start of conscription the average weekly enlistment fell to 10,000, only half the figure it had been under the voluntary system.

The shortfall in enlistments was eventually made up by raising the upper age limit from 41 to 50 and by including married men. Aside from the military considerations, what exemption from the call-up highlighted was how dependent Britain was on its workers for its survival. The nation's heroes were not confined to the battlefield. Nor were its heroines.

KEY TERM

Starred workers From 1914, volunteers who were already doing vital war work had a star put against their name and were exempted from military service.

The role of women

The banners carried down London's Whitehall, in July 1915, in the last suffragette demonstration did not demand votes for women. Instead, they read, 'We demand the right to serve'. In many respects, their wish was granted. A huge number of women entered the workforce during the course of the war. The following figures indicate the scale.

Direct war work

- 100,000 women joined auxiliary (non-combative) units of the armed services.
- 100,000 became military nurses in such units as the First Aid Nursing Yeomanry (the FANYs).

Other work

- 200,000 women worked in government departments.
- 500,000 did clerical work in the private sector.
- 250,000 became land workers.
- 50,000 women worked in public transport as tram and bus conductors and drivers.
- 800,000 females were employed in engineering workshops.

To these figures should be added the many thousands who worked on a voluntary, unpaid basis in hospitals, canteens and welfare centres.

Between 1914 and 1918, 4.9 million workers left their jobs to join the armed services. The gap this created in the workforce was filled in the following ways:

- natural increase in population of young people of working age – 650,000
- delayed retirement of existing workers – 290,000
- foreign workers – 100,000
- wounded men who did not return to active service – 700,000
- through overtime and longer hours the equivalent of – 1,000,000
- women workers taken on – 1,700,000.

SOURCE J

? How did the work of the FANYs help to advance the status of women?

Three drivers of the First Aid Nursing Yeomanry in 1917.

The women who entered the factories to replace the enlisted men became an indispensable part of British industry. Without them, the output of the munitions factories, on which the war effort depended, could not have been maintained. Yet the large influx of women into the factories created a particular problem for the trade unions. Few of the female workers were members of a union. Not unnaturally, the women felt entitled to the same level of pay as had been received by the men they replaced. However, the unions were reluctant to press for this. Since most women were classed as unskilled, union officials worried that if their claims were pushed it would weaken the claims of men for higher wages. The broad result was that although workers' pay certainly rose during the war, women did not share proportionally in this. The principle of equal pay was still many decades away.

It is clear that women had made an unprecedented contribution as workers to the war effort and that their status and reputation were greatly enhanced in consequence. However, historians are wary of seeing this as a permanent social advance since, once the war was over, the great majority of women gave up their jobs to the returning male workers. It is true that female shorthand typists had come to stay; they largely took over from the ink-stained male clerks who had been such a feature of nineteenth-century offices. However, it was a different story in the factories. The rush of women into the factories in wartime proved a blip on the graph. As Table 2.7 shows, by 1920 the proportion of women in the industrial workforce was little higher than it had been before the war.

Table 2.7 Percentage of women to men in the workforce 1914–20

Date	Industry (%)	Transport (%)	Agriculture (%)	Commerce (%)	All workers (%)
July 1914	26	2	9	27	24
July 1918	35	12	14	53	37
July 1920	27	4	10	40	28

Nevertheless, in more subtle ways women had made advances that they were not subsequently to give up. Their clothing and hairstyles became more practical. It was not so much that hemlines were raised (that would not happen until the 1920s) as that dresses became lighter and more adapted to the needs of regular physical movement that work demanded. The need for women to travel between home and work on a daily basis, or live away from home altogether, produced a sense of independence. This was sometimes expressed by women going into public houses on their own, something which only those regarded as 'floozies' had dared to do before the war.

The trade unions

Between 1914 and 1918 trade union membership rose from 4 million to 6 million. The stronger position of the unions resulted in higher wages and improved working conditions for workers. Yet this did not mean peace on the industrial front. Having declined during the first two years of the war, strike action increased during the last two (see Table 2.8). This was evidence of a powerful feeling among workers that the burden of winning the war was falling disproportionately on them. They were the class that was having to make the greatest sacrifice, and they doubted that the government, despite the many public tributes it paid them, fully understood this.

Table 2.8 Industrial strikes 1913–19

Year	Working days lost	Number of strikes	Number of strikers
1913	9,804,000	1459	664,000
1914	9,878,000	972	447,000
1915	2,953,000	672	448,000
1916	2,446,000	532	276,000
1917	5,647,000	730	872,000
1918	5,875,000	1165	1,116,000
1919	34,969,000	1352	2,591,000

The wartime economy

Four years of war altered Britain's economy in a number of key areas.

Government spending and borrowing

By the end of the war, spending by the government amounted to 62 per cent of **GNP**. The remarkable change this represented can be understood by noting that in 1813, at the height of the Napoleonic Wars, British government spending amounted to only seven per cent of GNP:

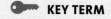

KEY TERM

GNP Gross national product. The annual total value of goods produced and services provided by Britain at home and in trade with other countries.

- The government raised the capital needed by borrowing from banks at home and in North America. About two-thirds came from such loans. The remaining third was raised from increased taxation.
- This resulted in income tax being quadrupled between 1914 and 1918.
- Overall, government borrowing increased the **national debt** from £650 million to £8000 million. At the end of the 1914–18 war Britain owed so much that a quarter of the revenue raised by the government had to be spent on paying the interest charges (£325 million) on the national debt.

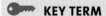 **KEY TERM**

National debt The total amount owed by the government to its domestic and international creditors.

The staple industries

Measured by output, the war years were a period of growth for British industry as production expanded to meet the huge demand for goods and materials. But it was an unnatural growth that hid an underlying downward trend. The fact was that Britain's staple industries were in long-term decline. For many decades British industry had been seriously weakened by foreign competition, notably from Germany and the USA (see page 5). It had been handicapped by its own inability to adapt to new trends; the failure to introduce up-to-date machinery and the reluctance to modernise traditional work practices were examples of this. Industry had also failed to reinvest or attract new investment. This meant that it lacked the capital to buy new machines or develop modern production techniques.

For Britain, the war created a damaging trend in the countries which before 1914 had been major purchasers of British goods. Wartime blockade had obliged many of these countries to produce for themselves since they could no longer import supplies. They developed their own manufacturing industries and simply stopped buying from Britain. Having been forced to become self-sufficient, these countries after 1918 protected their gains by tariffs and trade embargoes.

Britain's staple industries (see page 4) found it difficult to adjust sufficiently to meet this change in the economic world order. Old-fashioned production methods left British manufacturers with high overheads. This made them reluctant to drop their prices since this would cut their profits. The consequence was a lack of competitiveness and a fall in demand for British-made goods. The rest of the world no longer wanted the products of Britain's traditional manufacturing industries at the prices British manufacturers were now forced to set. What the First World War did, therefore, was to hasten a decline that had already begun.

End of free trade

Equally significant was the commercial disruption caused by the war. The economic blockades to which nearly all the warring countries resorted destroyed the normal international trading patterns and made it impossible for Britain to follow a free-trade policy. In an attempt to maintain vital imports, the government increasingly interfered in the operation of the ports and docks to impose restrictions on the flow of goods. Although free trade had not been destroyed as a theoretical principle, the government's involvement in the wartime running of the economy had seriously undermined it as a practical proposition. The right of government to a central place in the planning of economic affairs had been established as a precedent. How far that right should be exercised in peacetime was now the controversial question.

Culture

Culture is an area in which it is difficult to be precise about the effects of war, but the following developments deserve attention:

- *Religion*. In many ways the suffering and loss that the war brought intensified religious feeling. Military chaplains who accompanied the troops to the front reported that the men often took solace from the religious services that were held. There was a saying that 'there are no atheists in a fox hole', a reference to the phenomenon that when men are facing imminent death they tend to cling to the idea of a God.

  It was also observable at home that families fearing for their loved ones, husbands, sons and brothers, turned to religion for comfort. Attendance at church services markedly increased and there was a notable turning to spiritualism, the belief that the grieving could make contact with the departed.
- *Relations between the sexes*. The emancipation that war brought to many women was expressed in their easier relations with men. The rigid rules of etiquette broke down in the face of war's dangers. Some moralists complained that the new informality led to the abandonment of restraint, and pointed to the increase in illegitimate births as evidence of this.
- *Class shifts*. In a similar way, the greater contact between people that followed from military and industrial conscription resulted in their meeting those from other classes, whom they would not have come across in ordinary times.
- *Music*. The flowering of poetry in wartime is well known (see page 50). What is sometimes overlooked is the great resurgence in British music in the same period. The haunting works of the composer George Butterworth, who volunteered for service, take added poignancy from the fact that he died at the Battle of the Somme in 1916. Ralph Vaughan Williams, who, although over age, volunteered to serve as a stretcher bearer, composed some of his most elegiac music in response to his wartime experience. Sir Edgar Elgar is renowned for his stirring patriotic music, such as his 'Pomp and Circumstance' marches, used as a call to arms during the war. However, musicologists consider his later works to be a lamentation for the dead of the First World War, an outstanding example being his heart-rending cello concerto.

Summary diagram: The Home Front 1914–18

The impact of war casualties on ordinary families
↓
The Treasury Agreement, 1915, gave status to unions
↓
Conscription resulted in gains for the industrial workers

Status of women
↓
Indispensable to the war effort
↓
Failure to achieve equal pay
↓
Majority of women factory workers gave up their jobs at war's end
↓
Lift in social status, steps towards fuller emancipation
↓
Enfranchised in 1918

The trade unions not entirely co-operative – strikes continued in wartime

Economic impact of the First World War

Rise in government spending

60% of GNP spent on war

Large increase in national debt

War distorted international economy – weakened Britain's already declining staple industries

War stimulated cultural response

Chapter summary

Having struggled between 1911 and 1914 to contain the domestic crises that confronted it – the Lords–Commons conflict, suffragette protests, industrial strife and a divided Ireland – Asquith's government had to adjust itself to the great demands of war. The military conflict had the effect at home of splitting the Liberal Party; Asquith was ousted by Lloyd George, whose dynamic premiership was a major factor in Britain's ultimate victory in 1918. The four years of war profoundly influenced the political balance: the Conservative and Labour parties made major gains at the expense of the Liberals, who found it increasingly difficult to balance their traditional libertarian values with the growth of State power which the war effort required. Lloyd George's success as coalition prime minister in the 1918 election was a personal triumph but it broke his Liberal Party. Equally important changes occurred on the social and economic fronts; among the most significant of these were the advancement of women and the strengthening of the trade unions. The economy suffered, however. Britain's need to borrow heavily in wartime left it in debt while the commercial disruption of war accelerated the decline of the staple industries. Free trade was one of the casualties of war.

Refresher questions

Use these questions to remind yourself of the key material covered in this chapter.

1 On what grounds did the Lords resist the 'people's budget' and the Parliament Bill?

2 Why was female suffrage a politically difficult issue for all the parties?

3 Why did the years 1911–14 witness severe industrial strife?

4 Why was Ulster on the verge of civil war in 1914?

5 Why was a coalition formed in 1915?

6 Why was the overthrow of Asquith such a significant political development?

7 What special contribution did Lloyd George make to the war effort as prime minister?

8 In what ways did Lloyd George break from traditional parliamentary government?

9 What was the political importance of the 'coupon election'?

10 How did electoral reform in 1918 work to the disadvantage of the Liberals?

11 What did the Labour Party gain from the war years?

12 How had the war years worked to the benefit of the Conservative Party?

13 How was the position of women affected by the war?

14 How did the war affect the staple industries in Britain?

15 Did the 1914–18 war create a new economic situation or simply accelerate existing trends?

 Question practice

ESSAY QUESTIONS

1 'The industrial unrest in Britain between 1911 and 1914 was a grave threat to the Liberal government.' Explain why you agree or disagree with this view.

2 Assess the reasons why Lloyd George replaced Asquith as prime minister in 1916.

3 How successful was the Representation of the People Act 1918 in extending democratic rights?

4 How important was the role played by British women on the Home Front during the First World War?

SOURCE ANALYSIS QUESTIONS

1 With reference to Sources C (page 43) and H (page 53), and your understanding of the historical context, which of these two sources is more valuable in explaining the reaction of the British people to the First World War?

2 With reference to Sources C (page 43), D (page 50) and H (page 53), and your understanding of the historical context, assess the value of these sources to a historian studying the way the British people responded to the First World War.

3 Study the three Sources C (page 43), D (page 50), H (page 53), and then answer both questions. a) Use your knowledge of the Labour Party during the war to assess how useful Source H is as evidence of their attitude towards the First World War. b) Using these three sources in their historical context, assess how far they support the view that the mass of the British people supported the war effort.

CHAPTER 3

Post-war Britain 1918–29

When peace came in 1918, there were great hopes that Britain would reap the rewards of victory, but the post-war years proved troubled times. Lloyd George's coalition government was defeated in 1922 having been judged to have failed to meet the challenges facing Britain. There followed two years of undistinguished Conservative government. In 1924, a minority Labour Party found itself in office. But after less than a year, the Conservatives were back in power, a position they held until 1929. These developments are examined under the following headings:

★ The post-war coalition 1918–22

★ The conservative government 1922–4

★ Labour in office 1924

★ Baldwin's government 1924–9

The key debate on *page 112* of this chapter asks the question: What caused the 'The Strange Death of Liberal England'?

Key dates

1916	**April**	Easter Rising	1924	**Jan.**	Labour government formed under Ramsay MacDonald
1919	**June**	Versailles Treaty		**Oct.**	Zinoviev Letter
1921	**Dec.**	Irish Treaty	1924–9		Baldwin's Conservative government
1922	**Sept.**	Chanak crisis			
	Oct.	Lloyd George resigned	1925	**April**	UK returned to gold standard
	Nov.	Election returned Conservatives to power			Red Friday
			1926	**May**	General Strike
1923	**May**	Baldwin replaced Bonar Law as prime minister	1927	**May**	Trade Disputes Act
			1928	**April**	Reform Act granted full suffrage to women
	Nov.	Lloyd George rejoined Liberal Party	1929	**May**	General election

The post-war coalition 1918–22

▶ *What problems stood in the way of post-war reconstruction?*

Reconstruction

Reconstruction, which had begun during the war, was continued into the post-war period. A massive demobilisation programme, involving the return of over a million men to civilian life, was set in motion by Winston Churchill as war secretary. Ambitious proposals were drawn up for improved health facilities, unemployment, pay and pensions. However, the grim economic circumstances in post-war Britain, caused by high inflation and declining orders for British goods, largely thwarted these schemes, but there was some success in regard to housing.

Housing

A particular feature of Lloyd George's 1918 election campaign had been his repeated promise to provide homes fit for heroes. He was sincere in his desire to improve living conditions for ordinary people and entrusted the task to **Christopher Addison**, the minister of health. Addison was responsible for introducing in 1919 the first Housing and Town Planning Act. The aim of the measure in regard to housing was for the local governments to clear slums and to construct low-rent homes (referred to as council houses) specifically for the working class. In one respect the Act was a major success: by 1922, over 200,000 such houses had been built.

Yet, while there was no doubting Addison's enthusiasm, he had a limited understanding of the economics involved. Unlike the situation in wartime, when as Lloyd George's successor as minister for munitions he had had the power to direct the relevant industries, he had no control over the post-war building industry. His response was to spend as much government money as possible. This worked insofar as houses were built, but the cost was excessive. His ministry paid for houses at the rate of £910 per unit whereas the true building cost was only £385. The government was using public money to pay a huge subsidy to the building industry.

Faced with an outcry, Lloyd George had no option but to remove Addison and apologise in the Commons for the mess that his sacked minister had made. By 1922, government grants for new housing were withdrawn altogether. The scandal was that by that time the increase in population meant there was a shortage of over 800,000 homes among the poorer sections of the community.

Yet despite the embarrassment for the coalition government over its housing policy, an important social principle had been established. What Addison's Act had laid down was that housing was now, like education, considered a necessary public service which the local authorities were responsible for providing. Later

KEY FIGURE

Christopher Addison (1869–1951)

Liberal minister of munitions 1916–17, president of Local Government Board 1919, minister of health 1919–21.

measures illustrated that this was now a working principle of government (see pages 99 and 118).

National Insurance

A development for which Lloyd George was personally responsible was the extension of National Insurance. The Liberals' measure of 1911 had covered only 3 million workers (see page 26). During the war another million munitions workers had been added to this number. Between 1920 and 1921 Lloyd George extended the provisions to cover 8 million more workers, 12 million in all. The aim was to protect workers against short-term unemployment, which at a time of high demand for labour seemed the only cover that was likely to be necessary.

What neither Lloyd George nor anybody else could know at this time was that in a few years the problem would not be casual short-term unemployment but persistent long-term joblessness. It was this development that has tended to divert attention from the post-war coalition's considerable achievements in the area of social services.

Post-war industrial problems

Throughout the coalition years of 1918–22, Lloyd George continued with his aim of improving industrial relations. He maintained links with both employers and trade unions and encouraged them to think in terms of conciliation rather than confrontation. Unfortunately, these successes were overshadowed by the larger drama of the post-war breakdown in industrial relations. It was coal mining that attracted the greatest attention. Coal, once one of Britain's staple exports and the basis of the country's nineteenth-century industrial strength, was becoming increasingly difficult to mine profitably. Germany's wartime blockade of Britain and the general disruption of international commerce that war had brought had greatly reduced foreign orders, which were not renewed after 1918. In addition, even their most sympathetic supporters found it difficult to deny that the mine owners were out of touch with the real economic world. The mining unions demanded that the industry, which had been brought under government control during the war, should not be returned to the owners, but should be **renationalised**.

Lloyd George was unable to satisfy them on this; nor could he sanction government interference in order to meet the miners' wage demands. He was able, however, to use his negotiating skills to defuse the situation in 1921 when it appeared likely that the railwaymen and transport workers would join the miners in a **General Strike**. However, the embers of syndicalism had been fanned in the South Wales coal fields and the coalition had to face continuing unrest and disorder there and in the industrial areas of Britain that were suffering from the post-war **recession**, or slump as it was often described by contemporaries.

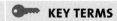 **KEY TERMS**

Renationalised Brought back into public ownership (in effect, government control).

General Strike All the unions affiliated to the TUC calling their members out on strike.

Recession A slowing down of economic growth, caused by a fall in demand for manufactures, followed by falling profits, lowered wages and job losses.

It was Britain's inability to cope with the effects of the worldwide industrial slump that undermined Lloyd George's promise that the workers of Britain would be well rewarded for their heroic wartime efforts. By 1922, unemployment had risen to over a million, inflation had leapt ahead of wage levels, and the existing social services were stretched beyond their capacity. Worse still, by 1922 the economic recession had become so bad that the government, rather than expand social welfare provision, had to cut back. The withdrawal of resources, known as the **'Geddes Axe'**, applied to education, hospitals and housing.

All governments tend to be judged primarily on their economic record. The evident failure of the social and economic policies of the coalition tended to dwarf its successes in other spheres. The mistakes seemed too many, suggesting that the problems of post-war Britain had proved too great for Lloyd George's government to cope with effectively. Even an apparent social-policy success, such as the Addison Act which resulted in 200,000 new homes, brought it little public approval, since the measure was thought not to go far enough and any real improvements were attributed to the Labour-controlled local councils, who were largely responsible for implementing the policy.

KEY TERM

'Geddes Axe' Named after Sir Eric Campbell-Geddes, chairman of the special government committee which recommended the spending cuts.

The Anglo-Irish question

In 1914, the Act granting home rule to Ireland had been suspended for the duration of the war (see page 47). It was, therefore, an issue with which Lloyd George's post-war coalition had to deal when peace came. But things had not stood still in Ireland after 1914. Another dramatic twist in the story had occurred in the form of the Easter Rising.

The Easter Rising 1916

The suspension of the Home Rule Act at the start of the war had not solved the Irish problem; it had only shelved it. This became very apparent in April 1916 when a breakaway group of Irish nationalists, led by **Patrick Pearse**, seized the General Post Office in Dublin and posted up a signed proclamation announcing the establishment of the Irish Republic. The rebels, as they were immediately dubbed by the British authorities, had hoped for two things: an invasion of Ireland by German forces and a nationwide rising by the Irish people. Neither took place.

After four days of desperate fighting, the republicans were overwhelmed by a British force and their ringleaders rounded up. Yet what had begun as an ill-organised, poorly supported and failed rising soon took on the proportions of a great modern Irish legend. This had less to do with the romantic self-sacrifice of the republicans than with the severity, as perceived by the Irish, with which they were then treated by the British. Fifteen of the most prominent participants in the rising, including the seven individuals who had signed the proclamation, were tried and shot. Seventy-five others were sentenced to life imprisonment. Many Irish people saw these punishments as a vicious overreaction on the part

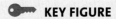

KEY FIGURE

Patrick Pearse (1879–1916)

Young idealistic, deeply patriotic Irish poet, a charismatic figure whose execution immediately turned him into a martyr in Irish eyes. On the night before he was shot, he wrote to his mother, 'This is the death I should have asked for if God had given me the choice of all deaths'.

of the British authorities. The rebels who had lost their lives became posthumous Irish heroes.

Anxious not to allow the failed rising and its aftermath to create further problems in Ireland, Asquith turned to Lloyd George to contain the situation. Lloyd George immediately entered into discussions with Redmond, the Irish Nationalist leader, and Carson, leader of the Ulster Unionists. His main object was to prevent the Irish problem from undermining the British war effort. He confided to Carson that he feared that in six months the war might well be lost. 'The Irish-American vote will go over to the German side. They will break our blockade and force an ignominious peace on us, unless something is done, even provisionally, to satisfy America.'

In his urgency to prevent this, Lloyd George was not above giving contradictory promises to both Redmond and Carson, which persuaded them to accept a compromise, referred to as the 'Heads of Agreement'. This granted immediate home rule for the 26 counties of southern Ireland while the six counties of Ulster remained part of the United Kingdom until after the war, when their permanent constitutional status would be decided by an imperial conference.

Lloyd George gave Redmond the impression that the separation of Ulster from the rest of Ireland was purely temporary; at the same time he reassured Carson that it would be permanent. Lloyd George's manoeuvring came to nothing for, when the Heads of Agreement was put to the coalition cabinet, the Unionist members refused to ratify it. They claimed Lloyd George had gone too far to appease the Irish Nationalists. The most stubborn opponent was **Lord Lansdowne**, who insisted that the agreement be modified so as to satisfy Unionist objections. When Redmond learned of this he broke off negotiations and the agreement became a dead letter.

Sinn Féin and the IRA

The failure of Redmond's moderate Irish MPs at Westminster to reach a settlement in their 1916 negotiations with the Unionists had put a powerful propaganda weapon into the hands of the extremists, who argued that force was the only way to achieve Irish independence. The parliamentary party began to lose ground to the more extreme Sinn Féin party, which had come to prominence in 1914. In 1917, led by **Éamon de Valera**, who had played a major role in the Easter Rising, Sinn Féin won two by-elections.

Matters became still more strained in 1918 when Lloyd George's coalition attempted to extend conscription to Ireland. Irish anger at this led to Sinn Féin's winning 73 seats in the 'coupon election', seats which it pointedly refused to take up at Westminster. Instead, in 1919 it defiantly set up its own *Dáil Éireann* (Irish parliament) in Dublin. In the same year Sinn Féin's military wing, the Irish Volunteers, reformed itself as the Irish Republican Army (IRA), dedicated to guerrilla war against the British forces.

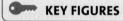

KEY FIGURES

Lord Lansdowne (1845–1927)

Foreign secretary 1900–5, Conservative leader in the House of Lords 1903–16.

Éamon de Valera (1882–1975)

Leader of Sinn Féin 1917–26, president of Ireland 1959–73; avoided execution after the Easter Rising by claiming American citizenship.

IRA activists became so disruptive that Lloyd George sanctioned the recruitment of a special irregular force, known as the **'Black and Tans'**, to deal with the situation. The tough methods used by this force soon led to their being hated by Irish nationalists, who accused Lloyd George of recruiting them from violent prisoners in British military gaols in order to terrorise the civilian population in Ireland. Indeed, Lloyd George was accused of applying the same methods in Ireland that twenty years earlier he had denounced as barbarous when used against the Boers (see page 12).

Moves towards a political settlement

When it became apparent that military force was not bringing peace to Ireland, Lloyd George's thoughts turned again to the idea of a constitutional settlement acceptable to both Nationalists and Unionists. After decades of bitterness over home rule, this would not be easy, but the atmosphere of the times encouraged change. The **Versailles Treaty** had enshrined the principle of national **self-determination**. Indeed, it was during the treaty negotiations that Lloyd George had led the British delegation in pressing for the principle to be accepted. It was inconsistent, therefore, for Britain to continue to deny self-determination to Ireland. There was also the undeniable fact that home rule had been law since 1914, even though it had yet to be implemented.

There were signs also that the Conservative Party was ceasing to be as rigidly attached to the Unionist cause as it had been before 1914. The Conservatives had grown weary of the strife in Ireland. Accordingly, in 1921 Lloyd George gathered together a team of negotiators that included the new Conservative leader, **Austen Chamberlain,** as well as **Lord Birkenhead**, previously one of the staunchest opponents of home rule. He then offered de Valera a truce and invited him and the other Irish leaders to London to discuss the drafting of a treaty of settlement.

When they arrived, Lloyd George shrewdly played on the idea that he represented the last hope of a just settlement for Ireland. He suggested that if they could not reach an acceptable agreement under his sympathetic leadership it might well be that he would have to resign, to be replaced by Bonar Law, whose unyielding resistance over home rule would destroy any chance of settlement. His argument persuaded them to accept the appointment of a boundary commission charged with the task of detaching Ulster from the rest of Ireland. What this acceptance meant was that Irish Nationalists had given ground on the critical issue; they had dropped their previous insistence that Ulster must be part of an independent Ireland.

With this as a bargaining factor, Lloyd George was able to convince the Unionists that the rights and independence of Ulster had been safeguarded. It was essentially the same position as had been reached in the 1916 negotiations, but on this occasion the Unionists did not scupper the talks. As Lloyd George had perceived in 1916, a settlement depended ultimately on Unionist acceptance.

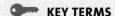

KEY TERMS

'Black and Tans'
An irregular British force specially created to contain the violence in Ireland; it was so-called from the colour of its outfits, which were made up from a job lot of police and military uniforms.

Versailles Treaty The post-war peace settlement drawn up by the major Allied victors, Britain, France, Italy and the USA; it redrew the map of Europe and sought to create the conditions for the future settlement of international crises.

Self-determination
The right of people to form a nation and government of their own choice.

KEY FIGURES

Austen Chamberlain (1863–1937)

Chancellor of the exchequer 1919–21, foreign secretary 1924–9; son of Joseph Chamberlain and half-brother of Neville Chamberlain.

Lord Birkenhead (1872–1930)

MP 1906–19, attorney general 1915–19, lord chancellor 1919–22.

In December 1921, after a long, complicated series of discussions, in which all Lloyd George's arts of diplomacy, if not duplicity, were exercised, the parties finally signed the Irish Treaty.

The Anglo-Irish Treaty 1921

The essential feature of the treaty was partition:

- southern Ireland was granted independence as the Irish Free State
- Ulster remained part of the United Kingdom.

In the event, the treaty split the Irish parties and a savage civil war broke out in Ireland, fought between the pro-treaty Nationalists, led by **Michael Collins**, and the anti-treaty Republicans, led by de Valera.

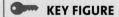

KEY FIGURE

Michael Collins (1890–1922)

A charismatic IRA military organiser, whose willingness to accept the 1921 treaty led to his assassination by anti-treaty republicans in 1922.

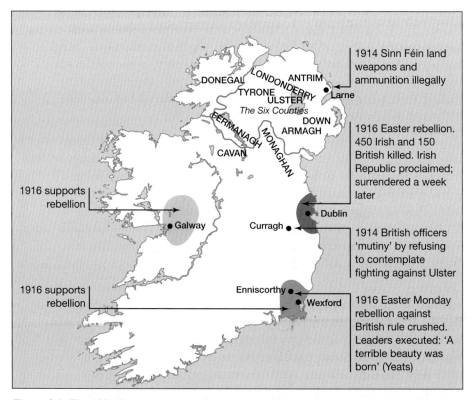

Figure 3.1 The 1921 Treaty settlement partitioned the island of Ireland into the Irish Free State and Northern Ireland (comprising the Six Counties). Northern Ireland is sometimes loosely referred to as Ulster, although historically Ulster had been made up of nine counties – the six shown, plus Donegal, Cavan and Monaghan. The fact that Northern Ireland did not include these last three was of immense importance, since it left the Protestants in a majority in the north. Why did the treaty not provide a permanent settlement of the Ulster question?

In retrospect, the settlement of 1921 can be seen as both a remarkable historical achievement and a contemporary political failure. A British politician had had the vision, the skill and the luck to undertake successfully something which, since the 1801 Act of Union, had evaded all other statesmen who had approached it, a workable solution to the Anglo-Irish question. Subsequent events were to show it was far from being a perfect solution; nevertheless, judged against the scale of the problem confronting him, Lloyd George's achievement was formidable.

The political failure lay in the fact that the treaty was necessarily a compromise. The Unionists were left feeling betrayed by Lloyd George's willingness to give in to what they regarded as republican terrorism. The Nationalists could not forget his use of the 'Black and Tans'; neither could they regard the treaty as anything other than a concession belatedly extracted from a British government who granted it only when all other means of maintaining the Union had failed.

The end of the post-war coalition in 1922

One of the repercussions of Lloyd George's Irish policy was that it finally killed off the idea of a permanent coalition or centre party. To be workable this would have had to include Labour as well as Conservative and Liberal members. Labour had found the methods that Lloyd George sanctioned in Ireland distasteful and, therefore, unsupportable.

It is doubtful in any case whether a genuine fusion of Liberals and Conservatives was possible. At Lloyd George's suggestion, talks had been held between the **chief whips** of the parties in 1920, but these had broken up with nothing substantial agreed. The reality was that Conservative support for Lloyd George was a matter of expediency, not principle; it did not imply any real desire to make that support permanent. The chances of a lasting coalition were always slim. Lloyd George did not really have enough to offer either the Conservative or Labour parties for them to consider a permanent coalition. They entertained thoughts of union only as a means of having a say in affairs until they felt sufficiently secure to strike out on their own.

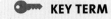 **KEY TERM**

Chief whips The MPs who perform the vital function of organising their party in Parliament.

The coalition's declining reputation

After four years, the commonly held view of the coalition was of a tired, ineffectual, administration, led by an individual who was past his best and was sustained in office by a combination of his own love of power and a Conservative Party which would continue to support him only as long as it served its own interests. Commentators and newspapers began to express distaste for the low tone of the coalition, a reference to the unattractive mixture of economic shortcomings, political expediency and financial corruption that had come to characterise it.

Lloyd George and corruption

The charge of corruption took particular strength from the so-called 'Lloyd George Fund', which provided an easy target for those wanting to blacken his name. Unashamedly, Lloyd George had used his power of patronage as prime minister to employ agents to organise the sale of honours and titles on a commission basis. **Maundy Gregory** was the most notorious of these salesmen. It was said that the asking rate during the coalition years was between £10,000 and £12,000 for a knighthood, and between £35,000 and £40,000 for a baronetcy.

During this period, some 90 peerages and 20,000 Orders of the British Empire (OBEs) were purchased by well-heeled, if not always well-born, social climbers. Lloyd George justified the practice by referring to the long tradition of patronage in Britain; the sale of titles, he suggested, was not new to British history. He argued that it was a justifiable means of raising political funds, given that he did not have access to the donations that the Conservatives regularly received from the business world or the Labour Party from the trade unions.

Whatever the validity of this claim, it did not prevent opponents from likening the honours sale system to the pre-war **Marconi scandal** as yet another example of Lloyd George's dishonesty. It provided a powerful additional argument for those Conservatives who had begun to question their party's continued support for Lloyd George. They pointed out that that support had always been conditional and suggested that the corruption of the coalition, added to its policy failures, was now beginning to taint the Conservative Party itself.

Chanak crisis 1922

More damaging for Lloyd George was a major problem abroad – the Chanak crisis. The trouble arose from the resentment of the defeated Turks at the dismemberment of their country under the terms of the 1920 **Treaty of Sèvres**. Under their new leader, **Mustapha Kemal**, the Turks threatened to recover by force the territories they had lost to their old enemy, Greece. Lloyd George, in the tradition of Gladstone, sided with the Greeks against their former oppressors. In September 1922, he ordered British reinforcements to be sent to Chanak on the Dardanelles, a likely area of confrontation. War threatened, but diplomacy eventually prevailed and the Turks withdrew. At home, Lloyd George's action was condemned by many Conservatives as an unnecessary and irresponsible piece of sabre-rattling that might well have led to a major war.

The Conservatives abandon Lloyd George

The Conservatives' chance to undermine Lloyd George came shortly afterwards, when Lloyd George announced his intention of calling a general election. This posed a critical question for the Conservatives. Should they, in the light of the obvious unpopularity of the coalition, continue to support Lloyd George? This demanding issue was discussed at a decisive meeting of the Conservative Party, held at the Carlton Club in October 1922. **Stanley Baldwin**, soon to be the leader of the party, joined Bonar Law in urging their colleagues to disassociate themselves from a prime minister who was no longer worthy of their trust. In his influential speech at the meeting, Baldwin spoke of Lloyd George as 'a dynamic force which had already shattered the Liberal Party and which was well on its way to doing the same thing for the Conservative Party'. Baldwin's words helped to swing the concluding vote: the Conservative MPs voted by 187 to 87 to abandon Lloyd George and the coalition by standing for election as a party in their own right.

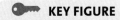

KEY FIGURE

Stanley Baldwin (1867–1947)
Conservative leader 1923–37; chancellor of the exchequer 1922–3; prime minister 1923–4, 1924–9, 1935–7.

The 1922 election

The Conservatives' wisdom in withdrawing from a tired and unpopular coalition reaped the benefits in the general election held a month later. The Liberals, who went into the election as a party divided between the respective supporters of Lloyd George and Asquith, suffered a heavy defeat. They were never again to be in government as a party. The defeat of the coalition ended Lloyd George's ministerial career and also destroyed the possibility of his building an effective centre party in British politics.

The Liberals lost a large number of seats, dropping from a combined figure of 161 for the two sections of the party in 1918 to a combined figure of 116 in 1922 (see Table 3.1). This contrasted sharply with the Conservatives holding their own, with 345 seats in 1922 compared with 358 in 1918. The most impressive feature was Labour's achievement in doubling its seats from 73 to 142.

Yet, as was noted in regard to the 1906 election (see page 19), the number of seats won and lost can blind one to the actual figures of popular support for the parties. In an electorate that had been more than doubled by the 1918 Representation Act, the Conservatives increased their vote by 1.6 million and Labour by 1.8 million. What is often overlooked is that the combined Liberal vote also rose significantly by 1.4 million. This could hardly be described as a massive rejection of the Liberals. The critical factor was not loss of popular support, but the unevenly distributed votes in the constituencies. Although Labour had won 26 more seats than the Liberals it had done so with only 0.4 per cent more of the popular vote. In proportional terms it had taken:

- 15,943 votes to elect each Conservative MP
- 29,868 votes to elect each Labour MP
- 36,116 votes to elect each Liberal MP.

Table 3.1 The November 1922 general election result

Party	Votes	Seats	Percentage of vote
Conservatives	5,500,382	345	38.2
Labour	4,241,383	142	29.5
National Liberal (Lloyd Georgians)	1,673,240	62	11.6
Liberals (Asquithians)	2,516,287	54	17.5

Obviously the divisions within the Liberal Party had seriously weakened it politically, but it was the imbalance in the electoral system that made a recovery by the Liberals after 1922 an impossibility. The Liberals were destroyed as a party of government not by the will of the people but by the workings of the system. Of course, this was not the result of some malign plan by the Liberal Party's opponents. It just happened that way. It was the accidental outcome of the unplanned way in which the electoral pattern operated.

Assessing the coalition

The coalition of 1918–22 has not had a good press. Lloyd George has often been criticised for running a cross-party government that did not conform to the normal pattern of party politics and, therefore, could not survive. The suggestion is that by governing in peacetime without a genuine party majority, Lloyd George made himself 'the prisoner of the Tories'. He could carry on only as long as the Conservatives backed him. His final defeat in 1922, following the withdrawal of Conservative support, is thus interpreted as in some way marking a return to normal two-party politics which had been disrupted by the war and Lloyd George's wish to stay in power.

What this line of argument assumes is that the two-party system is normal and necessary to British politics. However, what brought Lloyd George down was not his defiance of two-party politics, but the decision of the Conservatives to abandon him. Had it served their purpose to continue supporting him they would have done so. They were looking after their own interests, not defending some abstract principle of party politics. Moreover, the notion of Lloyd George as 'prisoner' was the interpretation of later observers. Few contemporaries saw it that way. Indeed, historian Martin Pugh (2012) has suggested that it suited the Conservatives after 1922 to portray Lloyd George as having been not their prisoner but as a dictator over them. In this way, they were able to absolve themselves from the mistakes of the coalition years.

Lloyd George

David Lloyd George was the dominant British politician of the first quarter of the twentieth century and ranks with Churchill as one of the greatest figures of the age. Such was the range of his activities that in studying him one is studying all the major events of his time.

Lloyd George's political significance 1905–22

Lloyd George was a keen advocate of coalition politics, believing that a pooling of the finest minds and talents from all the parties would serve Britain best. He appreciated that 'party' was an unavoidable feature of the political structure, but he tried to move towards a position in which consensus politics would replace strict party alignments. It has often been said that Lloyd George's natural home was the Labour not the Liberal Party. He always rejected this notion.

David Lloyd George

1863	Born in Manchester
1864–77	Brought up in Wales
1890	Became Liberal MP
1905	President of the Board of Trade
1908	Chancellor of the exchequer
1915	Munitions minister
1916	War minister then prime minister
1918–22	Prime minister of coalition government
1926	Liberal Party leader again
1945	Died

As a young radical Liberal MP, Lloyd George became a national figure with his onslaughts on the Conservative–Unionist government's mishandling of the Anglo-Boer War. He added to his reputation by vigorously defending free trade against the protectionist policies of the Conservatives. The period 1905–14 was when he was most active as a social reformer. As a dynamic member of Asquith's pre-war cabinet, first as president of the Board of Trade and then as chancellor of the exchequer, he was responsible for promoting a range of measures that marked the first steps towards the Welfare State.

During the first two years of the war, Lloyd George held in turn the offices of chancellor of the exchequer, minister of munitions and war secretary. His unique contribution to the war effort reached its climax when he became prime minister in 1916. During the next two years he worked indefatigably and inspiringly for victory over Germany. His immense personal contribution led to his reputation as 'the man who won the war'.

After the war, Lloyd George continued as the head of a peacetime coalition government, a decision which widened the growing split in the Liberal Party. He added to his renown as a statesman by personally leading the British delegation at the Versailles Peace Conference in 1919 and by achieving the Irish Treaty of 1921, the nearest that any single politician has come to solving the Anglo-Irish question. However, his attempts to fulfil his wartime promise to make Britain 'a land fit for heroes' made little headway. Growing domestic problems and increasing disenchantment with Lloyd George led the Conservatives, the main prop of the coalition, to withdraw their support from him in 1922. This effectively ended his premiership. Lloyd George was never again to hold office.

Yet, judged purely in terms of the policies he followed, it is sometimes difficult to see where he differed from the Labour Party. His work as a social reformer in the pre-1914 period was very much in tune with the programme of the Labour Party of that time. Furthermore, his widening of central government authority during the war extended the powers of the State to an unprecedented degree and took him way beyond anything the old Liberal Party would have contemplated.

This connects with the central dilemma created by the Liberal Party's attempt to modify its policies. Precisely because it was a halfway stage, the progressive but still limited form of social-service programme that the new Liberalism advanced between 1906 and 1914 was bound to be superseded by the full-blown Welfare-State socialism of the Labour Party. Some historians have seen this as the basic explanation for the decline of Liberalism in the twentieth century. They have argued that the Liberal Party fell between two stools:

- In trying to be socially progressive it forfeited its claim to represent traditional values.
- Yet, despite its apparent radicalism it did not go far enough along the road of State control.

It was thus unable to provide an effective challenge to either the Conservatives, representing the force of tradition, or the Labour Party, standing for nationalisation and State direction of the economy.

Contemporaries and later critics condemned Lloyd George for treating his party in so cavalier a way, as effectively to destroy it as a political force. Since it was during the most active period of his career that the Liberal Party declined in importance some of the blame must fall on him. His challenge to Asquith in 1916 led to a permanent split in the party. After 1922 there was never to be another Liberal prime minister or a Liberal government.

Lloyd George: a dictator?

The charge of dictatorship rests on Lloyd George's neglect of Parliament and his use of a personal secretariat to bypass the normal political channels. The fact is, however, that the electoral structure in Britain prevented dictatorship. No matter how strong Lloyd George's authority may have appeared to be, he was always dependent on the support of the Conservatives in Parliament. This was amply demonstrated in 1922 when his governmental power-base ceased to exist once the Conservatives chose to withdraw their support from him.

Lloyd George and industrial relations

Lloyd George devoted much of his time to negotiating with bosses and workers, endeavouring to achieve settlements that were not simply compromises but recognitions that employers, employees and government had a common interest. There are strong grounds for saying that it was Lloyd George who made the trade unions an integral part of British politics. His direct appeal to them in 1915 to suspend their agitation for the duration of the war and to enter into partnership with the government in running the wartime economy was a recognition of their indispensability to the national war effort and gave the unions a consciousness of their status that they were never to lose.

Lloyd George's legacy

It is difficult to deny that Lloyd George weakened the Liberal Party to the point of political impotence. At the same time, it is also arguable that he proved the most creative British politician of the twentieth century. He, more than any other single individual in British public life, laid down the basic political agenda for much of the rest of the twentieth century. The key aspects of that agenda were:

- the State as economic planner
- the redistribution of wealth through taxation
- social reform and the Welfare State
- the acceptance of trade unions as part of the political and industrial framework.

These were to remain the essential issues in British domestic politics throughout the twentieth century.

Summary diagram: The post-war coalition 1918–22

The problems of post-war reconstruction

Demobilisation
Health facilities
Unemployment
National Insurance and pensions
Housing
↓
Set against grim economic circumstances
– high inflation and falling demand for British goods

The Anglo-Irish issue

Legacy of the Easter Rising
IRA vs 'Black and Tans'
The Anglo-Irish Treaty 1921
↓
A major achievement but essentially a compromise
Mutual bitterness remained
Civil war in the new Ireland

↓

End of the 1918–22 coalition

Its fall the result of:
↓
Policy failures – economic, social, foreign affairs
Lloyd George's tarnished reputation
Corruption
Abandonment of Lloyd George by the Conservatives
Continued split in Liberal ranks meant certain defeat in 1922 election

↓

Lloyd George's political significance 1905–22 assessed

The Conservative government 1922–4

▶ *Why were the Conservatives in office for such a short period?*

▶ *How had Labour come to replace the Liberals as the second largest party by 1923?*

Despite the Conservatives' decisive break with Lloyd George and the reassertion of their separate identity as a party, their period in office between 1922 and 1924 was disappointingly short of achievement. The poor economic situation and growing unemployment stifled any major initiatives. An inhibiting problem was that Britain had emerged from the war heavily in debt to the USA. The government's attempts to reduce this resulted in an agreement that verged on the humiliating. At the end of his negotiations with the Americans in 1923, Stanley Baldwin, the chancellor of the exchequer, had committed Britain to repaying £46 million annually for 62 years.

Chamberlain's Housing Act 1923

One of the few bright notes for the government was the 1923 Housing Act.

Introduced by **Neville Chamberlain**, the minister of health, the Act laid down that:

- housing subsidies would take the form of a central government grant
- this was to be paid annually to local authorities over a twenty-year period
- the amount of the subsidy was £6 for each property erected for council housing by private builders.

The 1923 election

Seriously unwell with throat cancer when he became prime minister, Bonar Law had to retire in May 1923 after only eight months in office. His place was taken by Stanley Baldwin, who judged that the best way to reverse the recession and tackle unemployment was to return to a policy of tariff reform (see page 15). He called a general election, hoping to gain a mandate for his plans.

Lloyd George meanwhile had decided that the collapse of the coalition had left only one course open him: to rejoin the official, although much reduced, Liberal Party. He and Asquith agreed to ignore their differences and reunite their supporters in a single party with free trade as their election rallying cry.

Although the Conservatives emerged from that election as singly the largest party, their decline from an overall majority of 75 to a minority of nearly 100 represented a serious electoral rebuff and could be read as a final rejection of tariff reform. Following a defeat on a vote of confidence in the Commons, Baldwin resigned in January 1924.

Despite increasing their strength from 116 to 159 seats between the 1922 and 1923 elections (see Table 3.2), the Liberals were now the third party and obviously could not form a government on their own. Neither the Conservatives nor the Liberals were prepared to consider forming a coalition. Given this impasse, Labour, as the larger opposition party, was entitled to take office even

KEY FIGURE

Neville Chamberlain (1869–1940)

MP 1918–40, chancellor of the exchequer 1923–4 and 1931–7, minister of health 1924–9, prime minister 1937–40; son of Joseph Chamberlain and half-brother of Austen Chamberlain. It was said of him that he was an easy man to respect, but a difficult man to like.

Table 3.2 The 1923 general election result

Party	Votes	Seats	Percentage of vote
Conservatives	5,538,824	258	38.1
Labour	4,438,508	191	30.5
Liberals	4,311,147	159	29.6

though it lacked an overall majority. So it was that, after less than twenty years as a parliamentary party, Labour found itself forming a government.

By 1923 Labour had pushed the Liberals into third place in British party politics. Why this had occurred can be conveniently summarised by comparing the reasons for the decline of the Liberals with those for the rise of Labour.

Liberal decline

- The split between Asquith and Lloyd George during the 1914–18 war created a breach in the Liberal Party that was never properly healed.
- The Liberals did formally reunite in 1923 but it was an unconvincing affair. Lloyd George kept his own party premises and staff, and he and Asquith remained suspicious, if respectful, of each other. The result of the disunity was that the Liberals never again held office in their own right.
- Liberal values, such as the freedom of the individual, had been compromised by restrictive government measures during the war, particularly the introduction of military conscription. Liberalism could be said to have lost its moral authority.
- The Liberals had, in a sense, legislated themselves out of existence. Impressive though their pre-1914 reform record was, it marked the limit to how far they were prepared to go in changing the roots of society. They may have been radical but they were not revolutionary.
- Party politics in the twentieth century was an increasingly expensive affair. The Liberal Party was strapped for cash. As Lloyd George was fond of pointing out, his party had neither donations from the business world that the Conservatives received nor funds from the trade unions that Labour enjoyed.
- Before 1914 the party had always been able to rely on the parliamentary support of the Irish Nationalists. This was no longer available after Sinn Féin boycotted the House of Commons in 1918 and home rule for southern Ireland was implemented in 1922.
- Despite, or perhaps because of, its long period in office after 1905, there was a distinct decline in enthusiasm among the party's grass-roots workers in the constituencies.
- The 'first past the post' electoral system proved a destroyer of Liberal hopes of recovery. The party was unable to spread its popular support in such a way as to win key marginal seats. Knowing that the Liberals were unlikely to win an election, the party's supporters began to ebb away.

Labour's rise

- Working-class voters defected from the Liberal Party to the more radical Labour Party.
- Labour's strong trade union links provided it with a sound financial base.
- The Labour Party had a good war record. After initial misgivings, it played a major role in the patriotic war effort. This did much to dispel fears that it would be an unreliable defender of British interests.

- Its senior politicians had gained experience as cabinet ministers in the coalition governments, thereby showing that the party was as capable of government as any of the other parties.
- It improved its constituency organisation during the war and in 1918 adopted a formal constitution setting out its programme.
- As a young party, there was a freshness and enthusiasm about its constituency workers that the established parties found hard to match.

Conclusion

It should be stressed that none of the reasons and explanations in these two lists should be taken to mean that the rise of the Labour Party was inevitable. Without the war, there is no reason to suppose that the Liberal Party would have been irrevocably divided or that the State would have moved so far towards controlling society, a development that undermined the Liberal Party's traditional defence of the liberty of the individual.

Summary diagram: The Conservative government 1922–4

- A government burdened by debt
- Chamberlain's Housing Act (1923) was the only major measure
- Baldwin fought election on protection ticket
- 1923 election left Labour as larger opposition party

Why had the Liberals declined? – Why had Labour risen?

 # Labour in office 1924

▶ *Why were the other parties willing to accept the formation of a Labour government in 1924?*

Labour's taking office under Ramsay MacDonald in 1924 was a truly remarkable turn of events, yet in a sense it was on sufferance. Asquith was prepared to commit his Liberals to conditional support of the Labour Party for three reasons:

- He saw it as a way of ousting the Conservatives from power.
- He calculated that, since Labour would be dependent on Liberal support, he would be able to exercise effective control over the new government, bringing it down altogether should he choose.
- Asquith also reckoned, as did the Conservatives, that the inexperience of Labour would lead it to fail in office and thus discredit itself as a party of government.

As a realist, Ramsay MacDonald was well aware of how tightly he was restricted. The composition of his cabinet, which contained few left-wingers and a number of non-Labour Party personnel, was an indication that he appreciated the limitations of his position. It was for this very reason that some of his party colleagues had advised against taking office.

MacDonald's decision to press on was based on his belief that to decline office would look like cowardice and that the very act of assuming power, even if only for a limited time and with little chance of following radical policies, would make the vital point that Labour had arrived as a party that could govern responsibly. In this respect, Ramsay MacDonald's was a notable achievement.

Labour's record

Throughout Labour's nine months of office in 1924, its minority position denied it the opportunity of implementing radical measures. It introduced only three main domestic measures and those were non-controversial:

- Restrictions on unemployment benefit were eased.
- More public funds were directed to educational provision.
- Wheatley's Housing Act.

Wheatley's Housing Act

As minister of health in the first Labour government, **John Wheatley** developed Chamberlain's 1923 scheme (see page 96) in the following ways:

- the subsidy paid to private builders for each property they erected for council housing was raised from £6 to £9
- the annual payment to local councils was extended from 20 to 40 years.

Wheatley impressed on local authorities that the council housing subsidised in this way was to be rented, not sold. His fear was that if the properties became available for purchase they would be bought by the relatively prosperous, whereas the whole point of the scheme was to provide homes for the poorest at affordable rents. The success of this Act was clear in the statistic that showed that by 1933 half a million council houses had been built.

The Campbell case, September 1924

The short life of the government came to a premature end in September 1924, largely as a direct consequence of the Campbell case. The government was accused of interfering with the justice system by using its influence to have a prosecution withdrawn against a left-wing journalist, J.R. Campbell, who had been charged with promoting mutiny by urging troops to disobey orders if ever they were called on to fire on striking workers.

Although the Conservatives roundly attacked the government over this, they were not out for blood. Nor were the Liberals; Asquith was quite willing for a committee of inquiry to consider the matter, which would have meant many

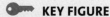

KEY FIGURE

John Wheatley (1868–1930)

Born in Ireland, raised in Scotland, worked as a miner and became a strongly left-wing Labour MP for a Glasgow constituency; minister of health 1924.

months passing before a report appeared. However, for some reason best known to himself, Ramsay MacDonald chose not to use the time he had been offered. Instead, he made the vote on the setting up of the inquiry a matter of confidence in the government. He announced that if the Commons voted in a majority for the inquiry he would resign. When the House duly did so, the prime minister kept his word and thus brought about the end of the first Labour government over a legal trifle.

It was an extraordinary move on Ramsay MacDonald's part. Yet, while he had made a strange tactical error, he showed shrewdness on a broader political front. He judged that the Liberals were a spent force. He believed that, although his own party was not yet strong enough in the Commons to sustain itself for a long period in office, the very fact that it had come into government showed that Labour had replaced the Liberals as the only realistic alternative party to the Conservatives.

The soundness of this analysis was borne out by subsequent events. Although the Labour government had gone out of office after only nine months, largely because of the Campbell case, popular support for the Labour Party actually increased in the election that followed in October 1924. It is true that it lost 40 seats while the Conservatives gained 151, but it was the Liberals who suffered most, losing 119 seats and nearly 1.4 million votes. This was the clearest sign yet that Labour had superseded the Liberals as the second main party in Britain. Labour's success in increasing its support was even more remarkable when set against the crisis which confronted it at the time of the election.

Table 3.3 The October 1924 general election result

Party	Votes	Seats	Percentage of vote
Conservatives	8,039,598	419	48.3
Labour	5,489,077	151	33.0
Liberals	2,928,747	40	17.6
Communist	55,346	1	0.3

The Zinoviev Letter 1924

On 25 October 1924, four days before the election, the *Daily Mail* carried the following headline: SOVIET PLOT: RED PROPAGANDA IN BRITAIN: REVOLUTION URGED IN BRITAIN.

Beneath the headline it printed a letter purportedly from Grigor Zinoviev, chief of the **Comintern**. It was addressed to the **British Communist Party**, urging its members to infiltrate the Labour Party and use it to bring down the British State. The letter is believed by historians to have been a forgery, concocted by **White Russian** *émigrés* to suggest that the Labour Party was a front for Soviet subversion.

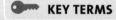

KEY TERMS

Comintern The Communist International, the Soviet agency for fomenting revolution in other countries.

British Communist Party Set up in 1921, it was always subservient to the Comintern, which provided the bulk of its funds.

White Russian *émigrés* Anti-Communists who had fled from Russia following their defeat by the Communists in the civil war there (1918–20).

The reason why the letter created such excitement was that Ramsay MacDonald's government had negotiated trade and diplomatic agreements with the Soviet Union. An Anglo-Russian Treaty had been drawn up containing the following main terms:

- Britain agreed to advance a £30 million loan to the Soviet Union
- in return the Soviet Union would pay compensation for the British financial assets it had seized after the Russian Revolution in 1917.

SOURCE A

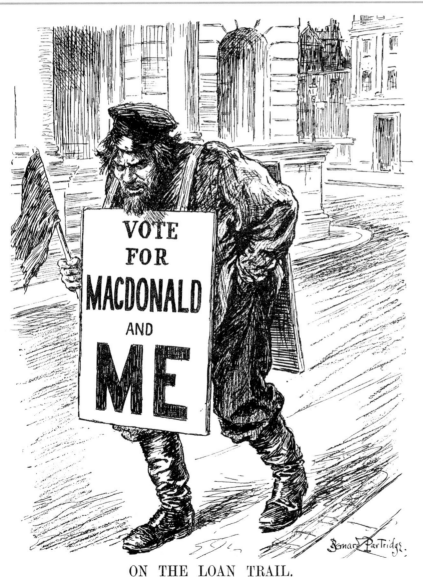

ON THE LOAN TRAIL.

Why might many people in Britain at this time have been willing to accept the Zinoviev Letter as authentic?

'On the Loan Trail'. A cartoon from *Punch*, a satirical British magazine, of October 1924 ironically summed up the attitude of large sections of the press towards the affair of the Zinoviev Letter. The text below the caption read: 'In a document just disclosed by the British Foreign Office (apparently after considerable delay), M. Zinoviev, a member of the Bolshevik dictatorship, urges the British Communist Party to use "the greatest possible urgency" in securing the ratification of Mr. MacDonald's Anglo-Russian Treaty, in order to facilitate a scheme for "an armed insurrection" of the British proletariat.'

While the treaty was never put into operation, since the government went out of office before it could be ratified, it provided ammunition for those in Britain who believed that relations between Ramsay MacDonald's government and **revolutionary Russia** were far too close for Britain's good. Yet, in answer, Ramsay MacDonald could refer to his far from negligible record in foreign affairs, where he had been concerned with promoting more than just better relations with the **USSR**.

Foreign affairs

During Labour's brief period of office, Ramsay MacDonald made a considerable contribution to the improvement of international relations generally and those between France and Germany in particular. He was the first and only British prime minister to attend the **League of Nations** in Geneva. While there, he was instrumental in the drafting of the Geneva Protocol, whose main proposals were that nations should:

- agree to accept that disputes would be settled by collective decisions
- consider active ways of achieving disarmament
- act together to prevent or deal with unprovoked aggression.

The Protocol was not formally accepted by the League but it was an interesting restatement of the principle of **collective security** and one which was particularly pleasing to the pacifists, who were still an important part of the Labour movement. In more practical terms, it encouraged France and Germany to lessen their animosity. At a conference in London which he chaired, Ramsay MacDonald persuaded both countries to move towards a settlement of the reparations issue. Up to this point, France had consistently demanded that Germany pay the full amount originally laid down in the Treaty of Versailles; Germany had equally consistently argued that the reparations were unrealistically heavy and so could not be paid.

The Dawes Plan 1925

The readiness of France and Germany to reconsider their positions led to international acceptance of the Dawes Plan. This was a scheme devised by General Dawes, an American banker, based essentially on Ramsay MacDonald's earlier proposals. Its main terms were:

- France agreed to lower the reparations figure to a level which would not cripple Germany.
- Germany was to be allowed to pay the lower rate for five years, which would give its industry the chance to recover.
- Germany was to be entitled to raise international loans to help it recover economically.
- Britain was to act as go-between, collecting the sums paid by Germany.

Since the Dawes Plan was not agreed on until 1925, nearly a year after Labour lost office, Ramsay MacDonald was not accorded as much credit as he deserved. Nevertheless, it may be justifiably claimed as one of the major achievements of the first Labour government.

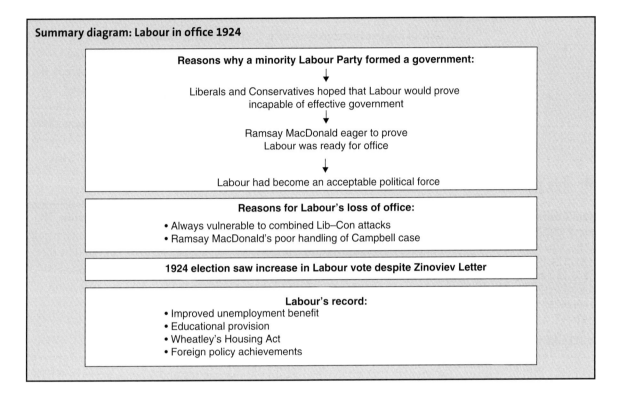

Summary diagram: Labour in office 1924

Reasons why a minority Labour Party formed a government:
↓
Liberals and Conservatives hoped that Labour would prove incapable of effective government
↓
Ramsay MacDonald eager to prove Labour was ready for office
↓
Labour had become an acceptable political force

Reasons for Labour's loss of office:
- Always vulnerable to combined Lib–Con attacks
- Ramsay MacDonald's poor handling of Campbell case

1924 election saw increase in Labour vote despite Zinoviev Letter

Labour's record:
- Improved unemployment benefit
- Educational provision
- Wheatley's Housing Act
- Foreign policy achievements

 # Baldwin's government 1924–9

▶ *How successful was Baldwin's government in this period?*

Back in office in November 1924, following Labour's resignation, Stanley Baldwin formed a government that over the next five years introduced a number of important measures. His chancellor of the exchequer was Winston Churchill, who after twenty years as a Liberal had now returned to the Conservative Party. Defending himself against a charge of having twice ratted on the parties he belonged to, he remarked that, while anybody could rat, it took a special person to 're-rat'. Baldwin accepted that tariff reform was no longer a viable policy and he quietly dropped it. Instead, he adopted a broad policy aimed at improving British trade and finances; he also gave attention to a number of social reforms. However, one underlying problem – the sluggish economy, which had failed to recover from wartime, and one particular event – the General Strike, have tended to overshadow his administration.

The path to the General Strike

From the beginning, the Baldwin administration was confronted by looming problems in industrial relations.

Red Friday, July 1925

One of the few direct moves of the Labour Party in office in favour of the workers in 1924 had been its backing for an agreement that protected the wages of the miners. However, the mine owners, who had originally accepted the agreement, soon went back on their word. In June 1925, they declared that they were obliged to cut wages, citing as justification the desperate state into which the British coal industry was sliding; orders were falling and production costs were increasing. Not surprisingly, the miners' national union (the Miners' Federation) resisted bitterly. When the TUC supported them, a General Strike was planned for 31 July (nicknamed Red Friday).

Baldwin's government bought itself time by offering a temporary subsidy to maintain miners' wage levels and by setting up the **Samuel Commission**. The move prevented a strike but the basic problem had not been solved. Much would hang on the Commission's report, which was scheduled to be delivered by the spring of the following year, 1926. In the intervening months British industry began to experience the harmful consequences of a fateful financial decision made by Winston Churchill at the Treasury.

Return to the gold standard

Before 1914 Britain's currency had been on the **gold standard**. This had given it a strength that led foreign investors to buy sterling and use it as a common form of exchange. Nearly all major trading nations had followed Britain and adopted their own gold standard, which brought stability to international commerce. It was the economic disruption caused by the First World War that made it impossible for countries to keep to this. In 1919 Britain suspended the operation of the gold standard for a period of six years.

The gold standard would begin to operate again in 1925. The big consideration for Churchill was at what rate to value the pound sterling when it returned to the gold standard. He decided to strengthen the pound by restoring it to its pre-war parity with the **US dollar**. This meant raising the pound's exchange rate from $3.40 to $4.86.

While this bold step helped British financiers, it deepened the plight of British exporters, who found it even harder to sell their goods abroad at the newly inflated prices required by the increased value of the pound. This was because the real gold value of Britain's pound sterling raised its exchange rate against all other currencies as well as the dollar. Foreign traders had to pay larger amounts of their own currency when purchasing British goods. This was an obvious

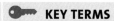

KEY TERMS

Samuel Commission
A body of inquiry, 1925–6, under the chairmanship of Herbert Samuel with the remit to examine the problems of the mining industry and put forward solutions.

Gold standard The position in which a nation's currency is kept at a high value by tying it to the price of gold.

US dollar As the world's strongest currency, the dollar was taken as the financial benchmark. All other currencies were measured in terms of their exchange value against the dollar.

disincentive to buying British. The return to the gold standard in 1925 thus added to the growing tendency for British goods to be priced out of the market.

The General Strike 1926

It was in this depressed atmosphere of falling sales that the Samuel Commission presented its report in March 1926. Its main recommendation was that the coal industry be totally restructured, but it urged that in the meantime the miners should accept a cut in wages, a proposal that the mine owners rushed to implement. The owners also tried to divide the Miners' Federation by offering deals to the miners at district branch level. The Federation reacted angrily and called on the TUC again to support them. The TUC did so, passing a key resolution (Source B) committing itself to a **General Strike**, to begin on 30 April. Meanwhile, the mine owners had begun to impose **lock-outs**.

 **KEY TERM**

Lock-outs Preventing workers from attending work by locking the gates to workplaces.

SOURCE B

From the TUC's Industrial Committee resolution, 14 April 1926, quoted in C.L. Mowat, *The General Strike*, Edward Arnold, 1969, p. 22.

This Committee protests against the action of the mine-owners in abandoning national negotiations and in attempting to open negotiations with the districts. This, in the opinion of the Committee, is calculated to create ill-feeling and suspicion at a critical time, and is a course of action contrary to the spirit of conciliation and the expressed views of the Royal Commission, and prejudicial to the prospect of an amicable settlement.

The Committee reiterates its previous declaration to render the miners the fullest support in resisting the degradation of their standard of life, and in obtaining an equitable settlement of the case with regard to wages, hours and national agreements.

According to Source B, on what grounds did the TUC support the Miners' Federation?

From the beginning, there was poor liaison between the TUC and the miners. Moreover, none of the TUC leaders genuinely wanted a strike on this scale; they hoped that, as had happened a year earlier, the government would back down rather than risk conflict. However, unlike 1925, the government was now prepared to call the TUC's bluff. Indeed, many in the cabinet, most notably Churchill, wanted a showdown with the labour movement. Nonetheless, talks in Downing Street between government officials and TUC leaders seemed, by Saturday 1 May, to be on the verge of success. A compromise, by which the employers would withdraw their lock-out notices and the workers would lift their strike threats, was close to being agreed.

But then there occurred an episode that destroyed the negotiations and made a strike unavoidable. On the evening of 2 May, news broke that the printers at the *Daily Mail* had refused to typeset a provocative editorial by the paper's editor. The key passage to which the printers objected read:

What does the editorial in Source C mean by saying that 'The general strike is not an industrial dispute'?

SOURCE C

From an editorial in the *Daily Mail*, 3 May 1926.

The miners, after weeks of negotiation, have declined the proposals made to them, and the coal mines of Britain are idle.

The Council of the Trades Union Congress, which represents all the other trades unions, has determined to support the miners by going to the extreme of ordering a general strike.

We do not wish to say anything hard about the miners themselves. As to their leaders, all we need say at this moment is that some of them are (and have openly declared themselves) under the influence of people who mean no good to this country.

The general strike is not an industrial dispute; it is a revolutionary movement, intended to inflict suffering upon the great mass of innocent persons in the community and thereby put forcible constraint upon the Government.

This was just what the government hawks, such as Winston Churchill and Lord Birkenhead, had been waiting for. When he heard of the printers' action, Birkenhead declared delightedly, 'bloody good job!' Baldwin and his cabinet were pressed into delivering an ultimatum to the TUC stating that no further talks could take place unless the 'overt action' of the printers was condemned by the TUC and all strike notices were withdrawn. The TUC protested that it had not been consulted by the printers at the *Mail* and that it was still willing to negotiate. But by declining to wait for the TUC's reply, the government closed the door to a settlement. The next day, 3 May, the government declared a state of emergency and the TUC began its long-threatened strike.

The *British Gazette* was the government's official newspaper produced daily between 5 and 13 May 1926. Edited by Winston Churchill, it took a firm line in condemning the strike. On 6 May it printed a 'Message from the Prime Minister' (Source D).

What tone is discernible in Baldwin's message in Source D?

SOURCE D

From the *British Gazette*, issue 2, 6 May 1926, p. 1.

'Constitutional Government is being attacked. Let all good citizens whose livelihood and labour have thus been put in peril bear with fortitude and patience the hardships with which they have been so suddenly confronted. Stand behind the government who are doing their part confident that you will co-operate in the measures they have undertaken to preserve the liberties and privileges of the people of these islands.

'*The laws of England are the people's birthright. The laws are in your keeping. You have made Parliament their guardian. The General Strike is a challenge to Parliament and is the road to anarchy and ruin.*' STANLEY BALDWIN

The strike is intended as a direct hold-up of the nation to ransom. 'This moment', as the Prime Minister pointed out in the House of Commons, 'has been chosen to challenge the existing Constitution of the country and to substitute the reign of force for what now exists.'

Baldwin's message aroused an immediate response (Source D) from the TUC General Council, which produced its own newspaper, the *British Worker*, every day of the strike.

SOURCE E

From the *British Worker*, 7 May 1926, p. 1.

The General Council does not challenge the Constitution. It is not seeking to substitute unconstitutional government. Nor is it desirous of undermining our Parliamentary institutions. The sole aim of the Council is to secure for the miners a decent standard of life. The Council is engaged in an industrial dispute. There is no Constitutional Crisis.

It is fantastic for the Prime Minister to pretend that the Trade Unions are engaged in an attack upon the Constitution. Every instruction issued by the General Council is evidence of their determination to maintain the struggle strictly on the basis of an industrial dispute. They are not attacking the Constitution. They are not fighting the community. They are defending the mine workers against the mine-owners.

In Source E, how does the TUC defend itself against the accusation that by operating a general strike it was acting unconstitutionally?

Baldwin, with a keen sense of public relations, made a radio broadcast in which he stressed that it was not his intention to take sides in an industrial dispute; his only concern was the nation's well-being.

SOURCE F

From a transcript of Stanley Baldwin's radio broadcast, 8 May 1926, quoted in Keith Middlemas and John Barnes, *Baldwin: A Biography*, Weidenfeld & Nicolson, 1969, p. 415.

I am a man of peace. I am longing and working, and praying for peace. But I will not surrender the safety and security of the British constitution. You placed me in power 18 months ago by the largest majority accorded to any party for many, many years. Have I done anything to forfeit that confidence? Cannot you trust me to ensure a square deal to secure even justice between man and man?

As recorded in Source F, what technique does Baldwin use to put across his message?

The failure of the General Strike

Despite its apparent militancy, the TUC's threats were largely rhetoric; it did not want a strike. As a consequence, the workers' side had made few preparations. It was never, in fact, a General Strike. Only selected unions were called out, the main ones being:

- transport and railway workers
- printers
- workers in heavy industry
- gas and electricity workers.

While these would have made up a formidable industrial force if they had acted resolutely together, from the beginning there was a crippling lack of cohesion. Some workers in the unions and regions selected simply carried on working.

In marked contrast, the government were fully ready. Indeed, the reason for the government's climbdown, in July 1925, had been to give itself time to prepare for a confrontation. It was greatly aided here by the **Emergency Powers Act** of 1920. Under the terms of this six-year-old measure, the government had set up the Organisation for the Maintenance of Supplies (OMS), which created a national network of voluntary workers to maintain vital services should a strike occur. One of the key initiatives of the OMS was to do a deal with the road hauliers to keep food supplies moving.

Compared with the government's preparations, the organisation of the strike by the TUC was rudimentary and ineffectual. It was only on the eve of the strike, when the leaders of the Transport and General Workers' Union (TGWU) obliged their TUC colleagues to recognise what they had let themselves in for, that detailed plans were belatedly and hurriedly drawn up. There was little active support for the strikers from the general public. Many ordinary people sympathised but did little to help. Those who did become involved tended to be on the government's side. Ex-officers from the armed services enrolled as special constables, while university students volunteered as bus and train drivers. Such activities have been described as 'class war in polite form'. The **BBC**, which was officially neutral in its news bulletins, was careful to say nothing critical of the government or supportive of the strikers.

Ironically, it was a class war only for one side. Certainly there were some hotheads and left-wing extremists among the strikers who wanted to turn the affair into a blow against the capitalist system, but these were very much a minority. The behaviour of the mass of the strikers was peaceful and responsible. This has been movingly put by A.J.P. Taylor:

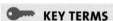 **KEY TERMS**

Emergency Powers Act Introduced during the days of the Lloyd George coalition, this measure granted the government wide authority and extraordinary powers in the event of a major disruption of essential services.

BBC Began in 1922 as the private British Broadcasting Company; in 1926 it became the British Broadcasting Corporation, funded by a compulsory licence fee paid by those with wireless sets.

SOURCE G

From A.J.P. Taylor, *English History 1914–45*, Oxford University Press, 1965, pp. 244–5.

These were the very men who had rallied to the defence of Belgium in 1914. The voluntary recruitment of the First World War and the strike of 1926 were acts of spontaneous generosity, without parallel in any other country … Such nobility deserves more than a passing tribute. The strikers asked nothing for themselves. They did not seek to challenge the government, still less to overthrow the constitution. They merely wanted the miners to have a living wage. Perhaps not even that. They were loyal to their unions and to their leaders, as they had been loyal during the war to their country and to their generals. They went once more into the trenches, without enthusiasm and with little hope.

What does A.J.P. Taylor mean when he says in Source G that the strikers 'asked nothing for themselves'?

Given the government's readiness, the TUC's reluctance and the general public's indifference, the strike stood no chance of success. There were violent clashes here and there between police and strikers but few unions were willing to support the miners in a fight to the finish. On 12 May, after ten days, the TUC called off the strike without winning any concessions from the employers or the government. The miners themselves carried on for another seven months before they, too, gave in unconditionally.

Trade Disputes Act 1927

In the aftermath of the General Strike, the government introduced a Trade Disputes Act aimed at making another General Strike impossible. It:

- outlawed general and sympathetic strikes
- restricted strike action to specific disputes
- forbade trade union funds being used for political purposes unless the individual member chose to contribute by 'contracting in'.

A particular government aim in the Act (Source H) was to restrict picketing:

SOURCE H

From the Trade Disputes and Trade Unions Act, July 1927, quoted in *Chitty's Statutes 1927*, Sweet & Maxwell, 1928, p. 1050.

It is hereby declared that it is unlawful for one or more persons (whether acting on their own behalf or on behalf of a trade union or of an individual employer or firm, and that notwithstanding that they may be acting in contemplation or furtherance of a trade dispute) to attend at or near a house or place where a person resides or works or carries on business or happens to be for the purpose of obtaining or communicating information or of persuading or inducing any person to work or abstain from working, if they so attend in such numbers or otherwise in such manner as to be calculated to intimidate any person in that house or place.

What restrictions are placed on trade union actions according to the clause in Source H?

To the opponents of the strike the Act seemed an appropriate way of forestalling further industrial troubles; to the strikers it appeared deliberately punitive.

Imperial issues

Britain and France were the only two empires to emerge intact from the First World War but the spirit of the times and the aspirations of the colonial peoples meant that imperialism was an obsolete idea. Pressure on Britain to grant independence to its colonies began to build. The most clamorous demand came for India (see page 121), but, at this stage, the most successful came from the white dominions – Australia, New Zealand, Canada and South Africa – which wanted recognition as fully independent states. In 1926 Britain bowed to this pressure and issued the **Balfour Declaration**, which acknowledged the dominions as wholly 'autonomous communities within the British Commonwealth of Nations'. Despite the language used, this was a significant step towards the dismantling of the empire.

Chief measures of Baldwin's government

As the following list shows, there was more to Baldwin's 1924–9 government in domestic affairs than the General Strike:

- 1925: a Pensions Act enabled contributors to draw their pension at 65. Britain's currency was returned to the gold standard (see page 104).
- 1926: an Electricity Act set up the national grid to provide power throughout Britain.
- 1927: BBC established a national radio broadcasting system.
- 1927: the Trade Disputes Act restricted trade union freedoms.
- 1928: Parliamentary Reform Act extended the vote to women on the same terms as men: all citizens over the age of 21. In terms of electoral rights, the granting of the flapper vote (see below) made Britain a full democracy.
- 1929: in an effort to stimulate production and commerce, a Local Government Act exempted all farms and 25 per cent of factories from local rates. The Act also effectively ended the old Poor Law (see page 2), by abolishing the Boards of Guardians and phasing out the workhouses.

The flapper vote

The extension of the full franchise to woman was sometimes said to have ushered in the flapper vote. The reference was to the emancipated young women between the ages of 21 and 30, known as 'flappers', whose self-confidence was expressed in their distinctive dress style and willingness to flout social convention by, for example, smoking in public. It was said that the flapper vote benefited the Labour Party in the 1929 general election, though there is no hard evidence for this.

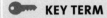

KEY TERM

Balfour Declaration
(1926) Stated that the dominions were 'equal in status, in no way subordinate one to another in any aspect of their domestic or external affairs, though united by a common allegiance to the Crown'.

SOURCE I

What are the distinctive features of the Flapper style of dress, as shown in Source I? **?**

Two young women in typical flapper outfits in 1925.

The 1929 election

The Conservative Party's 1929 election slogan 'safety first' was hardly an inspiring one after five years in office and its failure to control rising unemployment counted against it. In the election, its share of the vote dropped by ten per cent compared with 1924 (see Table 3.4). The Liberal Party staged a recovery by nearly doubling its aggregate vote. But its share of the vote was too thinly spread. The most impressive feature of the election was the increase in the Labour vote, sufficient to return it as the largest single party. It was time for a second Labour government.

Table 3.4 The May 1929 general election result

Party	Votes	Seats	Percentage of vote
Labour	8,389,512	288	37.1
Conservatives	8,656,473	260	38.2
Liberals	5,308,510	59	23.4

Summary diagram: Baldwin's government 1924–9

The path to the General Strike

	Development	TUC action	Government action
July 1925	Mine owners reduced wages. Miners agreed to await Samuel Report.	Backed miners' strike threat.	Offered miners a wage subsidy. Set up Samuel Commission. Made preparations to meet a strike.
Mar 1926	Samuel Commission urged miners to accept wage cuts. Miners' Federation called strike for 30 April.	Gave Federation uncertain backing.	
April–May 1926		Joined government in talks which seemed on verge of success.	Hawks pressed for a showdown.
2 May	Printers at *Daily Mail* refused to typeset editorial.	Denied knowledge of printers' action.	Delivered ultimatum to TUC.
3 May		TUC declared a general strike.	Declared a state of emergency.

Government's chief measures, 1925–9:

1925	Pensions Act
	Gold standard restored
1926	National Grid established
1927	BBC established a national radio broadcasting system
	Trade Disputes Act
1928	Granted the vote to women on same terms as men
1929	Local Government Act

 # Key debate

► *What caused the 'The Strange Death of Liberal England'?*

In 1934, a stimulating and provocative book appeared, entitled *The Strange Death of Liberal England*. Its author, George Dangerfield, sought to explain why, in the twenty years from 1914 to 1934, the Liberals had rapidly declined from being a party in government to being merely a fringe party. His essential answer was that the pre-war crises proved that by 1914 the Liberals were incapable of dealing effectively with the social and economic pressures of the early twentieth century, which was why by 1914 they were on the point of extinction.

EXTRACT 1

From George Dangerfield, *The Strange Death of Liberal England* (first published 1934), Granada Publishing, 1970, p. 14.

The year 1910 is not just a convenient starting point. It is actually a landmark in English history, which stands out against a peculiar background of flame. For it was in 1910 that fires long smouldering in the English spirit suddenly flared up, so that by the end of 1913 Liberal England was reduced to ashes. From these ashes, a new England seems to have emerged.

I realise, of course, that the word 'Liberal' will always have a meaning so long as there is one democracy left in the world, or any remnant of a middle class; but the true pre-war Liberal – supported as it still was in 1910, by Free Trade, a majority in Parliament, the ten commandments and the illusion of Progress – can never return. It was killed, or it killed itself, in 1913.

Other historians were keen to develop his thesis. They argued that the fierce confrontations between employers and workers, the violence of the suffragettes, the battle between Lords and Commons, and Ireland on the verge of civil war, were all signs that Britain had entered an era of 'class politics'. It was a new form of political warfare with which the Liberal Party was not equipped to cope.

Contrary views to Dangerfield's

Superficially, the extreme opposition to the Liberal governments does seem to indicate that their policies had failed to satisfy the major demands of the time. However, although Dangerfield's interpretation remains a very helpful starting point, it has been largely superseded by another school of thought which stresses that, difficult though matters were for the Liberals, they were still in office in 1914 after nine years of unbroken government:

- All challenges to their authority had been overcome.
- Asquith's cabinets had remained united throughout the troubles.
- The Conservatives, despite their gains in the 1910 elections, had not been able to oust Asquith's government.
- The Labour Party had made no serious inroads into the traditional Liberal strongholds.

It is the resurgence of the Liberal Party in this period rather than its decline that has been strongly emphasised by modern political historians Peter Clarke and Ross McKibbin. It is true that the Labour Party had grown in membership in the country at large, mainly through trade-union affiliation. Yet, on its own admission, it had been only a marginal political influence before 1914. Clarke suggests that the Labour Party had begun to see its future role not so much as a separate radical force but as a part of a Liberal–Labour 'progressive' movement.

All this tends to indicate that the problems of pre-1914 Britain were not a proof of the failure of Liberal policies between 1905 and 1914. The critical factor was the war. In a notable book, *The Downfall of the Liberal Party* (1966), historian Trevor Wilson suggested that the war was the essential reason for the decline in Liberal fortunes.

EXTRACT 2

From Trevor Wilson, *The Downfall of the Liberal Party 1914–1935*, Collins, 1966, p. 18.

The Liberal party can be compared to an individual who, after a period of robust health and great exertion, experienced symptoms of illness (Ireland, labour unrest, the suffragettes). Before a thorough diagnosis could be made, he was involved in an encounter with a rampant omnibus (the First World War), which mounted the pavement and ran him over. After lingering painfully, he expired. A controversy has persisted ever since as to what killed him. One medical school argues that even without the bus he would soon have died; the intimations of illness were symptoms of a grave disease which would shortly have ended his life. Another school goes further, and says that the encounter with the bus would not have proved fatal had not the victim's health already been seriously impaired.

However, other historians have argued that the war accelerated the decline rather than causing it. More recently, it has been suggested that the key factor was not so much that the war undermined the Liberals, but that it strengthened Labour. Diverted by the demands of war from their progressive policies, the Liberals gave ground to the Labour Party as the new force of reform. The reassessment of the reasons for the Liberals' strange death was memorably put by historian Alan Sykes.

EXTRACT 3

From Alan Sykes, *The Rise and Fall of British Liberalism 1776–1988*, Longman, 1997, p. 273.

The Liberal party was not, to re-work a familiar metaphor, run down by a rampant omnibus (the First World War) whilst loitering without intent. None of the parties was that passive. The Conservatives recognised the bus and jumped on board; the Liberals mistook the direction it was travelling and threw themselves in front of it; the Labour Party stepped aside, and stripped the Liberal corpse of its valuables when the bus was safely gone. The robbers were led by men who had been driven from Liberalism. The final verdict on the party is not inevitable decline through old age, nor accidental death, but suicide while the balance of politics was disturbed.

? How have interpretations of Liberal decline been adjusted since George Dangerfield's thesis first appeared in 1934?

The incontrovertible fact was that after 1918 the Liberals would never again form a majority government. The war had obliged the Liberals to abandon some of their most cherished libertarian values, as their acceptance of conscription indicated. Politically, the splitting of the party into its Lloyd George and Asquith factions left a division that was never truly healed. Favoured by the oddities of the electoral system, the Labour Party in the interwar years moved in to take the Liberals' place.

Chapter summary

David Lloyd George had promised to make Britain a land 'fit for heroes', but while it was true that his coalition government achieved some important social reforms, as, for example, in housing, the record overall was unimpressive. Britain's indebtedness and outdated industries did not allow Britain to make the necessary recovery. Despite Lloyd George's remarkable attempt to solve the Anglo-Irish question, his administration was also increasingly associated with corruption, a principal reason for the Conservatives' withdrawing their support from him. A short Conservative government under Stanley Baldwin (1922–4) was followed by an even shorter minority Labour government under Ramsay MacDonald in 1924. However, the true significance of Labour in office lay in the fact that it had held office at all. It was a sign that Labour had replaced the Liberals as an electoral force. The Baldwin government of 1924–9 did have some achievements to its name, but its reputation was overshadowed by its suppression of the General Strike of 1926, an event that indicated the troubles that were afflicting Britain's staple industries. Britain's growing debts, not helped by its reversion to the gold standard, and mounting unemployment were further signs that economic problems had come to dominate the political scene.

Refresher questions

Use these questions to remind yourself of the key material covered in this chapter.

1 What problems confronted the post-war coalition on the industrial front?

2 What difficulties faced the post-war coalition over Ireland?

3 Why had a crisis arisen in Ireland in 1916?

4 How close did the Anglo-Irish Treaty of 1921 come to solving the Anglo-Irish question?

5 Why did the post-war coalition break up in 1922?

6 In what sense were the Liberals the victims of the electoral system after 1918?

7 In what ways can Lloyd George be said to have damaged his party?

8 Did Lloyd George have any political principles?

9 Why was Ramsay MacDonald willing to form a minority government in 1924?

10 How did the Campbell case and the Zinoviev Letter affect the fortunes of the Labour Party?

11 What impact did Ramsay MacDonald have on foreign policy?

12 What part did the return to the gold standard play in increasing Britain's economic difficulties?

13 Was the General Strike of 1926 an 'avoidable folly'?

14 Why did the General Strike never become an effective challenge to the government?

15 What social and economic reforms of note had Baldwin's government introduced?

Question practice

ESSAY QUESTIONS

1 How successful was Lloyd George's post-war coalition in dealing with the problems that faced it?

2 How far did the Treaty of 1921 settle the Anglo-Irish question?

3 How important in the development of party politics was the formation of the first Labour government in 1924?

4 'The General Strike of 1926 failed because the government was better prepared for it than the strikers.' Explain why you agree or disagree with this view.

SOURCE ANALYSIS QUESTIONS

1 With reference to Sources C (page 106) and E (page 107), and your understanding of the historical context, which of these two sources is more valuable in explaining why a General Strike occurred in 1926?

2 With reference to Sources C (page 106), D (page 106) and E (page 107), and your understanding of the historical context, assess the value of these sources to a historian studying the General Strike in 1926.

CHAPTER 4

From Labour to the National Government 1929–39

Throughout its two years, Ramsay MacDonald's second government was troubled and then finally overwhelmed by economic problems. Having resolved to lead Britain through the financial crisis that struck it in 1931, the prime minister 'betrayed' his party by forming a National Government composed largely of Conservatives. This proved electorally popular and the National Government stayed in power until 1940. Economic problems persisted and it was against the background of the Great Depression that the new government operated in its early years. It also had to face growing threats on the foreign front. These developments are studied under the following headings:

★ The second Labour government 1929–31

★ The 1931 crisis

★ The National Government and domestic policies 1931–7

★ The National Government and foreign affairs 1931–9

Key dates

1929–31	Second Labour government	1931	Gold standard abandoned
1929–35	The Depression		Statute of Westminster
1930	Coal Mines Act	1933	Oxford Union 'King and Country' debate
	Housing Act	1935	Baldwin became prime minister
	Education Bill	1936	German occupation of the Rhineland
	Gandhi's salt protest		Abdication crisis
1931	The May Committee	1937	Chamberlain became prime minister
	End of Labour government	1938	Munich Agreement
	Ramsay MacDonald formed National Government	1939	German occupation of Czechoslovakia
	Ramsay MacDonald expelled from Labour Party		British guarantees to Poland
			Britain declared war on Germany

The second Labour government 1929–31

▶ *What economic and political constraints did Ramsay MacDonald's second government work under?*

It was with apparent reluctance that Ramsay MacDonald took office in June 1929. Despite its impressive showing in the election, Labour still did not have an overall majority and there was a fear in the party that, as in 1924, this would prevent its following genuinely radical policies. The prime minister seemed aware of this when he appointed a cabinet that was predominantly right wing and moderate.

But it was not concern over being defeated by a combined Conservative–Liberal vote that most restricted Ramsay MacDonald's government. The truth was that Labour's second period of office coincided with the onset of a severe international economic depression which began in the USA with the Wall Street financial crash of 1929 and spread worldwide. Whatever its reforming intentions may have been, the Labour government was eventually undermined by the economic problems that this created.

Government reforms

Despite the restrictive atmosphere in which it had to operate, Ramsay MacDonald's government attempted to implement a number of important reforms.

Housing Act 1930

Introduced by **Arthur Greenwood**, the minister of health, the Act built on the earlier work of John Wheatley (see page 99) by reintroducing government subsidies for council housing and granting greater powers to local authorities to enforce slum clearance. As a result of this measure, more slums were cleared between 1934 and 1939 than in the whole of the previous half century.

Education Bill 1930

As president of the Board of Education, **Charles Trevelyan** introduced a Bill that would have raised the school leaving age to fifteen. But even before the House of Lords rejected his Bill, it had met resistance from a seemingly strange quarter. Catholic MPs on the Labour backbenches complained that insufficient attention had been paid in the Bill to the particular needs of Catholic schools. Their objection was that Catholic parents who paid taxes that went towards the provision of State education still had to provide out of their own pocket for the upkeep of Catholic schools. The debate over faith schools and how far they should be financed by the State would still be an unresolved question in the twenty-first century.

KEY FIGURES

Arthur Greenwood (1880–1954)

MP 1922–31, 1932–54; minister of health 1929–31; as deputy leader of the Labour Party 1935–45 he opposed appeasement of Hitler's Germany and strongly supported Churchill's decision in 1940 not to consider peace terms with Germany.

Charles Trevelyan (1870–1958)

MP 1899–1918; as president of the Board of Education 1929–31 he tried to build on the work of extending educational provision that he had begun in the same post in the 1924 Labour government.

Coal Mines Act 1930

This measure attempted to lessen the bitterness that still hung over the mining industry in the aftermath of the General Strike four years earlier. Its main terms were:

- the miners' working hours were reduced from 8 to 7½-hour shifts
- the employers were entitled to fix minimum wages and production quotas
- a commission was set up to consider how unprofitable mines could be phased out with least damage to miners' livelihoods.

Agricultural Marketing Act 1931

In a similar attempt to provide an overarching authority that could improve the supply of food to the public, the Act set up boards of food producers with the power to fix prices and arrange supplies more efficiently. This was an extension of the government policy adopted after the war to assist farming by laying down quotas of production for the farmers accompanied by the payment of subsidies to them to guarantee their income in good or bad times. This policy also prevented food prices rising too high for the consumer since the farmer knew that any shortfall in profit would be covered by the subsidy he received. Interestingly, it was this same practice that the miners had asked to be applied to the coal industry after the war, only to be told that the adoption of regular subsidies to mining was uneconomic.

London Transport Bill 1931

This measure, introduced by **Herbert Morrison**, become law in 1933. It created a public corporation responsible for providing cheap and efficient bus and underground transport for London's population.

Where Ramsay MacDonald's second government proved especially disappointing to the left wing of the Labour party was in its failure to reverse the Trade Disputes Act passed in 1927 in the wake of the General Strike (see page 109). The original Act had been seen by many as a vindictive move against the unions and it was hoped that Labour in office would undo its main terms. However, when the Liberals let it be known that they would not support such an adjustment, the government left the Act unamended.

Foreign affairs

Interestingly, the government's record in foreign affairs was more impressive than its domestic performance. Ramsay MacDonald regarded foreign policy as his special forte. In 1924 he had combined the offices of prime minister and foreign secretary. He would have liked to have done the same in 1929 but he allowed himself to be persuaded to make Arthur Henderson foreign secretary, although he reserved the right as prime minister to involve himself in foreign policy when he thought fit.

KEY FIGURE

Herbert Morrison (1888–1965)

MP 1923–4, 1929–31, 1935–59; leader of the London County Council 1933–40; minister of transport 1929–31; home secretary 1940–5; foreign secretary 1951; a diligent worker, he was disappointed never to have become party leader or prime minister.

Henderson, who had insisted that he would not consider any government post other than foreign secretary, was justified in his self-confidence. After only two months in office, he played a key role as negotiator in a conference at The Hague which ended with the European nations agreeing to the **Young Plan**, which saw Germany accepted again as an equal nation in Europe.

Henderson also made a considerable impression at the League of Nations in Geneva. Both the French and the Germans found him amenable and dependable and he helped to bring the representatives of those two peoples closer together than at any point since 1918. Such was the sense of trust he engendered among his foreign counterparts that he was able to rejuvenate the disarmament talks that had stalled. In recognition of his achievement he was made president of the disarmament conference in 1932. It was no fault of Henderson's that the economic depression and the development of **Nazism** in Germany after 1933 would soon wipe out the advances he had made.

Ramsay MacDonald also worked for international conciliation. In October 1929, he visited the USA with whom Britain's relations had not always been warm in the 1920s, largely because the Conservative governments had feared that America's strong anti-imperialist stance was an implied threat to Britain's own empire. The main issue Ramsay MacDonald discussed during his visit was the relative strength of national navies. It was this question that had stymied talks on disarmament. The powerful maritime nations – USA, Japan and Britain – were reluctant to risk reducing their armed fleets.

Early in 1930, as a result of Ramsay MacDonald's American talks, Britain hosted a three-nation conference specially convened to seek a compromise on naval matters. The key agreement reached at the conference was the ratio principle. The USA, Britain and Japan agreed in their warship building programmes to accept a ratio of 5:5:3. For every five American vessels there would be five British and three Japanese. The three countries promised not to increase their navies outside these proportions. As with Henderson's work, subsequent events were to diminish Ramsay MacDonald's achievement. Japan was unhappy with the agreement and soon ceased to abide by it as it prepared for war (see page 144). However, the closer contacts which Britain had made with the USA were to have important consequences when the Second World War came in 1939.

Anglo-Soviet relations

There had been an understandable hope among the left-wing members of the party that with Labour in office there would be a major improvement in Britain's relations with the USSR, which had plummeted at the time of the Zinoviev Letter in 1924 (see page 100). It was believed that 'left could speak unto left', the notion being that socialist Britain was well fitted to understand Socialist Russia.

Yet Ramsay MacDonald's government never showed any inclination to follow a socialist path internationally. The prime minister believed sincerely in the need to pursue international co-operation as a principle, but at no time was he willing to risk national interests by aligning Britain with Soviet ideas of revolution. Indeed, a major part of Ramsay MacDonald's achievement as a political leader was that he made his party electable by showing the voters that no matter what a few hotheads on the fringe might say, the Labour Party was a responsible and committed upholder of the British parliamentary system.

This did not prevent diplomatic progress being made. In October 1929 the government formally resumed full relations with the USSR; ambassadors were exchanged and embassies established. But beyond the formalities little else was done. The proposals put forward at the time of the 1924 Labour government for an Anglo-Soviet treaty covering loans and trade were not resurrected.

India

Ramsay MacDonald could also justifiably claim that it was during his second Labour administration that the first tentative steps were taken towards the independence of India. This had been a stated aim of the Labour Party since its earliest days. In December 1929, the **Indian Congress Party**, not waiting for the outcome of talks on dominion status, made a declaration of Indian independence.

Knowing that the British would not recognise this, Mohandas Gandhi (see box below), regarded as the father of modern India, organised a 'salt protest' in 1930. Collecting thousands of followers along the way he led a 250-mile march to the coastal town of Dandi. There, he picked up a lump of salt from the beach and crushed it in his hands. It was a simple but hugely symbolic gesture. Gandhi was protesting against the way the people were forbidden to gather natural sea salt and forced to buy the heavily taxed government-owned variety. For this he was arrested and imprisoned.

 **KEY TERM**

Indian Congress Party
The main nationalist party in India, dedicated to ending British rule, which had formally operated since the Government of India Act of 1858.

> ### Mohandas Gandhi 1869–1948
>
> As a young lawyer in South Africa, Gandhi had organised passive resistance to the race laws there. On returning to India he set about employing the same techniques as a means of undermining the British hold on India. A devout Hindu, Gandhi nonetheless sought mutual respect and tolerance between all religions and castes. His simple, even saintly, lifestyle endeared him to the great mass of the Indian peasantry to whom he was the Mahatma (great soul).
>
> Gandhi was arguably the most influential revolutionary of the twentieth century; his philosophy of non-violent protest became the model for civil rights movements everywhere. He was certainly the single most important influence in the growth of Indian nationalism.

This was an embarrassment for Ramsay MacDonald's government. Supposedly dedicated to Indian independence, it now found itself in a situation where it was the ultimate authority suppressing the independence movement. Striving for a way out, Ramsay MacDonald called a round table conference in London in November 1930. At first, the Congress Party refused to attend. But after a series of complex manoeuvres, which included Gandhi's being released from prison and invited to the conference, they accepted. However, by the time Gandhi arrived for the talks, the Labour government had resigned from office.

It was the brevity of the Labour government's term of office and its sudden end that prevented it from achieving a settlement of the Indian question at this stage. Nevertheless, the government's contribution was far from negligible. It had shown a willingness to accept that any lasting settlement would have to be on Indian terms. India would have to be granted its freedom. The question was when and how that would come.

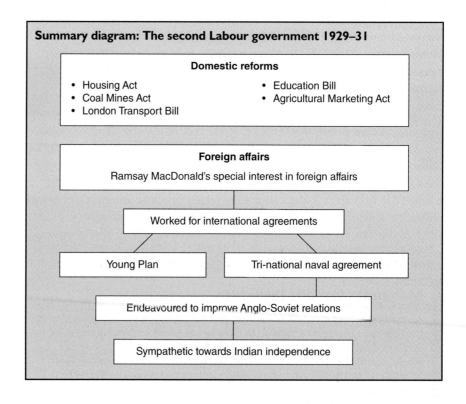

Summary diagram: The second Labour government 1929–31

Domestic reforms

- Housing Act
- Coal Mines Act
- London Transport Bill
- Education Bill
- Agricultural Marketing Act

Foreign affairs

Ramsay MacDonald's special interest in foreign affairs

Worked for international agreements

Young Plan

Tri-national naval agreement

Endeavoured to improve Anglo-Soviet relations

Sympathetic towards Indian independence

The 1931 crisis

▶ *Why was the Labour government brought down by the financial crisis of 1931?*

By 1931 Britain had begun to suffer severely from the effects of the worldwide depression which had begun two years earlier in the USA (see page 118). Unemployment had risen to nearly 3 million. To meet the hardship suffered by the victims, the Labour government raised unemployment benefit.

Financial problems

The decline in industrial production in Britain had caused a sharp fall in revenue from taxation, and the government simply began to run out of money. **Philip Snowden** as chancellor of the exchequer had no new ideas; there was nothing especially socialist about his budgets. Indeed, his approach to finance was a very conventional one. He was not prepared to take risks. He believed in **balanced budgets**, which entailed restricting public expenditure to essentials. It was this conservative attitude that so frustrated younger members of the Labour Party such as Oswald Mosley (see page 139), who believed that there were alternative economic and financial strategies that a Labour government ought to be trying.

The May Committee 1931

Still seeking a solution along traditional lines, Snowden, in February 1931, appointed a special committee under Sir George May as chairman, to consider ways out of the financial crisis. Declining to consider a new economic approach, the May Committee had nothing to suggest in the report that it presented in July other than cuts in public expenditure. It recommended a wide range of reductions in pay for teachers, civil servants and those in the armed services. The report's lack of originality and insight led to its being described by John Maynard Keynes (see page 185) as 'the most foolish document I have ever had the misfortune to read'.

The May Committee's proposal that aroused the most dissension within the government was the suggestion that unemployment pay be cut by ten per cent (the initial proposal was twenty per cent). Many in the cabinet believed that if this were to be done it would destroy the very principle for which the Labour Party had been created – the protection of the working class. But Ramsay MacDonald was also under pressure from the international bankers who were unwilling to advance further loans to Britain unless it reduced its welfare expenditure. He told his colleagues that there was no alternative but to make the cuts. When this proposal was put to a cabinet vote, ten of the 21 members rejected it.

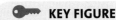 **KEY FIGURE**

Philip Snowden (1864–1937)
A Methodist, teetotaller, pacifist and supporter of the suffragettes; MP 1906–18, 1922–31; chancellor of the exchequer 1924, 1929–31.

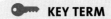 **KEY TERM**

Balanced budgets
Not allowing public expenditure to exceed income from revenue.

Ramsay MacDonald's 'great betrayal'

The cabinet split was the prelude to what became known in Labour Party history as 'the great betrayal'. Unable to carry a united cabinet with him, Ramsay MacDonald declared his intention of resigning on his and the government's behalf. However, although he went to Buckingham Palace for an audience with King George V, it was not to hand in his resignation. Instead, in the presence of the king, he entered into discussions with Stanley Baldwin and Herbert Samuel, the respective leaders of the Conservative and Liberal parties. The remarkable outcome of the talks was the formation of a new coalition or 'National Government' under Ramsay MacDonald, who would remain prime minister. The main details of the meeting were recorded by George V's private secretary (Source A).

SOURCE A

From a memorandum by King George V's private secretary, 24 August 1931.

At 10 a.m. the King held a conference at Buckingham Palace at which the Prime Minister, Baldwin and Samuel were present. The Prime Minister said that he had the resignation of the Cabinet in his pocket, but the King replied that he trusted there was no question of the Prime Minister's resignation: the leaders of the three parties must get together and come to some arrangement. His Majesty hoped that the Prime Minister, with the colleagues who remained faithful to him, would help in the formation of a National Government, which the King was sure would be supported by the Conservatives and Liberals. The King assured the Prime Minister that, remaining at his post, his position and reputation would be much more enhanced than if he surrendered the government of the country at such a crisis. Baldwin and Samuel said that they were willing to serve under the Prime Minister, and render all help possible to carry on the Government as a National Emergency Government until an emergency bill or bills had been passed by Parliament, which would restore once more British credit and the confidence of foreigners. After that they would expect His Majesty to grant a dissolution. To this course the King agreed. During the Election the National Government would remain in being, though of course each Party would fight the election on its own lines.

> From the description in Source A, how important a role would you judge George V to have played in the formation of the National Government?

'Country before party'

That afternoon, Ramsay MacDonald returned to tell his bemused colleagues in the last Labour cabinet meeting that he had agreed to stay on as prime minister at the head of a National Government. His explanation was that he was putting 'country before party'. He claimed that the economic crisis facing Britain was so serious that it could be met only by forming a cross-party government of national unity. Hugh Dalton, who had been a junior minister in the Labour government, gave an eye-witness account of the meeting (Source B).

SOURCE B

From Hugh Dalton, *Call Back Yesterday*, Muller, 1953, pp. 272–3.

At 2.30 the Cabinet Room is crowded … J.R.M. [James Ramsay MacDonald] sits alone on the other side of the long table. It is as though a martyr was speaking, just before a cruel death … he has to tell us that the Government is at an end. He is very sorry … But the gravity of the crisis is not yet widely understood. He is going through with this. … He realizes that he is committing political suicide. He is not going to ask any of us to do the same, or to put our heads into the noose into which he will put his. But perhaps some of us would be willing to travel the same road with him.

Ramsay MacDonald defended the bankers; he claimed that, far from acting improperly, they had offered the government 'the most valuable help'. It was the desperate financial circumstance, not malice, that had created the need to reduce welfare expenditure. Britain could not cope without an international loan. 'Otherwise, he said, 'sterling would have collapsed. There would have been a run on the banks, and then a run on the Post Office.'

The explanation did not satisfy the Labour ranks; it infuriated them. They protested that it had all been a plot on his part to retain personal power and that the National Government was already decided on long before he told the cabinet. He had gone behind the backs of his colleagues and plotted with the opposition leaders. Ramsay MacDonald was immediately expelled from his party and his name became reviled among succeeding generations of Labour supporters.

Beatrice Webb, a prominent Fabian, spoke for many Labour supporters (Source C) when she asserted that Ramsay MacDonald's decision was motivated by a love of office for its own sake.

SOURCE C

From Beatrice Webb's diary entry, 24 August 1931, quoted in M. Cole, editor, *Beatrice Webb Diaries*, Longman, 1942, p. 111.

My general impression is that [Ramsay MacDonald] feels himself to be the indispensable leader of a new political party which is bound to come into being within his life-time. He is no longer intent on social reform – any indignation he ever had at the present distribution of wealth he has lost; his real and intimate life is associating with non-political aristocratic society, surrounded with the beauty and dignity which wealth can buy and social experience can direct. Ramsay MacDonald is not distinguished either in intellect or character, and he has some very mean traits in his nature. But he has great gifts as a political leader, he has personal charm, he has vitality, he is assiduous, self-controlled and skilful.

Does Ramsay MacDonald emerge from the description in Source B a disgraced figure or a man of principle?

According to Beatrice Webb in Source C, in what ways do Ramsay MacDonald's personal failings outweigh his political gifts?

However, outside the outraged ranks of the Labour Party, there was considerable understanding and approval of Ramsay MacDonald's decision. *The Times*, arguably Britain's most representative newspaper, regarded the establishment of the National Government as a triumph for democracy (Source D).

SOURCE D

From *The Times*, 25 August 1931.

It is an interesting, dramatic and logical fact that the Labour Government has fallen in what has always been foreseen to be the acid test of democracy – namely, the capacity of its leaders to tell the people the truth and not to regulate their policy by the votes that it would bring. This is the test which Mr MacDonald, Mr Snowden, and those who supported them have triumphantly survived. That is the test to which their dissentient colleagues have ingloriously succumbed.

For his part, Stanley Baldwin was anxious to disassociate his Conservative Party from any suggestion of having been involved in a plot. He told the Commons (Source E) that he had been taken wholly by surprise by Ramsay MacDonald's decision to form a National Government.

SOURCE E

From Stanley Baldwin's speech in the House of Commons, 8 September 1931.

I became convinced that the Government were facing up to the situation. The co-operation of the other parties was willingly given to them for that purpose, and I indicated that, so far as our party was concerned, in any effort of that kind they might rely on our support in the House of Commons. I had no desire to see the government broken up – no one of us had – on this point we would vastly have preferred the Government to have carried on, and we would have assisted them and held ourselves responsible for whatever blame that might be attached to any difficult tasks … The last thing I should have thought of would have been to join a National Government.

In Source D, on what grounds does *The Times* give credit to Ramsay MacDonald?

In Source E, why was Baldwin so insistent that Ramsay MacDonald's decision had taken him by surprise?

The impact on the Labour Party

Since only three ministers and a handful of Labour backbenchers switched their loyalties to the National Government, there was a sense in which the Labour Party had undergone a purification. True, it took a pummelling at the polls in October 1931, losing 236 seats and seeing its popular support drop by 1.7 million votes (see page 129). But it was now free in opposition to redevelop its ideas and policies.

Yet, despite the condemnation of Ramsay MacDonald's behaviour in 1931, the younger brand of Labour politicians, including Dalton, Herbert Morrison, Ernest Bevin and Clement Attlee, who in the 1930s were to work for the recovery and growth of the Labour Party, did so along the lines that Ramsay MacDonald had laid down. Their aim was to make the party an electable force by working within the economic restraints that capitalism imposed and declining to move too far to the revolutionary left. This centrist position would create many bitter quarrels within the parliamentary Labour Party and in the movement as a whole; but it would also determine the essential structure and electoral politics of the Party. Notwithstanding his 'betrayal' in 1931, Ramsay MacDonald's legacy endured.

Following the general election of 1931, **George Lansbury** became Labour Party leader, taking over from Arthur Henderson who had filled the gap after Ramsay MacDonald's expulsion. Although he was a revered figure in the party, his advancing years meant that Lansbury had little to offer in terms of new ideas; his anti-war views inhibited him from adopting a strong stand on the rise of fascism and Nazism (see page 143).

Lansbury was succeeded in 1935 by Clement Attlee, known at this time by his military title, Major Attlee. In his characteristically quiet but authoritative way, Attlee, skilfully maintained the balance between the competing wings of the party and provided a leadership that helped the party to revive during a difficult period when the National Government remained electorally dominant.

The 'popular front'

A complication with which Labour had to contend was a turnabout in Soviet policy. During the 1920s and 1930s, the Soviet Union had taken a consistently contemptuous line towards the non-Marxist socialist parties of Europe, such as the Labour Party, dismissing them as 'social fascists', whose leaders had supinely co-operated with the corrupt governments of the day in suppressing the workers. But after 1935, Stalin, disturbed by the rise of an aggressive Nazi Germany, tried to gain some form of security by reversing his policy of non-alignment with the left. Through the Comintern (see page 100), he now appealed to the parties of the left in Europe to unite in a **'popular front'** against the evils of fascism.

Stalin's change of heart came too late. The European socialists were unwilling to switch direction simply to suit their previous abuser, the Soviet Union. Although the Communist sympathisers within left-wing parties threw themselves energetically into promoting the popular front, the mainstream parties, including the Labour Party in Britain, were understandably reluctant to respond to what they regarded as mere Soviet expediency in the face of German aggression.

This led to a series of struggles within the Labour Party between the advocates of the popular front and the party centre, which remained suspicious of Soviet intentions. The suspicions were borne out when Stalin made nonsense of the whole 'popular front' campaign by performing a still more extraordinary turnabout by entering into the **Nazi–Soviet Pact** in August 1939.

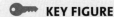

KEY FIGURE

George Lansbury (1859–1940)

Pacifist, very active in local politics; minister for works 1929–31, Labour leader 1932–5.

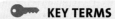

KEY TERMS

'Popular front' An alliance of all Communist, socialist and progressive parties.

Nazi–Soviet Pact A ten-year non-aggression agreement signed between Germany and the USSR in August 1939, which contained a secret protocol allowing the two countries to carve up Poland between them.

Summary diagram: The 1931 crisis

The 1931 crisis

- Rising unemployment
- Growing debts
- Government running out of money

Snowden's balanced-budget policy proved inadequate to meet crisis

May Committee

- Suggested public expenditure cuts as only solution
- These unacceptable to Labour cabinet, which resigned

But

Ramsay MacDonald's putting 'country before party':
- Declined to resign as prime minister
- Did a secret deal with opposition leaders
- Formed a National Government under him

Labour regarded this as 'betrayal' and expelled him from party

Ramsay MacDonald's legacy

- Left Labour as a centrist party
- Labour declined to accept Soviet 'popular front' policy

3 The National Government and domestic policies 1931–7

▶ *Was the National Government simply Conservative rule by another name?*

The Conservatives, knowing that they would fill the majority of the cabinet posts and that Ramsay MacDonald would be dependent on them as a party, fully backed the National Government. Although Lloyd George did not personally join the government, he did commit the official Liberal Party to the support of what was now a heavily Conservative-dominated coalition led by Ramsay MacDonald.

The 1931 election

Having formed his new government, Ramsay MacDonald immediately called a general election in order to confirm that what he had done had public acceptance. In the run-up to the 1931 election, voters were offered a clear choice between candidates who were willing to support the National Government and those who were not. As Table 4.1 shows, the labels defined the candidates' position, as in 'National Liberal' and 'National Labour'. Those without the label 'National' clearly did not support Ramsay MacDonald's new government.

Despite the extraordinary way it had come into being, the National Government proved popular at the polls. It gained over two-thirds of the aggregate vote, a figure unequalled in modern times. Clearly, the majority of the voters did not regard Ramsay MacDonald's action as betrayal. They broadly accepted that the exceptional crisis justified the creation of a new form of government whose first concern was, as Ramsay MacDonald put it, not party politics but national recovery. Notably, neither Oswald Mosley's New Party nor the Communist Party won any seats (see Table 4.1). Equally notable, as an example of electoral imbalance, was the revealing statistic that it took the Conservatives just 25,325 votes to return an MP whereas it took Labour 127,877.

Table 4.1 The October 1931 general election result

Party	Votes	Seats	Percentage of vote
Conservative	11,978,745	473	55.2
Liberal National	809,302	35	3.7
National Labour	341,370	13	1.6
Liberals	1,403,102	33	6.5
National Government (total)	**14,532,519**	**554**	**67.0**
Labour	6,649,630	52	30.6
Independent Liberal	106,106	4	0.5
Communist	74,824	0	0.3
New Party	36,377	0	0.2

The National Government's problems

One consequence of the formation of the National Government was a temporary easing of the financial crisis. A loan of £80 million (roughly equivalent to £1.7 billion in 2015) was immediately advanced by American bankers. The price for this was that Britain had to continue with the programme of cuts that had brought about the end of the Labour government. This produced strong opposition from those most directly affected by the tax hikes and pay reductions. For the government, the most disturbing example of this was the Invergordon Mutiny. In September 1931, in protest against the scheduled cuts in service pay, the 12,000 sailors from the fifteen ships of the Atlantic Fleet, moored at Invergordon in Scotland, declared that they would not obey orders. In a placatory move, the government limited the cuts to around half the original figures proposed. At the same time, it ordered that the ringleaders be arrested and imprisoned; a further 200 sailors were dishonourably discharged.

The hostile reaction to the cuts and the knowledge that the £80 million loan was fast being used up increased the pressure on the government to abandon the gold standard. This was duly done on 19 September, five days after the Invergordon Mutiny. The devaluation that this entailed did not have the disastrous effects that had been widely feared. The pound fell by a quarter of its value from $4.86 to $3.40, but this did not cause any major disruptions in the money markets and had the consequence over the longer term of making British exports cheaper and, therefore, more competitive.

The performance of the National Government in the 1930s tends to be judged by historians in relation to its handling of two major problem areas: the economy and foreign affairs (see page 144). The government that Ramsay MacDonald now led had to contend with the financial and economic problems that had helped to bring down his previous Labour government. These are best understood by reference to the Depression, the term that is still useful as a description of what Britain experienced for much of the 1930s.

The Depression

The year 1929 was critical in international history. It marked the beginning of a worldwide economic depression that was to last for a decade and affect nearly every country in the world, Britain included. It was in the October of 1929 that the USA, the world's most powerful economy, suffered the **Wall Street Crash**. This financial disaster was followed by a severe industrial decline between 1929 and 1932. In a desperate effort to limit the damage, the USA immediately introduced restrictive measures. It erected prohibitive trade barriers to keep out foreign goods and it recalled its foreign loans. Britain was one of the first countries to be harmed by these policies. Since the American market was now largely closed, the British manufacturing industries could not sell their goods in what had been their biggest outlet.

Already in decline (see page 78), Britain's staple industries were particularly badly hit. There was the added problem for Britain that its trade with the USA had previously been the major means by which it had raised the capital to pay off its loans. Unable now to trade with the USA, Britain found itself in an impossible position. It was saddled with debts and could not raise the capital to meet them. It is true that Britain was itself owed large amounts by France, Italy and other Allies from the wartime. However, since these countries were also victims of the international depression there was little prospect of their being able to pay what they owed to Britain.

 **KEY TERM**

Wall Street Crash
The collapse of the US stock market in 1929, which destroyed share values and investments.

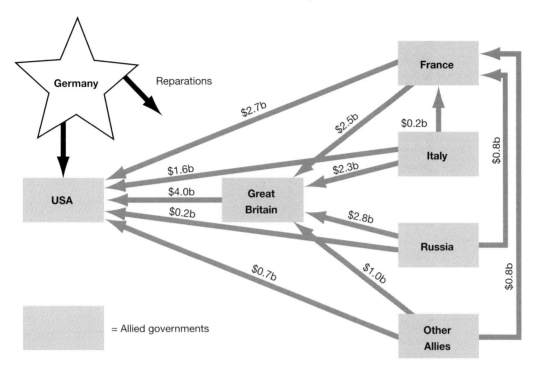

Figure 4.1 This diagram illustrates the links created by the loans and borrowings among the Allies during the First World War. The arrows point from the debtor to the creditor countries, showing how much was owed. In theory, Germany was committed to paying large reparations to the Allies. But the relatively small amounts it did pay came from loans advanced by the USA, which stood at the centre of the whole interlocking system. This was why the health or otherwise of the US economy was of such vital concern to Europe. How does the diagram support the notion that 'If the USA sneezes, Europe catches a cold'?

The following tables help to provide a picture of how the industrial depression, at its worst between 1930 and 1936, affected Britain.

Table 4.2 Unemployment in Britain 1921–40

1921	1.58 million	1931	2.64 million
1922	1.50 million	1932	2.64 million
1923	1.28 million	1933	2.40 million
1924	1.12 million	1934	2.10 million
1925	1.22 million	1935	2.00 million
1926	1.28 million	1936	1.90 million
1927	1.12 million	1937	1.49 million
1928	1.20 million	1938	1.70 million
1929	1.28 million	1939	1.60 million
1930	1.98 million	1940	1.10 million

Table 4.3 Percentage of unemployed in certain trades in 1936

Sector	Percentage
Shipbuilding	30.6%
Coalmining	25.0%
Shipping	22.3%
All textile trades	13.2%
Commerce and finance	3.8%
Printing and paper	6.2%
Skilled building crafts	6.3%
Chemical trades	7.9%
Engineering	8.3%
Average for all UK trades	12.5%

Table 4.4 Percentage of unemployed according to region in 1936

Region	Percentage
South-east England	5.6%
London	6.5%
South-west England	7.8%
Midlands	9.4%
North-west England	16.2%
North-east England	16.6%
Scotland	18.0%
Northern Ireland	23.0%
Wales	28.5%

Tables 4.3 and 4.4 illustrate the blight affecting the staple industries in Britain. In 1936, the overall unemployment figure for all British trades was 12.5 per cent. However, shipbuilding, mining, shipping and textiles all showed much higher figures. In contrast, the service industries all had single-figure rates of unemployment. The service industries were those enterprises developed after the First World War to meet the growing demand for modern convenience and leisure goods, such as radios, refrigerators and vacuum cleaners, newspapers and magazines. The building, electrical engineering, printing and chemical trades rapidly expanded to provide these commodities, which were directly aimed at stimulating consumer demand.

The 'hungry thirties'

The discrepancy between the decline of the staple industries and the boom in the consumer industries is striking. It indicates that there was no single trend that could be observed. Whether one saw growth or decline depended on where one looked. This is clearly evident in the statistics in Table 4.4. Low in the relatively prosperous London and the south-east, unemployment was noticeably higher in the areas where the staple industries were concentrated, principally:

- the manufacturing centres of Birmingham and the Black Country
- coal and steel in Yorkshire and Wales
- textiles in Lancashire
- shipbuilding on the Tyne and in Scotland and Northern Ireland.

The term the 'hungry thirties' came into common use after 1945 to describe the high unemployment and depression that had afflicted Britain in that decade. However, revisionist historians suggest it is inaccurate to speak as if the 'Depression' had been a common experience in Britain. They regard it not as a single phenomenon but as several. What observers see depends on where they stand. Table 4.4 indicates that the Depression was very much a regional affair. In those areas of Britain dependent on the old industries for their livelihood, the Depression was severe and enduring. If, however, the focus is shifted to such regions as the Thames Valley or the Home Counties, the picture becomes one of remarkable growth. The increase in house-building and in the purchasing of cars and domestic commodities could be taken as both cause and effect of the good times prevailing in these areas.

Living standards between the wars

As the previous section noted, the Depression was a patchy affair. It did not impact on the whole of Britain equally. Unemployment and decline were not universal. Indeed, in a number of areas there was spectacular growth. However, that was of little comfort to those in the depressed regions. They complained that a southern-dominated Parliament and government did not fully appreciate the sufferings of the workers in the north. It was part of a north–south divide often described as the '**two nations**'. It was little consolation to the victims of the Depression to be told that things were better elsewhere in the country.

Yet, after acknowledging the poverty that so many in the regions experienced, the fact remains that for many of the population the interwar years were a time of genuine economic advance. Figure 4.2 (page 134) is instructive here. It shows that at no time did **retail prices** move ahead of wages; the lines of the graph remain parallel throughout the 1920s and 1930s, indicating that purchasing power (the means to buy goods) was maintained even when wages appeared to fall. This meant that **real wages** increased. For those in work, times were better, not worse, during the Depression.

Growth in consumerism

The plight of the laid-off workers in the staple industries was only too real, but it was far from being the whole story. Between 1924 and 1935 real wages rose as a national average by seventeen per cent. This gave the majority of people in Britain greater purchasing power, a fact proved by the expanding sales of consumer goods, known popularly as '**mod cons**'. The women's cosmetics industry also experienced a very rapid growth as working-class women began to use the lipsticks, powders and perfumes that previously had been exclusive to

KEY TERMS

Two nations The term was first used in the nineteenth century to define the division of Britain between the rich and the poor, between the areas of Britain which were flourishing and those which were in decline.

Retail price The price paid for goods by the purchaser in the shops.

Real wages The purchasing power of earnings when set against prices. When prices are high money will buy less; when prices are low the same amount of money will buy more.

Mod cons Short for modern conveniences, for example household accessories such as vacuum cleaners, refrigerators and wirelesses.

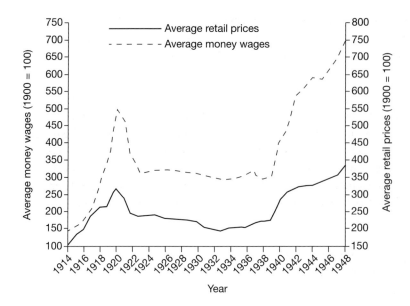

Figure 4.2 A graph comparing prices and wages in Britain 1914–48.

more privileged women. Access to popular entertainment became widespread. Reading tabloid newspapers and magazines, listening to the wireless, going to the cinema and watching professional sport became the main leisure activities of the British people. One measure of this is that between 1924 and 1935 cinema audiences grew from 36,000 a year to 8 million.

A housing revolution

In this same period one and a half million houses, many having indoor lavatories and hot running water, were provided at low rent by the local authorities (see page 99). In addition to these council houses, two and a half million homes were provided by the building industry for private sale. A major factor enabling people of fairly modest incomes to buy houses was the increase in the 1930s of the number of **building societies**.

Key measures in the provision of homes for ordinary people were the National Government's Housing Acts of 1933 and 1935, which were a development of the measures introduced by Greenwood in 1930, during the 1929–31 Labour government (see page 118). The National Government's housing legislation granted increased subsidies to those local councils who were prepared to tackle the problems of slum clearance and overcrowding. The subsidies were put to effective use. In 1936 the average weekly rent paid by council house tenants in Britain was an affordable 11s. (55p).

Housing was one of the success stories of the National Government. By 1939, a third of the 4 million houses in Britain had been constructed in the twenty years since 1918, many of those during the 1930s. The developments in the provision of both private and council house building in the interwar years began a housing

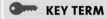
KEY TERM

Building societies Finance companies which advanced mortgages (loans) over long periods of time (for example, 25 years), making it possible for those on regular incomes to buy houses knowing that they would be able to pay back the capital and interest.

revolution in the provision of homes, which was to be a notable aspect of social advance in the twentieth century. In 1914 only ten per cent of the population owned their own homes. Fifty years later this proportion had grown to sixty per cent.

An impressive feature of many new homes was their use of electricity as the chief source of power. By 1939, the spread of the **national grid** was providing electricity to nearly all of urban Britain, a development that largely explains the rapid rise in living standards that occurred across the nation. This was of particular significance for women. By tradition, they were the workers in the home. The installation of a domestic electricity supply gave women access to the mod cons (see page 133), which provided the potential for making life less burdensome.

The National Government's policies

Despite its presiding over such important modernisations, the National Government had no genuine answer to the economic problems of the day. Its essential response was to return to protective tariffs in an attempt to stimulate industrial recovery. This was unimaginative; protection of itself would not have ended the Depression. It can be said fairly of the National Government, as of all the interwar governments, that they did not develop economic policies that were realistic enough for the problems they faced.

This was most obviously the case in regard to unemployment. The government's strategy for combating it was to cut public expenditure in the hope that this would limit inflation, and so encourage manufacturers to continue producing and, therefore, employing workers. It shied away from the intervention advocated by John Maynard Keynes and Oswald Mosley (see page 139). The strongest criticism of the government's failures tended to come from outside Parliament. Memorable examples were the hunger marches, invariably peaceful, not to say poignant, protests by the unemployed, who felt they had no other way of drawing attention to their desperate condition than by taking to the streets. The most famous of these was the Jarrow March of 1936, which involved 200 unemployed Tyneside shipyard workers walking from Jarrow to London.

Literary response

It was not the Jarrow March but an earlier workers' march in Salford that had been broken up by the police that inspired what became regarded as the outstanding literary response to the Depression. *Love on the Dole* was a novel written by Walter Greenwood in 1933. In its depiction of lives blighted by economic deprivation following factory closures, it offered a powerful and moving insight into the experience of ordinary working people. Greenwood said that in his novel, which was later made into a play and film, he had sought 'to show what life means to a young man living under the shadow of the dole, the tragedy of a lost generation who are denied consummation, in decency, of the natural hopes and desires of youth'.

KEY TERM

National grid A nationwide network of high-voltage lines carrying electricity from generating stations to homes and factories.

Recovery

What ultimately helped the National Government was not its own policies but the recovery in world trade that occurred towards the mid-1930s and which was sustained by large-scale rearmament in the late 1930s. Although unemployment remained high for peacetime and was the outstanding domestic issue of the time, it did fall from its peak of 2.6 million in 1932 to 1.7 million in 1938.

The 1935 election result showed that, despite the inability of the National Government to deal with unemployment, it had largely maintained its support. The Liberals were clearly no longer a political force, and although the Labour Party had increased its popular support, it was not yet able to convert that into seats in the Commons.

An interesting statistic is that this was the last election in Britain in which the winning party polled more than 50 per cent of the vote. All governments since then have been minority governments.

Table 4.5 The 1935 general election result

Party	Votes	Seats	Percentage of vote
Conservatives (including National Labour and National Liberal)	11,810,158	432	53.7
Labour	8,325,491	154	37.9
Liberals	1,422,116	20	6.4
Communists	27,117	1	0.1

Ramsay MacDonald's legacy

Age and declining health led to Ramsay MacDonald's retirement in 1935. He had already gone on too long; in his last years he often became rambling and incoherent. But it would be unfair to let this last image dominate his reputation. It is true that he had split the Labour Party and that he had no genuine answer to the economic problems that dogged all three of his administrations, 1924, 1929–31 and 1931–5. Yet his constructive contribution to political life far outweighed his failings. The development of the Labour Party as an electable and acceptable part of the political system was largely his work, and his attempts to create harmony in international relations won him the admiration of many in Britain and abroad.

> ## Ramsay MacDonald's record
>
> - His decision to lead his minority parliamentary party into office showed Labour had arrived as a party of government.
> - His pursuit of moderate policies freed Labour of the accusation that it was a front for Marxist extremists.
> - He broke the party over his decision in 1931 to stay in office and form a coalition, which resulted in Labour's being out of office for the next fourteen years.
> - In putting 'country before party' and leading the National Government, he was advancing the notion of consensus politics.
> - In none of his three administrations was he prepared to abandon orthodox traditional financial and economic policies.
> - He earned a deserved reputation as a peacemaker in international affairs.

Imperial issues

A feature of Ramsay MacDonald's years that is sometimes lost sight of is the development in imperial affairs. It was under him that, only a few months after the formation of the National Government, the Statute of Westminster was passed. This measure, in effect, ended the British Empire at least in name. From now on it was to be a commonwealth of independent states. Britain still had its colonies, as Ramsay MacDonald's dealings with India had illustrated (see page 121), but the dominions were entirely free of British control and could withdraw from the Commonwealth if they so chose. It was a logical development of the 1926 Balfour Declaration (see page 110).

Imperial preference

The more immediate concern in the early 1930s was not the constitutional question but economics. There were many on the Conservative side who argued that the Depression made the retention of any element of free trade impractical. They pushed for the adoption of imperial preference. This was essentially a return to the ideas of Joseph Chamberlain, who had argued for the formation of a self-contained common market between Britain and its overseas territories (see page 22). Two steps were taken towards this in 1932:

- Britain introduced an Import Duties Act which imposed a ten per cent levy on non-imperial goods.
- An Imperial Economic Conference in Ottawa adopted imperial preference as a trading principle.

The outcome was disappointing. The agreement did not apply to all the colonies, only to the dominions, which, in the event, were reluctant to tie themselves strictly to the letter of the Ottawa agreement. The result was that although there was some increase in inter-dominion trade this was never enough to meet the expectations of those who had put their faith in imperial preference as a way of curing Britain's economic ills.

Baldwin as prime minister 1935–7

Ramsay MacDonald was followed as prime minister by the Conservative leader, Stanley Baldwin, who formed his third government. Much to the annoyance of his political opponents, Baldwin's policy of 'masterly inactivity' appeared to suit the situation. He continued to present the image he had developed as prime minister in the 1920s of the pipe-smoking Englishman who loved his country and its people and who could be relied on in a crisis. This had been evident in his handling of the General Strike in 1926, where his calmness had prevented his government colleagues from going to extremes (see page 107).

The abdication crisis 1936

Baldwin's phlegmatic approach was also apparent in his handling of the abdication crisis in 1936, a situation created by the wish of Edward VIII to marry Mrs Wallis Simpson, an American divorcée. Baldwin took a consistently constitutional approach, refusing to be drawn into the moral issues that many others thought were at stake. He advised the king that for him to take a divorced woman as his marriage partner would be incompatible with his position as head of the Church of England, which did not recognise divorce. He informed Edward that the government would have to consider resigning if he pressed on with his marriage plan.

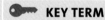

KEY TERM

King's Party An unofficial grouping of some 60 MPs, including Winston Churchill, who argued that Edward VIII should be allowed to make his own decision free from political pressure.

Although a group of Conservatives formed an unofficial '**King's Party**', the majority of MPs, the whole of the Labour Party and, as far as can be judged, public opinion, supported the prime minister's principled stand. Baldwin's view prevailed. In December 1936, after just 325 days as uncrowned king, Edward VIII put his personal desires before his sense of duty and announced his abdication. Six months later he married the woman without whom, as he told the nation in his abdication broadcast, he could not live.

Stanley Baldwin

Baldwin was a deeply respected parliamentarian and was admired for his lack of pettiness and his generosity of spirit towards his political opponents; for example, he always made a point of personally welcoming new MPs in the Commons, whatever their party. It has been suggested that his calm leadership and lack of vindictiveness played no small part in Britain's avoiding the political extremism that marred so many European countries between the wars (see page 143).

Like Ramsay MacDonald, he appears genuinely to have believed in putting country before party when Britain's interests were at stake. It is doubtful that the National Government could have worked at all had Baldwin not backed it from the beginning with his special brand of moderation and absence of political rancour. Such were the political uncertainties after 1931 that traditional politics might have fractured altogether had he not been there to hold things together.

His readiness to serve loyally under Ramsay MacDonald was a stabilising influence in the early 1930s.

Baldwin wanted class divisions to be eradicated from politics and society. It was for that reason that some of the right-wing Conservatives sometimes disapproved of him. Having in mind Baldwin's desire to see welfare schemes extended and funded by central government, they complained that his notions were 'half-way to socialism'. At times he also received strong criticism from the press, whose proprietors found his 'safety-first' approach unattractive. It is an interesting reflection of the less-than-clear political divisions between the parties that Baldwin should have been regarded as too socialist in his approach while Ramsay MacDonald was considered not socialist enough.

Baldwin's record as prime minister

Strengths:

- His calm but firm leadership was of great value in Britain at a time of political extremism elsewhere in Europe.
- His lack of small-mindedness and respect for opponents made him a figure around whom compromise and conciliation could develop.
- He rode major domestic crises ably, for example the 1926 General Strike and the abdication crisis.
- He made the National Government work when there was a risk of politics fracturing.

Limitations:

- His lack of insight in economic matters meant that he made no significant contribution to resolving unemployment.
- His detachment from foreign affairs limited his understanding of the character of developments in Nazi Germany and fascist Italy.

Challenges to traditional parliamentary politics

One of the claims for Baldwin was that his non-confrontational style was an important factor in preventing Britain from gravitating towards the extreme form of politics that developed in so many countries in Europe in the interwar years. Significant parties of both the left and right extremes did emerge in Britain, largely in reaction to the economic difficulties of the time, but they never became more than fringe movements.

Oswald Mosley

One of Ramsay MacDonald's interesting ministerial appointments in 1929 was an able and ambitious young man, **Oswald Mosley**, who was made chancellor of the Duchy of Lancaster. Although this was a non-cabinet post, Mosley was one of a group entrusted with the task of examining ways of tackling unemployment. He found, however, that when he presented his own formal

 **KEY FIGURE**

**Oswald Mosley
(1896–1980)**

Variously a Conservative, an independent, a Labour MP and a Fabian; he found none of the parties satisfied his particular political notions, which was why he turned to a form of politics outside the mainstream.

set of proposals on the matter they were turned down by the cabinet on the grounds that they were either too impractical or too expensive. Among Mosley's suggestions were:

- greater use of tariffs to raise revenue
- the money raised through tariffs to fund pensions and unemployment cover
- funded early retirement schemes in industry to open up jobs for younger workers
- government control of the banks to prevent financial problems arising.

The New Party

Frustrated by his rejection, and in spite of being very well received at the 1930 Labour conference, Mosley decided to go it alone. He resigned from Labour and founded his own New Party based on the proposals he had put to the cabinet. The New Party fielded 24 candidates in the 1931 election, on a programme of curing joblessness. It failed to attract public support, each of the 24 who stood gaining an average of only 1500 votes.

British Union of Fascists (BUF)

The dismal electoral performance intensified Mosley's despair of parliamentary politics, which, he claimed, were no longer capable of answering Britain's needs. In 1932 he founded the British Union of Fascists (BUF). While the BUF was prepared to contest elections, its ultimate aim was the establishment of a **corporate state** in which Parliament would cease to exist or have only a minor role to play.

Mosley took as his model the Italian Fascist leader, Benito Mussolini (1883–1945). A former socialist who became embittered by the effete character of the Italian political system, Mussolini had led his followers, the Fascists, to power in 1922 and ruled as *il Duce* (the leader) until 1943. Mosley was impressed by Mussolini's intense nationalism and his hatred of communism. He was also taken with Mussolini's reorganisation of the Italian state along corporatist lines, which, he believed, had rid Italy of the type of economic problems that still threatened Britain. As with all the Fascist parties in Europe at this time, there was a strong racist element in Mosley's BUF. It vehemently denounced the Jews, asserting that it was their malign control of international finance that was principally responsible for the economic depression.

Although Mosley himself was an interesting character with many striking ideas, his Fascist movement never gained truly popular support. That is not to deny that it was not capable of frightening the authorities by causing serious disorder, as witnessed in the Battle of Cable Street in October 1936. Declaring its hatred of immigrants, the BUF planned a provocative march through London's East End, an area that was home to many Jews and Irish. This was met with barricades and fierce and violent resistance from locals, who forced the march to be diverted away from the area.

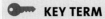

KEY TERM

Corporate state Power concentrated at the centre, entitling the government to direct the running of society and the economy without reference to a Parliament.

While creating disturbance was relatively easy, becoming a credible party was altogether more difficult and the BUF never advanced beyond the periphery of politics. Although Mosley's ideas on economics attracted people as diverse as **Aneurin Bevan** and Harold Macmillan, his political notions tended to alienate rather than attract responsible opinion. The only people with any sort of social standing who joined the BUF were some second-rate writers and minor aristocrats. It is true that the *Daily Mirror* and the *Daily Mail* showed some initial sympathy for Mosley's plans to lessen unemployment, but, as soon as the latent racism of his movement became overt, the newspapers dropped him.

The BUF had some success in local politics, but it is highly doubtful that it would ever have been an electoral force nationally. This was never actually put to the test as there were no general elections between 1935 and 1945. However, since the highest recorded number of BUF members in the 1930s was 50,000, the party's chances of a winning any seats appeared negligible.

KEY FIGURE

Aneurin ('Nye') Bevan (1897–1960)
Labour MP 1929–60, minister of health 1945–51, minister of labour 1951; of Welsh coal-mining stock, he became the outstanding voice of left-wing Labour.

Reasons for the BUF's lack of success in 1930s' Britain

- The party was dependent on Oswald Mosley and never had a separate identity as a credible political movement.
- Mosley's undoubted abilities were not matched by any other members of the party.
- His style of leadership, based on Mussolini in Italy and Hitler in Germany, was alien to British politics and won him few admirers outside his own Fascist ranks.
- Apart from its ideas on unemployment, the BUF had no real plan of action. It relied too greatly on stirring up hatred and emotion without knowing how to use these in a sophisticated political form.
- It was only in the grim economic atmosphere of the early 1930s that the BUF had any attraction. Once the economy began to pick up British fascism began to wither.

- Unlike Italy and Germany, Britain had a stable political system which, despite the Depression of the 1930s, never came under serious threat from extreme movements like the BUF.
- Notwithstanding the personal wealth which Mosley and some of his aristocratic associates put into the BUF, the movement never raised enough funding to sustain it as a powerful force.
- As the threat of war increased in the 1930s (see page 148), the BUF's sympathy for Nazi Germany made it very suspect in the eyes of ordinary members of the British public.
- The social and economic breakdown for which the BUF longed never occurred. Mosley remained 'an opportunist for whom no opportunity came'.

The Communist Party of Great Britain (CPGB)

Many of the limitations from which the BUF suffered also applied to the other extreme political movement in Britain, the Communists. Established in 1920, the Communist Party of Great Britain (CPGB) depended for its funds largely on secret grants from the Soviet Union. An intriguing detail that has come to light is that the Communist Party received more money in this way than the official Labour Party was able to raise for itself by legitimate means. Yet, in political terms the Soviet payments were a waste. As Table 4.6 illustrates, at no point, even in the grimmest days of the Depression, did the Communist Party ever make sufficient ground to be more than a minority pressure group.

Table 4.6 The CPGB's electoral performance

Year	Candidates	Votes	Seats	Percentage of vote
1924	8	55,346	1	0.3
1929	25	50,614	0	0.3
1931	26	74,824	0	0.3
1935	2	27,117	1	0.1
1945	21	102,780	2	0.4

It is true that Communists made a bigger impression in local government. Parts of Glasgow, for example, and some London boroughs saw Communists play a prominent role in the 1930s in protests over rent payment and housing conditions. But such local following as the party gained never translated into a national movement of note. The same was true of its efforts in the workplace. Communists were often behind the strikes and industrial disruptions of the time, but they failed to exploit the troubled economic circumstances well enough to make themselves a major political force or become a real threat to the political order whose overthrow they sought.

Unable to gather support on its own terms, the CPGB tried to affiliate to the Labour Party. It made four separate applications, in 1924, 1935, 1943 and 1946, but was rejected on each occasion. At the time of the first application in 1924 the Labour Party ruled that anyone belonging to the CPGB could not join the Labour Party as an individual member. Consequently, the only way Communists could directly influence Labour was by '**entryism**', joining the party without declaring their real allegiance.

Such tactics undoubtedly intensified the struggle over policies between the left and the right of the Labour Party. Significantly, however, Labour under Attlee, following the pattern established by Ramsay MacDonald, always sought the moderate centre ground when presenting his case to the electorate. One of Attlee's major achievements during his twenty years as leader after 1935 was to prevent the Marxist left from imposing its revolutionary policies on the Labour Party.

Intellectual influence of communism

Interestingly, where Communist ideas were strong was not among the workers but among intellectuals. University lecturers, writers and poets, such as **W.H. Auden** and Stephen Spender, found Marxist anti-capitalist ideas appealing. Dismayed by the Depression and the rise of fascism, they concluded that Soviet communism offered a better way. That was why the Spanish Civil War attracted their interest (see page 146). It was during the 1930s that a coterie of some of the brightest young men at Cambridge University, known as the 'Cambridge Five', were recruited by the Comintern (page 100) to spy for the Soviet Union. The most notorious of these were **Guy Burgess** and **Donald Maclean.**

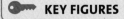

KEY TERM

Entryism Infiltrating a political party with the aim of subverting its policies.

KEY FIGURES

W.H. Auden (1907–73)

A prolific poet and essayist whose themes included politics, religion and human relationships; his accessible style made him a popular left-leaning commentator on his times.

Guy Burgess (1911–63) and Donald Maclean (1913–83)

Both worked in the 1940s in the Foreign Office, from where they leaked British State secrets before fleeing to the Soviet Union in the 1950s.

It is now clear that British intellectuals turned to communism largely as a reaction against the existence of the right-wing regimes in Hitler's Germany, Mussolini's Italy and Franco's Spain. Fascism and communism are now seen as mirror images, which explains the deep mutual hatred between them as ideologies. But in the 1930s it was their differences that were emphasised by contemporaries. To be a supporter of the one was to be the bitter enemy of the other. The aggression and brutality of Nazi Germany gave a form of acceptability to Soviet communism, which was seen as being intellectually respectable in a way that fascism could not be.

Intellectuals convinced themselves that the excesses of communism were occasional lapses brought about by desperate circumstances, whereas the viciousness associated with Nazism and fascism was an integral and definitive part of their character. This readiness to be forgiving of communism was boosted by the entry of the Soviet Union into the war as an ally of Britain in 1941 (see page 150).

The poet W.H. Auden memorably described the 1930s as 'a low, dishonest decade', and it is certainly true that historians have tended to find the period of the National Government a dispiriting one. The politicians of the day had no answer to the economic difficulties that confronted them; domestic policies seemed to be a matter of drift rather than direction. However, in the end it is not the National Government's domestic policy but its record in foreign affairs that has come in for the strongest criticism.

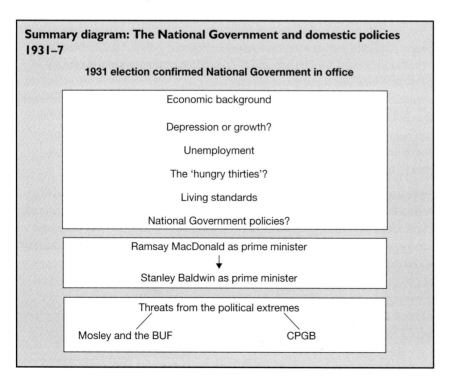

Summary diagram: The National Government and domestic policies 1931–7

1931 election confirmed National Government in office

Economic background

Depression or growth?

Unemployment

The 'hungry thirties'?

Living standards

National Government policies?

Ramsay MacDonald as prime minister
↓
Stanley Baldwin as prime minister

Threats from the political extremes

Mosley and the BUF   CPGB

The National Government and foreign affairs 1931–9

▶ *Why did the National Government adopt a policy of appeasement in its foreign relations?*

▶ *What part did public opinion play in the conduct of the National Government's foreign policy?*

In the first half of its period of office, the National Government was preoccupied with the major economic problems that confronted Britain. In the second half, it was crises in foreign affairs that demanded its attention.

Public opinion

An interesting feature of the foreign policy followed by the National Government was the influence public opinion had on it. The 1930s were a period when public attitudes began to be measured more accurately and given greater attention by parties and politicians. The Gallup Organization, an American body, began to make studies of British public opinion in the 1930s. Although the methods and techniques were unsophisticated by later standards, they were obviously the beginning of something significant. There were signs that the National Government became aware of public opinion and began to be influenced by it.

Where public opinion was most noticeable was in the marked reluctance of people to regard war as a legitimate step in national policy. This derived from a profound horror of military conflict, drawn from memories of the carnage of 1914–18. Moreover, there was a general belief, strengthened by newsreels of the terrible effects of bombing, that a future war would be still more appalling since the civilian population would be at the mercy of aerial attack. British audiences had been shocked by films showing the devastation caused by the **Axis powers'** bombing of civilian targets in Spain (see page 146) and by similar Japanese attacks on the cities of China in the **Sino-Japanese War**.

Since war was too horrible to contemplate, its avoidance became a demanding necessity and, therefore, the government's chief objective. None of the political parties felt free to advocate a rearmament programme. Furthermore, in a time of economic depression, it was not easy to argue the merits of arms expenditure at the expense of welfare. In November 1936, Baldwin showed how sensitive the decision-makers had become to the power of public opinion: 'supposing I had gone to the country and said that we must rearm, does anybody think that this pacific democracy would have rallied to the cry? I cannot think of anything that would have made the loss of the election more certain.'

🔑 KEY TERMS

Axis powers Germany and Italy, the main opponents of the Allies in the Second World War in Europe.

Sino-Japanese War A struggle fought from 1937 to 1945 in which the Japanese deliberately terrorised Chinese civilians by bombing raids.

SOURCE F

From a speech by Stanley Baldwin in the House of Commons, 10 November 1932, quoted in Keith Middlemas and John Barnes, *Baldwin: A Biography*, Weidenfeld & Nicolson, 1969, pp. 269–70.

I think it is well also for the man in the street to realise that there is no power on earth that can protect him from being bombed. Whatever people may tell him, the bomber will always get through. The only defence is in offence, which means that you have to kill more women and children more quickly than the enemy if you want to save yourselves … If the conscience of the young men should ever come to feel, with regard to this one instrument [bombing] that it is evil and should go, the thing will be done … But when the next war comes, and European civilisation is wiped out, as it will be, and by no force more than that force, then do not let them lay blame on the old men. Let them remember that they, principally, or they alone, are responsible for the terrors that have fallen upon the earth.

According to Baldwin, in Source F, why are civilians so vulnerable in modern warfare?

The 'King and Country' debate 1933

Baldwin had good grounds for describing Britain as a 'pacific democracy'. There were striking occasions when the British people were regarded as having very clearly expressed their refusal to contemplate war. In February 1933, the Oxford Union voted by a large majority in favour of the resolution 'That this House will in no circumstances fight for its King and Country'. Given that Oxford University supposedly contained some of the brightest young people in the nation, who would provide the next generation of leaders in public life, the debate was interpreted by many in Britain and abroad as evidence of how powerful a hold pacifist feelings had in the country at large.

The peace ballot 1934–5

In a remarkable measurement of public opinion, the first ever attempted on such a scale, a nine-month, house-to-house poll was organised by the **League of Nations Union**. Eleven and a half million people answered a series of questions regarding their views on disarmament. Most responded strongly in favour of Britain's remaining a member of the League of Nations and backed the notion of an 'all-round reduction of armaments'. However, to arguably the most important question, whether they supported international armed resistance against an aggressor, nearly 7 million replied yes, 2 million said no, with another 2 million abstaining.

The answers revealed a basic confusion of thought in the majority of those questioned. They were in favour of disarmament while at the same time believing in the legitimacy of international armed resistance to aggression. This was a contradiction to which many held without perhaps realising they were supporting two mutually exclusive positions. A remarkable example of such thinking were the words of the leader of the Labour Party, Clement Attlee.

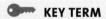 **KEY TERM**

League of Nations Union
Formed in October 1918 with the aim of educating the public to the need for supporting the League, as the only guarantor of peace through collective security.

In 1935 he defined his party's approach to international questions. He told the Commons: 'We stand for collective security through the League of Nations. We reject the use of force as an instrument of policy. Our policy is not one of seeking security through rearmament, but through disarmament.'

Attlee's assertion is an interesting expression of the basic paradox in British attitudes at this time. He declared his support for the League of Nations and collective security, but, at the same time, he rejected the use of force and appealed for disarmament. Attlee's critics in the Commons suggested that his position defied logic. If collective security was to be workable, it had to encompass the use of force, albeit internationally organised and employed only as a last resort. It was, therefore, inconsistent to be for collective security but against the use of force. Nevertheless, regardless of its logic, the anti-war stance was a predominant attitude for much of the 1930s. The government was conscious of this and largely acted in accordance with it until German aggression finally undermined it (see page 149).

The Spanish Civil War 1936–9

The belief in collective security and disarmament was put to the test during the Civil War in Spain (1936–9). In 1936, General Franco led his Nationalist forces, representing Catholic conservative Spain, in rebellion against the Republican government, which had the support of a combination of anarchists, regional separatists and Communists. A bitter three-year conflict followed. Italy and Germany, eager to test their new weapons and military tactics in a real war, aided Franco's armies while Stalin's USSR backed the Republicans.

The National Government in Britain remained officially neutral throughout the struggle. It joined with the French government in formally declaring a policy of non-intervention. But this was an occasion when there was a detectable gap between the governments and the peoples of France and Britain. The Republicans in Spain appealed for help to the peoples rather than the governments of Europe. This provided a great rallying call for those who had been frustrated by the successes of fascism in Italy and Nazism in Germany, and by the apparent indifference of their own governments to all this.

There was a sense in which the Spanish War came just at the right moment for such people, trade unionists, liberals, Marxists and idealists, referred to broadly as the left. A.J.P. Taylor captured the importance for them of the conflict: 'the Spanish question far transcended politics in the ordinary sense. The controversy provided for the generation of the thirties the emotional experience of their lifetime.' Seeing Spain as a simple struggle of democracy versus fascism, they responded eagerly to the Republican appeal and rushed in their thousands to enlist in the **International Brigades**. Intellectuals such as George Orwell, Stephen Spender and W.H. Auden viewed the Spanish War as the perfect arena for a death struggle with fascism.

KEY TERM

International Brigades
The pro-Republican forces made up of foreign volunteers who fought in the Spanish Civil War.

The enthusiasm of the idealists did not receive universal approval. The fact was that the war produced divided responses in Britain. There were those, and not merely those in government, who argued that, in their eagerness to fight for a good cause, the pro-Republican volunteers had disregarded the historical and regional subtleties that had caused the Spanish conflict. It was an oversimplification to interpret it in terms of good versus evil; the war was more complex in its origins than that.

The strongest criticism was that the Republican supporters had been duped into becoming pawns of the USSR. While it was true that the Soviet Union had given direct assistance to the Republicans, it had done so at a high price. Stalin took the whole of Spain's gold reserves and claimed the right to direct the Republican war strategy. When it became clear to the non-Communist members of the International Brigades that the Soviet Union was as cynically exploitative of the situation in Spain as was Nazi Germany, much of the heart went out of their struggle.

The Spanish Civil War, which was eventually won by Franco's Nationalists after three bitter years of fighting, clearly showed the unwillingness of the National Government to take risks in foreign affairs. No matter how passionately interested in the conflict many of its people were, Britain stood militarily and diplomatically aloof. It was this same reluctance to be involved that was to bedevil the National Government's attempts to deal with the mounting threat of Nazi expansionism in Europe.

Chamberlain and appeasement 1937–9

Following Baldwin's retirement in 1937, Neville Chamberlain became prime minister. He inherited as his greatest problem a Europe dominated by an expansionist Germany. Until the last moment, he continued to believe that war was avoidable and that Adolf Hitler and Germany could be appeased or pacified if their genuine grievances were met. In taking this line, Chamberlain knew he had the approval of the bulk of the British people. **Appeasement** already existed as the received wisdom of the day. It was one of the clearest examples yet of government policy being in tune with the wishes of the people.

> **KEY TERMS**
>
> **Appeasement** A conviction that the main duty of government is to avoid war. If that means granting aggressors some of their demands in order to satisfy them, that is preferable to armed conflict.
>
> **Anschluss** German for union or incorporation.

German expansion under Hitler 1933–9

- 1933: Germany withdrew from both the disarmament talks at Geneva and the League of Nations.
- 1935: conscription began to expand Germany's armed services in direct defiance of the restrictions imposed in 1919.
- 1936: German troops reoccupied the Rhineland, which had been demilitarised under the Versailles Treaty.
- 1938: the **Anschluss** incorporated Austria into the German State, a move expressly forbidden by the Treaty of Versailles.
- Sudetenland area of Czechoslovakia occupied by Germany.
- 1939: the remainder of Czechoslovakia was seized.
- Germany invaded Poland.

The outstanding example of Chamberlain's approach was his handling of the Czech crisis in 1938, the event which may be said to have led directly to the outbreak of war a year later, and the one by which the policy of appeasement is invariably judged.

The Czech crisis 1938

Under the Versailles Treaty, an area known as the Sudetenland had been incorporated into the newly created state of Czechoslovakia. However, the Sudetenland was overwhelmingly German in population. Hitler eagerly exploited the demand of the 3 million Sudeten Germans for 'self-determination', the right to be reincorporated into Germany. He subjected the Czech government to a set of impossible demands, threatening war if they were not accepted.

To avoid war, which Britain had begun to prepare for by digging shelters and distributing gas masks, Chamberlain took it on himself to make direct personal contact with Adolf Hitler. A series of meetings between him and Hitler, which involved Chamberlain's flying to Germany on three separate occasions, culminated in September 1938 in the signing of the Munich Agreement. Under its terms, the European powers, Britain, France and Italy, acknowledged Germany's claims to the Sudetenland and obliged the Czechs to accept its loss. In a radio broadcast Chamberlain justified his sacrifice of the Czechs: 'How horrible, fantastic, incredible it is that we should be digging trenches and trying on gas-masks here because of a quarrel in a faraway country between people of whom we know nothing.'

Although those words came later to be regarded as notorious, at the time they were accepted by the majority of the British people as being the only proper response to the crisis. Before Chamberlain entered the plane on his first visit to Hitler, he quoted Shakespeare, declaring to loud cheers that 'out of this nettle, danger, we pluck this flower, safety'. The cheers were even louder on his return from Munich, when he waved a copy of the agreement he had signed with Hitler declaring their nations' commitment never to go to war with each other again. He had, he said, brought back 'peace in our time'. That evening, crowds filled Downing Street to shout Chamberlain's name and applaud him long and enthusiastically when he appeared at the window to acknowledge their cheers. Cinema audiences also broke into spontaneous applause when they saw the newsreels and heard the commentator praise Chamberlain for his consummate statesmanship. Formal prayer services were held in Westminster Abbey and Canterbury Cathedral in which the prime minister was lauded as a saviour of world peace.

Appeasement and public opinion

It should be stressed how big a step in the manipulation of public opinion Chamberlain's visits to Hitler were. They were a study in public relations. The whole thing was meant to impress the British people and keep them on his side. That was why he was careful to make sure his departure and return were major press occasions, covered by the cameras. He well knew that the newsreels would be shown to the millions of the nation's cinema-goers. What has sometimes been lost sight of is how successful Chamberlain was in this. Because his appeasement diplomacy towards Hitler eventually proved futile, it is too easy to forget how hugely popular it initially was. Chamberlain had carried the people with him. Of equal significance was the **attitude of the British military**, who did not regard the nation as being in a position to fight a major war.

It all ended in failure, of course; Hitler had no intention of being bound by his promise given at Munich that the recovery of the Sudetenland marked his last territorial demand. In 1939, he went on to dismember the rest of Czechoslovakia and then to prepare to do the same to Poland. Reluctantly admitting that Hitler could not be stopped by diplomacy, Britain gave Poland guarantees of protection. It was hoped the guarantees might make Hitler pause. But they did not. Chamberlain's capitulation to German demands over Czechoslovakia had convinced Hitler that Britain was neither willing nor able to fight over Poland. He was half right. The Polish guarantees were essentially a gesture since Britain simply did not have the physical means to defend Poland. Nonetheless, it was in accordance with those guarantees that Britain, its patience exhausted, declared war on Germany in September 1939.

The collapse of his appeasement diplomacy made Chamberlain appear inept and foolish, an image that was quickly spread by his opponents and one that has remained the common view taken of him by posterity. Yet what has to be emphasised is that, until appeasement became an obvious and tragic failure, it had expressed the will of the great majority of the British people. In seeking by every means to avoid war, Chamberlain was pursuing a policy that matched the public mood.

Sympathy for Germany

A further key consideration is that, until the post-Munich period, moderate political opinion was markedly sympathetic towards Germany. The harshness of the Versailles settlement in regard to Germany was commonly acknowledged as giving that country the right to redress its legitimate grievances. There were those in Britain who regarded the reoccupation of the Rhineland, the *Anschluss* with Austria and the reclamation of the Sudetenland as all being in keeping with the principle of self-determination which the Allies had made the basis of the peace talks in 1919.

Fear of Soviet communism

There was also an ideological dimension to the problem. Since 1917, Bolshevik (Communist) Russia had called for the violent overthrow of the capitalist nations of Europe. It is now known that there had been no possibility of this. The Soviet

KEY TERM

Attitude of the British military Throughout the 1930s, the chiefs of the British armed services consistently warned the government that their forces were too overstretched and underfunded to be able to engage successfully in a major European conflict.

Union did not have the strength, even if it had the will. But at the time the threat seemed real enough and it was taken seriously in Western Europe. That was why many in Britain welcomed the growth of a strong, anti-Communist Germany. They saw it as a barrier to the spread of Bolshevism westward. The perceived Soviet menace predisposed Britain to being conciliatory towards Nazi Germany. It was only when the USSR became perforce an ally of Britain, following the German invasion of Russia in June 1941, that suspicion of Soviet communism lifted, and then only for the duration of the war.

Churchill and appeasement

Since Winston Churchill, within a year of the failure of appeasement, would be prime minister, his attitude to Germany in the 1930s deserves attention. After 1931, when Ramsay MacDonald found no place for him in his government, Churchill, in his own words, was 'in the wilderness'. He tended to be distrusted for his habit of changing parties and his dated, not to say reactionary, imperialist views. He refused, for example, to acknowledge the legitimacy of India's claim for independence, arguing that it was Britain's duty and destiny to remain an imperial power.

The suspicions harboured towards Churchill meant that when he attempted to warn Parliament and people about the growing German threat, he was not given the attention a less suspect messenger of doom might have received. There was also the more uncomfortable consideration that he was not an entirely consistent opponent of aggrandising dictators:

- In 1933, he declined to speak out against the Japanese occupation of Manchuria.
- In 1935, he said little against the **Italian invasion of Abyssinia**.
- In 1936, he remained silent when Franco's Fascists overthrew the Spanish Republic.

Where he was consistent was in his condemnation of German expansion. He tried to warn the British and French politicians and people that Germany's rearmament under Hitler was a threat to the peace of Europe. Of the Munich Agreement in October 1938, he was bitterly scathing and wholly rejected the notion of Chamberlain's having brought back 'peace with honour'. In the House of Commons he declared passionately: 'We have suffered a total and unmitigated defeat', and warned that it was the 'foretaste of a bitter cup which will be proffered to us year by year unless we rise again and take our stand for freedom.' They were words which added greatly to his moral authority when he became prime minister in May 1940.

KEY TERM

Italian invasion of Abyssinia In 1934–5 Mussolini's expansionist Italy had attacked and occupied parts of Abyssinia. Although Britain and France initially disapproved, they declined to take any military action against Italy and in 1936 formally recognised the Italian takeover.

Summary diagram: The National Government and foreign affairs 1931–9

ISSUES:

Abyssinia   Rhineland   Spanish Civil War   Czechoslovakia   Poland

• The influence of public opinion on decision making

REASONS FOR BRITAIN'S APPEASEMENT POLICY:

• Memories of the slaughter of 1914–18 created a powerful anti-war feeling in Britain.

• Many people put their faith in the League of Nations and backed the concept of collective security.

• A growing belief between the wars that Germany had been harshly treated in the Versailles settlement.

• A similar belief that, in accordance with the principle of self-determination, Germany had the right to recover the German territories taken from it.

• Fear of Soviet Russia made Britain more tolerant of Nazi Germany.

• The same fear made it attractive to have Germany as a buffer state in central Europe.

• Anglo-French mutual suspicions made effective co-operation difficult.

• The cost of Britain's existing defence commitments discouraged further military expenditure.

• The armed services chiefs warned the government in the mid-1930s that Britain was already overstretched militarily and was incapable of fighting a major European war.

• The severe economic depression made welfare spending a priority before rearmament.

Chapter summary

Beset by economic difficulties throughout its two years in office, Ramsay MacDonald's Labour government was finally brought down by an acute financial crisis. 'Betraying' his party, Ramsay MacDonald continued as prime minister of a coalition National Government. Popularly supported though it was throughout the 'hungry thirties', the National Government failed to develop economic policies to deal with the depression that afflicted Britain. The effect of the economic slump varied in its severity from region to region. The worst hit areas were those where the staple industries were sited, the least affected those which saw a boom in the new consumer industries.

Stanley Baldwin, who succeeded Ramsay MacDonald in 1935, gave an impression of solid dependability which helped to calm the abdication crisis and was a factor in Britain's unwillingness to resort to extreme politics; neither fascism nor communism making a major impact. Unable, however, to find a solution to Britain's persistent economic problems, the National Government eventually suffered an even greater loss of reputation over foreign affairs. Neville Chamberlain, whose appeasement policy for a time was hugely popular in Britain's 'pacific democracy', was misled and outmanoeuvred by Adolf Hitler. Eventually, an exasperated and disillusioned National Government took Britain into war in September 1939.

Refresher questions

Use these questions to remind yourself of the key material covered in this chapter.

1 What domestic reforms did Ramsay MacDonald's 1929–31 government attempt?

2 What approach did Ramsay MacDonald take as prime minister towards foreign affairs in 1924 and 1929–31?

3 How did Ramsay MacDonald endeavour to improve Anglo-Soviet relations during his administrations of 1924 and 1929–31?

4 How sympathetic was the second Labour government towards Indian independence?

5 Why did the May Committee's proposals in 1931 arouse controversy?

6 What form did Ramsay MacDonald's 'betrayal' of his party in 1931 take?

7 How did Britain become caught up in the USA's economic depression?

8 Was the Depression of the 1930s a national or a regional problem?

9 Did living standards rise or fall during the Depression?

10 Why did neither the BUF nor CPGB gain wide support in Britain in the 1930s?

11 How significant were Ramsay MacDonald's periods of office as prime minister?

12 What did Stanley Baldwin's personal qualities bring to the National Government?

13 How did the Spanish Civil War divide opinion in Britain?

14 Why did Neville Chamberlain persevere for so long with an appeasement policy towards Germany?

15 What influence did British distrust of the USSR have on appeasement?

 Question practice

ESSAY QUESTIONS

1 'The Labour government of 1929–31 failed because it was overwhelmed by Britain's financial difficulties.' Explain why you agree or disagree with this view.

2 Assess the reasons why a National Government was formed in 1931.

3 'The economic depression of the 1930s in Britain was a regional, not a national problem.' How far do you agree?

4 How far did living standards in Britain rise between 1931 and 1939?

SOURCE ANALYSIS QUESTION

1 With reference to Sources A (page 124) and B (page 125), and your understanding of the historical context, assess the value of these sources to a historian studying the political crisis of 1931.

CHAPTER 5

Britain at war 1939–45

Britain's 'phoney war' ended in April 1940 with military defeat in Norway, an event that led to the replacement of Chamberlain by Churchill, who went on to be an inspired wartime leader of a highly able coalition government. The Second World War produced a social revolution in Britain. So involving was the struggle that hardly any individual or institution escaped its effects. That is why is has been referred to as a total war. This great formative event is examined in this chapter under the following headings:

★ Churchill's coalition government 1940–5

★ The impact of the war on Britain

★ The growth in the power of the State

The key debate on *page 187* of this chapter asks the question: Did Churchill's wartime leadership strengthen or weaken Britain's position as an international power?

Key dates

1939	Military conscription introduced	1942	Beveridge Report published
1940	Churchill replaced Chamberlain as prime minister	1944	Normandy landings
			V weapons launched
1940–1	The Blitz	1945	Yalta Conference
1942	Fall of Singapore		German surrender
	Tobruk defeat		

1 Churchill's coalition government 1940–5

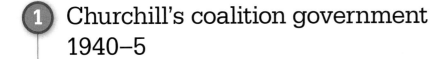

▶ *What style of leadership did Winston Churchill adopt as wartime prime minister?*

Although it had declared war on Germany in September 1939 on behalf of Poland, Britain was not in a position to take the offensive. The British busied themselves digging shelters, filling sandbags, trying on gas masks and organising the evacuation of children from the urban areas to the countryside. Much went on behind the scenes to prepare the armed services for war, but essentially it was a matter of waiting for Germany to make the first move. American journalists dubbed this period of relative calm 'the **phoney war**'.

Chamberlain's fall

The war began in earnest for Britain in April 1940 when Germany, anxious to gain vital iron-ore deposits, invaded Norway. Britain responded by sending a task force there, but it was too small to prevent the Germans overrunning the country. British troops made a humiliating withdrawal. Prime Minister Neville Chamberlain was angrily condemned for the campaign's failure by all parties in Parliament, including a large section of his own Conservatives. Churchill's less than successful role at the Admiralty in the naval part of the campaign tended to be overlooked.

During a two-day debate in the Commons, beginning on 7 May, a dramatic contribution was made by Conservative MP Leo Amery. Rounding on Chamberlain, Amery declared, in a direct quotation of the words used by Oliver Cromwell when dismissing an obstructive Parliament in 1653: 'You have sat here too long for any good you have been doing. Depart I say and let us have done with you. In the name of God, go.' Hardly less dramatically, Lloyd George, making his last major contribution in the Commons, weighed in with an equally destructive comment. Mockingly turning Chamberlain's earlier call for sacrifice against him, Lloyd George declared, 'The nation is prepared for sacrifice provided it has leadership. I say solemnly that the Prime Minister should give an example of sacrifice, because there is nothing which can contribute to victory in this war than that he should sacrifice the seals of office.'

Although the subsequent confidence vote gave Chamberlain a majority of 81, this compared badly with the 200 he could have expected had his party fully supported him. It was a moral defeat and convinced Chamberlain that he could not continue as head of government. The obvious question that now arose was who should replace him. There were two contenders: Lord Halifax, the foreign secretary, and Winston Churchill. Halifax was said to be the choice of the higher ranks of the Conservatives and also to be popular with King George VI. However, he suffered from three handicaps:

- As a peer, and, therefore, restricted to the House of Lords, his right to be prime minister was constitutionally unsound.
- Although a man of integrity, he had an uninspiring personality and doubted his own capacity to hold the highest office.
- The Labour Party leaders declared themselves unwilling to serve in a coalition with him as prime minister.

The outbreak of war with Germany had placed Churchill in a strong position. Throughout the 1930s he had consistently warned against the growing dangers of expansionist Nazi Germany and had urged Britain to rearm. Far from having been the warmonger for which his critics had denounced him, he could justifiably claim that events had vindicated his call for rearmament and his denunciation of appeasement.

Chamberlain's own choice was Halifax. However, having called the two men together, Chamberlain first asked Halifax whether he was willing to accept the premiership. Halifax gave a confused reply before saying no and that 'Winston would be a better choice'. Asked to comment on that reply, Churchill maintained a discreet silence that spoke volumes. Later that day Halifax related that Churchill had been 'very kind and polite, but showed that he thought that was the right answer'. Chamberlain duly recommended to the king that Churchill be asked to become leader of a new government. So it was that on 10 May Churchill became prime minister. He was to hold that office for the next five years. Later, in his writings on the Second World War, he recalled the critical meeting at which the decision had been made (Source A).

SOURCE A

From W.S. Churchill, *The Second World War*, Penguin, 1985, volume 1, pp. 597–8.

I have had many interviews in my public life, and this was certainly the most important. Usually I talk a great deal but on this occasion I was silent … As I remained silent a very long pause ensued … Then at length Halifax spoke. He said he felt that his position as a peer, out of the House of Commons, would make it very difficult for him to discharge the duties of Prime Minister in a war like this. He would be held responsible for everything but would not have the power to guide the assembly upon whose confidence the life of every government depended. He spoke for some minutes in this sense, and by the time he had finished it was clear that the duty would fall upon me – had in fact fallen on me. Then for the first time I spoke. I said I would have no communication with either of the Opposition parties until I had the King's Commission to form a government.

Why, as described in Source A, did Churchill remain silent for so long?

Rejection of peace talks

One of the decisions Churchill took soon after becoming prime minister proved the most momentous of the whole war. Late in May, with German forces having broken the French and British armies in northern France, thoughts naturally turned to the possibility of a negotiated peace with Germany. At a meeting of the inner war cabinet, Halifax and Chamberlain suggested that they should seize the opportunity provided by Mussolini, who had declared himself willing to act as intermediary between Britain and Germany. Churchill allowed the point to be made but then sharply rejected it, saying that he doubted that Hitler's Germany was morally capable of offering decent terms. Attlee and Greenwood, the two Labour members of the five-man inner cabinet, concurred entirely with Churchill's view.

Winston Churchill

1874	Born the son of Randolph Churchill, a leading Tory radical
1898	Fought in the Sudan under Kitchener
1900	Taken prisoner by the Boers in South Africa
	Entered the Commons as a Conservative MP
1904	Left the Conservatives to join the Liberals
1908–9	President of the Board of Trade; showed himself to be a progressive social reformer
1910–11	Home secretary
1911–15	First lord of the Admiralty
1916	Served on the Western Front
1917–19	Minister of munitions
1919	Fiercely anti-Bolshevik, he supported British intervention in Russia
1921–2	Secretary for the colonies
1924	Left the Liberals and declared himself a 'constitutionalist'
1924–9	Chancellor of the exchequer
1926	Strongly opposed the General Strike
1929	Formally rejoined the Conservatives
1939–40	First lord of the Admiralty
1940–5	Prime minister and minister of defence
1945	His party heavily defeated in the general election
1947	Helped to define the Cold War by his 'Iron Curtain' speech
1951–5	Prime minister
1965	Died

In many ways Churchill was a radical, but he was loathed by the left because of his strike-breaking and fierce anti-Bolshevism. He was too individualistic to be entirely at ease in any one party. In 1904, after only four years as a Unionist MP, he left the party to join the Liberals. His radical approach to social questions made him the great ally of Lloyd George in their creation of the pre-1914 social service State.

Twenty years later, having established an impressive record as a Liberal social reformer, he returned to the Conservative fold, but in a strange relationship. He called himself a 'constitutionalist' and despite being chancellor of the exchequer in Baldwin's government between 1924 and 1929 did not formally rejoin the Conservatives until 1929. Churchill remained out of office for the next ten years. His demand that Britain rearm, and his outspoken attacks on appeasement and independence for India made him unpopular with the Conservative establishment and he despaired of ever playing a major role in politics again. It is certainly hard to think that, had the Second World War not intervened, he would have reached the pre-eminence he then did.

As well as making history Churchill also wrote it. His deep historical sense was evident in his many books and in his brilliant speeches in which he used his speech impediment to great effect. One example was his deliberate mispronunciation of the word 'Nazi', with a long 'a' and a soft 'z', in order to show his contempt for the movement to which it referred. His feel for the dramatic and his ability to use elevated language without losing the common touch was evident throughout the remaining war years 1940–5. His inspiring leadership did not mean he went unopposed in Parliament. However, although faced by the occasional no-confidence motion, he was never in serious danger of being removed. At the war's end he was defeated in the general election in 1945. After that, he tended to live on his reputation, being fêted in the many countries as a statesman of unparalleled stature. Resisting suggestions that he should retire, he claimed that he could still contribute to world peace. Prime minister again between 1951 and 1955, his advancing years and ill-health meant that he was little more than a figurehead in his last years in government, a downbeat end to one of the most extraordinary political careers of the twentieth century. Clement Attlee described him as 'the greatest citizen of the world of our time'.

At a meeting of the full 25-strong cabinet that followed soon after, Churchill restated his reasons for refusing to consider suing for peace. In a rousing address he declared that it would be a dereliction of duty if he were even to consider negotiating with 'That man [Hitler]'. He later recalled what he had said to his colleagues and how they had responded.

SOURCE B

Churchill's comments to the cabinet in May 1940, quoted in Martin Gilbert, *Churchill: A Life*, Minerva, 1992, p. 651.

'I am convinced that every man of you would rise up and tear me down from my place if I were to contemplate parley or surrender. If this long island story of ours is to end at last, let it end only when each one of us lies choking in his own blood upon the ground.' …

Quite a number seemed to jump up from the table and come running to my chair, shouting and patting me on the back … Had I at this juncture faltered at all in leading the nation I should have been hurled out of office. I am sure that every Minister was ready to be killed quite soon, and have all his family and possessions destroyed rather than give in.

> According to Source B, why did Churchill receive such an enthusiastic reception from his cabinet colleagues?

Reasons for Churchill's becoming prime minister

- Churchill's years in the political wilderness worked in his favour since he was not associated with the appeasement failures of the National Government.
- The outbreak of war in 1939 vindicated his opposition to Nazism and his call for rearmament.
- In May 1940 he had no real challenger since Halifax was too diffident and lacking in support.
- The Labour Party's refusal to enter a government led by Chamberlain or Halifax meant that a coalition of national unity could not be formed unless Churchill was prime minister.
- The crisis facing Britain, with the French and British armies on the verge of defeat in northern France, was so grave that whatever their misgivings about Churchill's previous supposed warmongering, the majority of MPs of all parties accepted that his bullish qualities and self-belief made him 'the man of the hour'.

The tone and style of Churchill's powerful and uplifting wartime speeches can be gauged from Source C, one of his first broadcasts to the British people (page 158).

How does Churchill achieve his dramatic effects in the speech in Source C?

SOURCE C

From a BBC radio broadcast by Churchill, 19 May 1940.

This is one of the most awe-inspiring periods in the long history of France and Britain. It is also beyond doubt the most sublime. Side by side, unaided except by their kith and kin in the Great Dominions and by the wide Empires which rest beneath their shield – side by side, the British and French peoples have advanced to rescue not only Europe but mankind from the foulest and most soul-destroying tyranny which has ever darkened and stained the page of history. Behind them – behind us – behind the Armies and fleets of Britain – gather a group of shattered States and bludgeoned races: the Czechs, the Poles, the Norwegians, the Danes, the Dutch, the Belgians – upon all of whom the long night of barbarism will descend, unbroken even by a star of hope, unless we conquer, as conquer we must, as conquer we will.

Churchill's wartime leadership

Churchill wrote in his war memoirs that, on becoming prime minister in 1940 at the age of 64, he felt that the whole of his previous life had been a preparation 'for this hour and this trial'. As Lloyd George had done in 1916, he devoted himself totally to the task of winning the war. Every other consideration took second place. Despite the deep depression from which he frequently suffered, the 'black dog' as he called it, he never wavered in his conviction that Britain would prevail. His inexhaustible capacity for work, his nerve-tingling oratory and his extraordinary gift for inspiring others were used to rally the nation to a supreme effort. He later wrote that the British people were the lions; he merely provided the roar.

As Lloyd George had done in the First World War, Churchill chose to govern through a war cabinet, but remained the dominant figure throughout. He later admitted wryly: 'All I wanted was compliance with my wishes after reasonable discussion.' It was a benign dictatorship. There were mutterings against Churchill among backbenchers in Parliament at various times during the war but no sustained opposition.

Churchill's worst moments came in 1942 when a number of military reverses, including the loss of Singapore to Japan and Tobruk to the Germans (see the box on page 159), increased the pressure on him. There were strong criticisms of his conduct of war policy at this point. In July 1942, Aneurin Bevan complained in the House that while the Soviet Union was able to resist the enemy for months at a time in various campaigns, badly led British forces capitulated too easily. Yet opinion polls showed that Churchill's popularity with the public was at times as high as 88 per cent and even at the darkest moments never dropped below 78 per cent.

The fall of Singapore, February 1942

The 70,000 British troops stationed there surrendered to the invading Japanese, who thereby gained control of South-East Asia. It was one of the most shattering defeats of the war for Britain. Some historians see it as marking the end of the British Empire.

The Loss of Tobruk, June 1942

The surrender of 33,000 British troops to Rommel's Army marked the lowest point in the eventually successful North Africa campaigns that Britain fought between 1940 and 1943.

SOURCE D

ALL BEHIND YOU, WINSTON

How effectively does the cartoon in Source D capture the reaction to Churchill's becoming prime minister?

'All Behind You, Winston'. A cartoon by David Low published in the *Evening Standard*, 14 May 1940. To Churchill's left are Attlee, Bevin, Morrison and Beaverbrook. Among those in the second row are Chamberlain, Halifax and Eden.

Churchill's coalition colleagues

The following were among his most notable wartime government colleagues.

Clement Attlee (1883–1967): deputy prime minister 1940–5

In his own time and for years afterwards, Clement Attlee tended to be underrated. He suffered by comparison with Churchill. Attlee's unprepossessing physical presence and limited skills as a public speaker did not create the grand image. However, there was no doubting his loyalty, patriotism and courage. Churchill, who regarded his deputy as a 'gallant English gentleman', relied on Attlee greatly for much of the government's liaison and administration. The

Labour leader's contacts with the military, with the left generally and the trade unions in particular proved invaluable in the organisation of the war effort.

Ernest Bevin (1881–1951): minister of labour and national service 1940–5

Bevin ranks alongside Churchill and Attlee as one of the most influential British statesmen of the age. Between the wars, as a moderate Labour Party member and trade unionist, he fought against the Communist infiltration of the party and the unions. As minister of labour in the wartime government he had the enormous task of organising British industry to meet the demands of war (see page 183). This involved him in drafting output targets and in negotiating with the bosses and trade unions to reach compromises that both adequately rewarded the workers and maintained wartime production at its fullest. The powers Bevin had over workers and industry were unprecedented. Yet it is a striking tribute to the sparing and responsible way in which Bevin used them that he was criticised in some quarters for being too cautious in his approach.

Stafford Cripps (1889–1952): ambassador to USSR 1940–2, minister of aircraft production 1942–5

Cripps was regarded as the most intellectually gifted member of the Labour Party. His Marxist sympathies had led to his temporary expulsion from the party for attempting to impose Stalin's popular front policy on it after 1937. Judging that this specially qualified Cripps for the task, Churchill sent him as ambassador to Moscow in 1940 in the hope that he would use his influence to undermine the Nazi–Soviet alliance (see page 127). However, after the USSR entered the war in 1941 this was no longer necessary and Cripps' strong pro-Communist leanings now proved highly valuable in the development of the wartime Anglo-Russian alliance.

Churchill next sent Cripps on a special mission to India in 1942 to discuss the possibility of independence. Churchill's aim was to keep India in the war on the British side and to help protect it against possible Japanese invasion. The move showed how expedient the prime minister was prepared to be in wartime. To maintain the war effort, he was willing to accept the possible weakening of Britain's imperial links with India and swallow his distaste for Cripps' politics. On his return from India, having failed to negotiate an acceptable plan for independence, Cripps was given the post of minister of aircraft production. He performed without panache but with competence, building on the work laid down by his predecessor Lord Beaverbrook, the dynamic newspaper magnate whom Churchill had brought into the government.

Herbert Morrison (1888–1965): leader of the London County Council 1934–40, minister of supply 1940, home secretary 1940–5

Morrison's invaluable experience in local government politics and administration as leader of the London County Council during the previous six years was put to very effective use when he became home secretary under

Churchill in 1940. Morrison served with distinction throughout the war. Like Bevin's, his powers were extensive and his duties huge and formidable. To him fell the responsibility of organising home security. He oversaw the defence of London during the **Blitz**, which included the recruitment and training of **fire watchers** and **ARP** officers. An interesting personal note is that the protective indoor shelters that he ordered in 1941 to be built in every appropriate house became known as Morrison shelters. He was also responsible for the policy of **internment**, the arrest and detention in special areas of those in the population whose national or political background made them suspect (see page 183).

Again like Bevin, Morrison exercised his wartime powers with marked restraint during the five years he was home secretary. This did not, however, prevent his coming under attack on occasion. One row was over his threat to close down the *Daily Mirror* for publishing a particular cartoon in March 1942 (see Source E). Churchill and Morrison chose to view the cartoon not as a tribute to the heroism of British seamen, but as an undermining of the war effort by implying that British lives were being sacrificed to make money for the oil producers. Morrison described it as a 'wicked cartoon' and ordered MI5, Britain's counter-espionage agency, to investigate whether Philip Zec, the cartoonist, was a subversive. MI5 found only that Zec, as a Jew, was a passionate anti-Nazi.

KEY TERMS

Blitz Sustained German bombing raids, mainly at night, on London and other selected British cities; it was at its most intense between September 1940 and May 1941.

Fire watchers Members of the public who took up vantage points on high buildings to report outbreaks of fire.

ARP Air Raid Precautions.

Internment The holding in detention of those members of the population whose nationality or political views made them a potential risk to national security.

SOURCE E

Why might the cartoon in Source E have been open to an interpretation opposite to the one intended?

'The price of petrol has been increased by one penny – official'.
A cartoon by Philip Zec published in the *Daily Mirror*, 5 March 1942.

Common sense prevailed and Churchill and Morrison, realising they had misread the cartoon's intention, called off the dogs and withdrew their threat to the *Mirror*, a newspaper which was thereafter recognised as being unfailingly patriotic and supportive of the war effort.

Despite the fuss this particular incident caused, it was not typical of Morrison's policies at the Home Office. Although his security measures were often unpopular because of their necessarily restrictive nature, they were intended to be as fair and as widely protective of the civilian population as the circumstances of war allowed. However, at a personal level Morrison found it easy to make enemies. Neither Ernest Bevin nor Aneurin Bevan could get on with him. On hearing someone describe Morrison as being his own worst enemy, Bevin jumped in with, 'Not while I'm alive, he ain't'.

Hugh Dalton (1887–1962): minister of economic warfare 1940–2, president of the Board of Trade 1942–5

Dalton's time as economics minister under Churchill is fascinating for the example it gave of the way in which politics could interfere with war planning. The great domestic demand was for coal to fuel the factories and plants that produced the hardware of war. Yet coal production actually fell between 1939 and 1942, from 227 million tons to 200 million. A mixture of poor wage levels and the conscription of 80,000 young miners into the services saw the number of miners drop sharply.

Dalton's response was to prepare a national scheme of rationing intended to reduce the amount of coal available to domestic consumers, so that the armaments factories would not go short. News of the plan leaked out, however, and there was a Conservative revolt. Judging the scheme to be a move towards nationalisation (see page 201), since it would subject the mine owners to direct government control, the Conservatives threatened an all-out attack. Dalton backed down in the face of the threat and coal rationing was formally abandoned.

The affair has been described as the 'only successful Conservative revolt of the war'. Yet not a great deal was lost. Dalton asked a series of committees and advisers to find other ways round the problem. The eventual answer, which largely worked, was simply to reduce the amount of coal that consumers could buy – rationing by other means. At the same time the miners were awarded an across-the-board wage increase and the promise of a minimum wage. Although this brought workers back to the mines, it did not lead to a significant increase in coal production. Nevertheless, supplies to the factories were maintained, which had been Dalton's basic intention.

Anthony Eden (1897–1977): secretary of state for war 1940, foreign secretary 1940–5

It was Eden's fate to live the greater part of his political life in the shadow of Winston Churchill, the man he admired and whom he would succeed, but not until 1955 (see page 225). In the late 1930s Eden had supported Churchill in his attacks on the National Government's appeasement policies. When Churchill became prime minister in 1940, he made Eden his war secretary and later in the year his foreign secretary.

Given that Churchill in effect acted as foreign secretary, attending all the key international conferences himself and conducting his own brand of summitry with US President Roosevelt and the USSR's Josef Stalin, Eden's role was reduced to that of the ever-present loyal confidant and background figure.

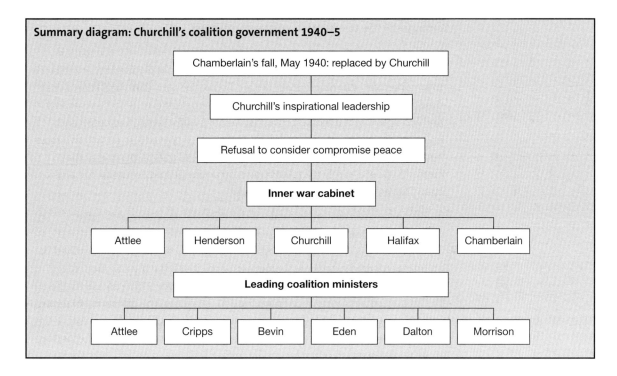

Summary diagram: Churchill's coalition government 1940–5

Chamberlain's fall, May 1940: replaced by Churchill

Churchill's inspirational leadership

Refusal to consider compromise peace

Inner war cabinet

Attlee | Henderson | Churchill | Halifax | Chamberlain

Leading coalition ministers

Attlee | Cripps | Bevin | Eden | Dalton | Morrison

2 The impact of the war on Britain

▶ *In what sense were the years 1939–45 a period of total war for the British people?*

The twentieth century has been described as the era of total war. So advanced had the world become technologically that warfare could no longer be limited to the military front. Modern war was now fought on an industrial scale. This meant that every citizen, combatant or not, became involved in the struggle. The civilian Home Front which provided the vast array of armaments and materials that sustained the war effort was equal in importance to the military front – a reason why all sides in the Second World War felt themselves morally justified in attacking civilian targets.

Total involvement

In Britain, the 1939–45 war was the greatest collective experience that the nation had yet undergone. War and its effects reached into every home and affected all sections of society. There was scarcely a family that was spared the anxieties that war entailed. Nearly everyone had a close relative in the armed services. The pain and worry of enforced separation between serving men and their families was a common experience. Fearful uncertainty about the fate of loved ones at home or at the front was an everyday shared reality. People carried on as best they could, but at home the war brought serious disruption to family and community life, to education and to employment.

Britain was the only warring country in Europe to avoid enemy occupation during the war. But there was another trauma it did not escape. It was subjected to long periods of bombing from the air. Before the war, there had been a deep dread that aerial bombardment of the civilian population would be so deadly and disruptive that it would prove insufferable. In the event, the bomb and rocket attacks directed on London and other cities proved less destructive than had been anticipated, but the constant threat to life and property that they created imposed barely tolerable strains on domestic and economic life and tested the emergency services to the limit.

To fight a six-year war on the scale of the 1939–45 struggle placed huge demands on Britain and its people. From the beginning it was realised and accepted that the war effort necessitated centralised direction. This resulted in an unprecedented extension of State authority, involving the sacrifice of legal and civil rights in the cause of national security. Between 1939 and 1945, the British government introduced conscription, rationing, the direction of labour, restrictions on the right to travel and evacuation. It is interesting to observe that Churchill's coalition government moved so far towards the regulated economy that the post-war Labour government, rather than being radical, was simply continuing the established pattern (see page 195).

The war had a lasting impact on social attitudes. Britain's collective effort as a nation in wartime narrowed the gap between the classes, or at least led to an understanding of how arbitrary and, by extension, how unacceptable class differences were. Privilege and deprivation would, of course, continue after the war, but the period 1939–45 proved a vitally formative period in the advancement of notions of political, social and economic equality. The war stimulated a widespread feeling that the people deserved something better than the grim economic uncertainties that had been the lot of so many in the 1920s and 1930s.

The mobilisation of resources

At the end of the war the Ministry of Information proudly declared: 'Britain has radically transformed her national existence by the extent of her mobilization for war.' It is certainly true that nothing illustrates the total **mobilisation of resources** of the British war effort more clearly than the statistics of the ways in which ordinary citizens were organised militarily, economically and socially during the six years 1939–45:

- UK's overall population – 51 million (32 million adults).
- Of the 15.9 million males aged between 14 and 64, 14.9 million (93 per cent) were registered for war service.
- Of the 16 million females aged between 14 and 58, 7.1 million (45 per cent) performed some type of war service.

The war service in which they were engaged took the following main forms:

- 5.5 million called up into the serving forces
- 3.2 million worked in the munitions industries
- 4 million in other essential war work
- 225,000 in full-time civil defence.

To be added to these figures were the 1.75 million in the **Home Guard** and 1.25 million in part-time civil defence. There were also many thousands involved in fire watching (see page 161), an activity that was compulsory for men who worked less than 60 hours a week and women who worked less than 50 hours.

During the war the government issued over 8.5 million Essential Work Orders. These were legal controls that directed workers to particular employment within designated vital industries and denied them the right to change their jobs or employers to dismiss them. Registration for employment was made compulsory in 1941.

Conscription

One of the divisive political debates at the beginning of the 1914–18 war had been over the morality of conscription (see page 69). The discussion in 1939 was much more muted; there was a widespread, if resigned, acceptance that the call-up was a necessity. From early 1938, growing fears of German expansion had led Britain to take some preliminary steps towards supplementing its 200,000-strong peacetime army. Under the terms of the Emergency Powers (Defence Act) of August 1938, physically fit males aged 20 and 21 had been obliged to undergo six months' military training. When war broke out in September 1939, Britain had 900,000 men available, a number which included the volunteers who came forward as soon as war was declared.

Judging that this fell well below Britain's military needs, the government in October rushed through a National Service Act which required all able-bodied males between 18 and 41 to register for armed service. Registration began with the youngest and continued in stages over the next ten months until it reached the 40-year-olds. Exempted from the call-up were men defined as being in **reserved occupations**, work judged to be crucial to the war effort. Those conscripted were allowed to choose to join one of the three services: army, navy

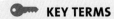

KEY TERMS

Mobilisation of resources
Drawing on and organising the whole of the nation's material and human potential.

Home Guard Local defence units largely made up of service veterans and those too old for the call-up; the movement was later lovingly caricatured in the BBC television series *Dad's Army*, which ran from 1968 to 1977.

Reserved occupations
Work done by dockers, farmers, merchant seamen, miners, scientists engaged in war projects, key transport workers (for example, railwaymen) and workers in the vital utilities (water, gas and electricity).

or air force. By the end of 1939, over 1.5 million had joined up: 1 million in the army and 250,000 in each of the other two services.

By the war's end, some 5.5 million Britons had been called up and over 4.5 million had seen active service. This represented nearly 60 per cent of all males aged between 18 and 40. As in the First World War, there was a number of conscientious objectors who asked for exemption from military service on moral grounds. They were treated with greater understanding than 25 years earlier, although they still tended to be regarded with disdain by the bulk of the population. Of the 60,000 who went in front of tribunals to plead their cause, 42,000 had their appeals against military service upheld.

Britain's wartime victims

It was revealed in May 1945 that the total number of casualties was very close to a million. This was broken down into the following categories:

- Armed services: 746,109 casualties
  - 287,859 killed
  - 274,148 seriously wounded
  - 184,102 prisoners of war.
- Merchant navy: 43,582 casualties
  - 30,589 killed
  - 12,993 missing or wounded.
- Civilians: 146,760 casualties (80,307 of these occurring in London)
  - 60,585 killed (27,570 men, 25,392 women, 7623 children)
  - 86,175 seriously injured.

Although Britain did not suffer the scale of war casualties experienced, for example, by Germany and the Soviet Union, the losses affected many millions beyond the immediate victims. Loss and bereavement became a common experience.

Food rationing

On the eve of war in 1939 Britain was importing around 55 million tons of food annually. This represented approximately a ton of imported food for each member of the population. Since the greater proportion of these supplies came via long sea journeys from regions as distant as Australia, the Caribbean, South Africa and North America, it soon became apparent that the supply routes were very susceptible to German U-boat attack. With vivid memories of the crisis produced by the German blockade during the 1914–18 war (see page 61), the government responded in two ways:

- It immediately drew up plans for food rationing.
- It began a campaign to encourage increased production of home-grown food on existing farms and to bring unused land into cultivation. The population was urged to plant and tend allotments on every available space. 'Dig for Victory' was one of the government's slogans.

Of all the hardships that war brought to the civilian population, rationing was arguably the one that was most consistently felt since it imposed itself on everybody's daily lives. It has been calculated that the topic that dominated the conversation of ordinary people was not the progress of the war, important though that obviously was, but rationing. This is not surprising; the food queues which formed daily, largely composed of housewives, were a constant reminder that putting food on the table was the most demanding need facing ordinary families.

SOURCE F

How do these posters in Source F help to give an impression of what the government regarded as the key issues and themes that the public should be informed about and urged to act upon?

A montage of wartime Ministry of Information posters, *c.* 1940, that became the backdrop to everyday life in the towns and villages.

It had been hoped that rationing itself would eliminate the need for long queues since everybody would be entitled to a prescribed allowance. However, in practice, food supplies were never so regular as to guarantee that the shops had what people wanted when they wanted it. Butchers, bakers and greengrocers could sell only what they were delivered. Queues often formed in anticipation of deliveries. A common joke among housewives was that if you saw a queue you joined it. It did not matter what it was for; it was bound to be for something you needed or could use.

The following list shows how food rationing was steadily extended over a range of basic items:

- January 1940: bacon, butter and sugar
- March 1940: meat
- July 1940: tea and margarine
- March 1941: jam
- May 1941: cheese
- June 1941: eggs
- January 1942: rice and dried fruit
- February 1942: tinned tomatoes and peas
- July 1942: sweets and chocolate
- August 1942: biscuits
- March 1943: sausages.

Vegetables and fruit were not put on ration, which meant they were invariably in short supply and occasioned some of the longest queues. Bread was also exempt but, since white bread flour was scarce, wholemeal loaves became the main type available. Milk was unrationed, which resulted in frequent shortages. Milk and egg powder in Ministry of Food tins was produced in an effort to make up for the shortfall in what many people regarded, along with tea, as the food they just could not do without. The government made a particular effort to supply children with essential vitamins. Infants and their mothers were entitled to cod-liver oil, concentrated orange juice and powdered milk. In 1941, State schools began to provide each individual pupil with a third of a pint of milk a day, free of charge, a practice which continued to operate until the 1970s.

The actual amounts of the rations to which each person was entitled varied slightly during the course of the war. Expectant or nursing mothers, infants, and people with special medical conditions were entitled to extra rations. The following list suggests the typical weekly allowances for the ordinary individual:

- bacon: 4 ounces (100 g), initially only 2 ounces (50 g)
- cheese: 4 ounces (100 g)
- eggs: 1
- fats (butter, margarine and lard): 4 ounces (100 g)
- meat: 6 ounces (150 g)
- sugar: 8 ounces (200 g), initially 12 ounces (300 g)
- sweets: 2 ounces (50 g)
- tea: 2 ounces (50 g).

Meat was often supplemented by Spam, a cheap processed form of ham, which a later generation of comedians found highly comical but which at the time was a godsend to families who concocted ingenious recipes to make it more palatable. Pigs (pork), cattle (beef) and sheep (mutton) were Britain's traditional sources of meat. But since wartime shortages had turned these into luxuries, the Ministry of Food urged people to consider alternative animal meats. Horseflesh was declared to be nutritious and, despite its toughness, fit for human consumption. A more notorious recommendation was snoek, a form of sea pike which proved tasteless and inedible. The public declined to be attracted by either of these strange delicacies and the government found itself with unsellable stocks on its hands.

The story goes that Churchill once asked to see an actual example of what a typical ration for one actually looked like. He was duly shown a set of plates with the various items on them. He remarked approvingly that he could comfortably survive for a day on that amount, only to be told that what he was looking at were the rations for a whole week.

Other forms of rationing

Food was far from being the only commodity to be rationed. Petrol sales were restricted immediately war was declared in 1939. Fuel shortages led to coal being rationed from July 1941. This was followed in March 1942 by the placing of severe restrictions on household consumption of gas and electricity. To save vital oil and fat supplies, soap was put on ration in February 1942. Price controls were introduced in an effort to make rationing fair and acceptable. The cost of rationed goods was fixed at a level that made them available even to the poorest families. There were protests from retailers who regarded this as an interference with the right to determine their own profits, but the government countered this by suggesting that in a time of national shortage rationing gave the shopkeepers guaranteed sales.

In a further effort to conserve materials needed for the war effort, rationing was extended to cover clothes in June 1941. As was the system with food, each individual was issued with a ration book containing colour-coded sets of coupons, denoting various amounts, which had to be presented to the shopkeeper when goods were being bought. The coupons were either cut out or marked with indelible pencil to prevent their reuse. At its lowest, the annual clothing allowance for each individual was 48 points. How restrictive that was is evident from the box below.

Examples of the points needed to buy each item of clothing

Men:

Overcoat: 18

Pair of shoes: 7

Vest and pants: 8

Pair of socks: 3

Pyjamas: 8

Shirt: 8

Women:

Coat: 14

Dress: 11

Skirt: 7

Stockings: 2

Nightdress: 6

Blouse: 5

Appreciating that rationing made it hard for ordinary families to buy new clothes, the government urged them 'to make do and mend' as a way of contributing to the war effort. The official line was that it was one's patriotic duty not to discard anything that could be reused. Women found ingenious ways of using old curtains to run up an apparently new dress. To give the impression that they were wearing stockings some girls applied gravy powder to their legs and then got someone they knew well to draw a pretend seam from the back of the thigh to the heel with an eyebrow pencil.

People, of course, grumbled about the ever-present strain and irritation of rationing. Yet, given the genuine national shortages that existed, the form of rationing that was introduced was probably as reasonable and efficient as could be achieved in the circumstances of war. It was based on the notion of fair shares and equality of sacrifice in a time of national emergency. One beneficial result of food rationing was that it encouraged an understanding of what constituted a proper balanced diet. In working out the necessary contents of the basic ration, the Ministry of Food's experts provided ordinary Britons with a valuable lesson in nutrition.

The black market

As with all rationing systems, there are always those prepared to exploit the situation for personal gain. A trade in forged ration books became widespread as people sought to circumvent the restrictions. This was one example of the illegal trafficking in food and goods that enabled people to buy more than their ration allowance permitted. Supplying and selling surplus goods became a highly organised and lucrative activity since the price asked was always highly inflated. Every city and town had its black marketeers – 'spivs' – and a large and eager clientele. How widespread the system was is evident in the statistic that during the war over 100,000 people were prosecuted by the Ministry of Food for black-market offences, and these were only the ones who were caught. The inspectors responsible for overseeing the rationing system worked with the police in making arrests and bringing charges against wrongdoers. Although the inspectors were acting for the general good, the public often resented them as government snoopers whose activities added to the cares and burdens of life in wartime.

The effects of bombing

In twentieth-century warfare, the line between combatant and non-combatant became increasingly blurred. The concept of total war and the technology of aerial bombardment made the terrorising of the civilian population possible and, arguably, legitimate. Yet one reason why the London Blitz proved bearable is that, grim though the bombing was, it never reached the scale anticipated in the gloomier pre-war forecasts. German cities, such as Dresden and Hamburg, were later to experience Allied bombardment that carried civilian suffering far beyond that undergone in British cities.

The death toll of 60,000 Britons killed as a result of bombing during the war was smaller than expected. Nevertheless, air raids created constant fear, as the diary of a housewife in Barrow recorded (Source G).

SOURCE G

From a diary entry for 4 May 1941, in *Nella Last's War*, 1981, quoted in Rex Pope, *War and Society in Britain*, Longman, 1995, pp. 106–7.

A night of terror, and there are few windows left in the district – or roof tiles! Land mines, incendiaries and explosives were dropped, and we cowered thankfully under our indoor shelter. I've been dreadfully sick all day, and I'm sure it's sheer fright, for last night I really thought our end had come … I've a sick shadow over me as I look at my loved little house that will never be the same again…. The house rocked and then the kitchenette door careered down the hall. I'll never forget my odd sensation, one a calm acceptance of 'the end', the other a feeling of regret that I'd not opened a tin of fruit salad for tea.

In what sense does Source G illustrate the reaction of both fear and resignation among the victims of bombing?

Destruction of property occurred on a large scale. Three and a half million houses were bombed out, necessitating 22.5 million people, nearly half the population, having to move house. The social disruption is further shown by the record of 60 million changes of address in Britain between 1939 and 1945. Damage to factories and production centres in cities such as London and Coventry was formidable, but the use of makeshift premises and the dispersal of industrial plants meant that production was not severely curtailed. Interestingly, worker absenteeism fell during the Blitz and again during the rocket attacks in 1944–5 (see below), which suggested that the systematic bombing had strengthened rather than weakened civilian morale.

There was some panic, particularly at the beginning of the Blitz, but this was not widespread and a mixture of resolution and resignation appears to have been the general response. The normal pattern of life and work was disrupted but not destroyed. People adjusted to the undoubted horror of it all and the sense of a shared common danger tended to maintain morale. A London journalist recorded in his diary in October 1914: 'We have got accustomed now to knowing we may be blown to bits at any moment. A family creeps out of its dug-out to get some supper. They sit down at table. Next minute they are all dead. We know this may happen to any of us. Yet we go about as usual. Life goes on.'

Hitler's terror weapons

Later in the war, the civilian population faced a new horror from the skies. In what proved to be Hitler's last desperate attempt to stave off defeat, he launched his use of terror weapons against Britain. **V1** raids, which began in June 1944, were followed three months later, by **V2** attacks. The weapons caused widespread death and damage in and around London and led to the evacuation of 1.5 million people. But, owing to sabotage by resistance groups in occupied Europe and Allied bombing of the launch sites, the destruction was never on the scale Hitler had originally planned.

🔑 KEY TERMS

V1 *Vergeltungswaffe* – retaliation flying bomb. A pilotless jet-propelled plane loaded with explosives.

V2 An armed rocket, launched from static or mobile sites.

> ## V1 and V2 attacks on Britain
>
> Number of V1s fired: 10,000. Of these:
> - 3676 hit London
> - 2600 failed to reach their target
> - 1878 were shot down by anti-air batteries
> - 1846 were destroyed in the air by RAF fighter planes.
>
> Total number of people killed by the V1s: 6184
>
> Total number of V2s launched: 1402.
>
> Total number of people killed by the V2s: 2754.

Evacuation

An interesting feature of the collective war effort in Britain was the way it increased social perception. The shared experience of the dangers of war helped to make people aware of each other in ways that had not happened before. Knowledge of 'how the other half lives' led to a questioning of the class differences that existed. Evacuation was especially influential in this respect.

At the outbreak of the war, the government, fearing large-scale air attacks on major urban centres, organised a migration of primary school children from the danger zones to the relatively safe rural areas. Although 4 million were planned for, only 1.5 million actually made the move. During the phoney war period most evacuees drifted back home, only to migrate again when the Blitz began late in 1940. A further evacuation occurred in 1944 at the time of the rocket attacks on London.

It was one of the largest movements of people in such a short time in British history; in terms of getting vast numbers of children from A to B and settled away from danger it was a huge success. However, the research into the effects of evacuation suggests that the majority of children suffered significant psychological disturbance as a result of being uprooted from home, family and environment. Acute homesickness and disorientation was the lot of most of the children. The culture shock on both sides is evident in the following report (Source H):

SOURCE H

From 'Town Children Through Country Eyes', National Federation of Women's Institutes, 1940, p. 5.

The state of the children was such that the school had to be fumigated after the reception. We have never seen so many verminous children. It appeared they were unbathed for months. One child was suffering from scabies and the majority had it in their hair and the others had dirty septic sores all over their bodies.

? What evidence is there in in Source H to indicate that evacuation was a traumatic experience for so many of those involved?

Their clothing was in a deplorable condition, some of the children being literally sewn into their ragged little garments …

Most of the children seemed under-nourished. Most of them seemed quite unaccustomed to ordinary everyday food and preferred a 'piece' or bag of chips on the doorstep.

Many of the mothers and children were bed-wetters …

Evacuation meant that town and country met for the first time. This came through strongly in the invaluable reports of the Women's Institute (WI), which organised much of the resettlement of the uprooted children. The astonishment of the country people at the habits of the evacuees they took in suggests that for the first time the middle and wealthier classes were learning how the other half lived. The WI's recording of the malnourishment and lack of social graces of the evacuees helped to create an awareness of the poverty and deprivation from which large sections of the urban population suffered (Source I).

SOURCE I

From 'Town Children Through Country Eyes', National Federation of Women's Institutes, 1940, p. 27.

Manchester. 'Few children would eat food that demanded the use of teeth. In almost every case they could only eat with a teaspoon. Practically all disliked fresh vegetables and puddings of fresh fruit were quite unknown to them.'

Liverpool. 'One little girl of 5½ remarked one day that she would like beer and cheese for supper. Most of the children seemed under-nourished yet some were troublesome to feed, not liking stewed fruit, vegetables and jam. Children had been used to receiving a penny at home to buy their own dinners. One used to buy broken biscuits, the other Oxo cubes.

What picture of deprivation emerges from Source I? **?**

Evacuation proved to be a remarkable social experiment. Designed as a protective measure for the young children of the cities, it led to a rethinking in social attitudes. In many instances, criticism and revulsion among the better-off turned into sympathy and brought a new sense of social concern. It was no coincidence that a major Education Act, aimed at widening educational opportunity for all children, was introduced in 1944 (see page 196). Privilege and deprivation would, of course, continue after the war but, insofar as Britain became a less class-divided society in the twentieth century, the impact of the Second World War was a major factor in making it so. This is not to argue that everybody pulled together as suggested by the Ministry of Information propaganda films or the patriotic BBC broadcasts. Social concern was not a universal response. While acknowledging that evacuation opened the eyes of many to the deprivation existing in Britain, a number of historians have stressed that there was an equal likelihood that it confirmed the prejudices of others. For example, modern historian John MacNicol suggests: 'For conservative social observers, [evacuation] confirmed the view that the bulk of the problems were caused by an incorrigible underclass of personally inadequate "cultural orphans" for whom a Welfare State could do little.'

As the flourishing black market indicated, people in Britain were far from being selfless saints totally committed to a united cause. It was not all **Dunkirk spirit**. Nevertheless, there was sufficient sense of common purpose engendered by the experience of war for historians to judge the period 1939–45 as having been a critical stage in Britain's development as a **socially cohesive nation**.

Industrial unrest

A further factor that challenges the notion that Britain was a wholly united society was the frequency of industrial disputes. Although these fell in number with the outbreak of war, by 1942 they were back at pre-war level (see Table 5.1). The disputes were over the traditional issues of pay and conditions. The workers, fully aware, as they had been in 1914–18, that the war had made them an indispensable part of the war effort, felt themselves entitled to press their claims. This was not lack of patriotism or disregard of those risking their lives at the front; it arose from a determination not to allow war needs to become an excuse for worker exploitation.

Table 5.1 Industrial strikes 1939–45

Year	Working days lost	Number of strikes	Number of strikers
1939	1,356,000	940	337,000
1940	940,000	972	299,000
1941	1,079,000	1,251	360,000
1942	1,527,000	1,303	456,000
1943	1,808,000	1,785	557,000
1944	3,714,000	2,194	821,000
1945	2,835,000	2,293	531,000

Women's role in the war

The remarkable contribution of women to Britain's war effort is immediately evident from the figures of their involvement:

- 1.85 million worked in the munitions industries
- 1.64 million were employed in other essential war work
- 3.1 million entered other full-time employment
- 467,000 entered the auxiliary armed services
- 56,000 served in full-time civil defence
- 350,000 served as part-time civil defence workers.

Women were not conscripted directly into the fighting services, but in December 1941 the compulsory enlistment of women into the **uniformed auxiliary services** was introduced. Britain was the first of the countries at war to do this.

KEY TERMS

Dunkirk spirit In June 1940, a volunteer armada of private vessels, helped transport 300,000 stranded British troops to safety from the beaches at Dunkirk. It was common thereafter to refer to this as an example of the spirit that would carry Britain through the war.

Socially cohesive nation A country whose people broadly agree on fundamental social principles, for example welfare provision.

Uniformed auxiliary services Auxiliary Territorial Service (ATS), Women's Auxiliary Air Force (WAAF), Women Royal Navy Service (WRNS or Wrens).

Those liable for call-up were widows without dependent children and single women aged between 20 and 30, later widened to 19–49 years.

Enlisted women could also opt to serve in the civilian Women's Land Army. By 1943 there were 80,000 'land girls' working, in effect, as poorly paid farm labourers in an unglamorous but vital part of the war economy.

On the industrial front, women workers were brought in to bridge the gap created by the conscription of millions of male factory workers. By 1943, nearly half of the females in Britain between the ages of 14 and 59 were employed in war work. A year later, women made up the following percentages of the workforce:

- 40 per cent in aircraft manufacturing
- 35 per cent in the engineering industries
- 50 per cent in the chemical industries
- 33 per cent in heavy industry (for example, munitions and shipbuilding).

This development appeared to give women increased status. Yet, within a few months of the war's end, 75 per cent of the female workers had left their jobs to return to their traditional role in the home. This makes it questionable whether the war had permanently altered traditional patterns of social behaviour. However, these things are often difficult to measure precisely. What was clear was that the contribution of women to the war effort had been enormous. Without their work in the factories. Britain could not have sustained itself.

Equally important, though less immediately visible, was the way, as effective heads of the family in their husbands' absence, a role thrust on them by the disruption of war, they had been the principal agents in the maintenance of social stability. It was wives and mothers who experienced the daily strain of trying to preserve family normality in a time of danger and shortages. Sadly, the strains did not necessarily end when the war ended. Indeed, wives, husbands and children who had been separated by war, often found it difficult to return to ordinary family life. David Kynaston, a modern social historian, has described the problem (*Austerity Britain 1945–51*, Bloomsbury, 2007, p. 97):

> The strains on marriage were severe. A couple might not have seen each other for several years; he expected to return to his family position as the undisputed head; she had become more independent (often working in a factory as well as running the home) – the possibilities for tension and strife, even when both were emotionally committed to each other, were endless.

The divorce figures may be taken as a mark of the disruption war had brought to ordinary people:

- 1939: 7012
- 1944: 12,314
- 1947: 60,190.

It remains a matter of lively controversy whether the war actually improved the lot of women. A group of distinguished French analysts has suggested that the abuse of women as industrial fodder far outweighed any gains from apparent emancipation. 'Women were liberated socially only to be enslaved economically.' Great though their contribution to the national effort was, it may be that in all countries, Britain included, women were more exploited than elevated.

The financial and economic impact of the war

The most immediate effect of the war was that it finally ended the Depression. Even before hostilities began in 1939, the threat of war in the late 1930s (see page 149) had led Britain to embark on a major rearmament programme. This re-created a huge demand for industrial products, which in turn led to a demand for workers. The problem was no longer a surplus of labour but a shortage. By 1941 an extra 2 million workers were needed to cope with the demands of war.

(see page 149)

KEY TERMS

PAYE Pay As You Earn. A system by which the tax due from workers is extracted from their wages before they have received them.

Lend-lease An arrangement that operated from 1941 under which Britain imported war materials from the USA with no obligation to pay for them until the war was over.

Balance of payments A measurement of the profit or loss on trade in a given period. When the price of imports outstrips the income from exports, financial crisis follows.

> ### The impact of the war on Britain's finances
>
> - Government expenditure rose from £1.4 billion in 1939 to £6.1 billion in 1945.
> - Income tax was levied from most workers by **PAYE** at the rate of 25 per cent of earnings in 1939, 50 per cent of earnings in 1945.
> - Government borrowed by direct loans and **lend-lease** from the USA. Between 1941 and 1945 Britain received $30 million worth of supplies under the lend-lease scheme.
> - In 1945 Britain owed £4 billion to overseas creditors.
> - The national debt rose from £500 million in 1939 to £3500 million in 1945.
> - The **balance of payments** deficit in 1945 was £870 million.

The Beveridge Report 1942

Since the nineteenth century a basic issue in British politics had been how far the State was responsible for the well-being of its citizens. The Second World War put the answer to that question beyond doubt. The war won the argument for all those who believed that for Britain the primary function of politics was to provide for the welfare of the people. All the parties came to accept that the efforts made by the British people in wartime required that reconstruction and welfare were now prime considerations. It is true that the parties would disagree about the speed with which welfare schemes should be implemented and how they were to be funded, but the principle had been established that the primary domestic purpose of government was to serve the economic and social interests of the people.

It is probable that Britain would have moved towards a Welfare State in peacetime. But what the war did was to increase the awareness of how much inequality and deprivation there was. This created a strong feeling that Britain owed its people protection and welfare. Economic well-being could not be left to the hazards of chance. The provision of a decent standard of living was the least that could be expected of a civilised nation duty bound to reward its people for their heroic efforts. The constant refrain of the government's message through its wartime propaganda agencies was that the nation was fighting for a better world.

The wartime coalition under Churchill gave considerable thought to post-war reconstruction. In political circles, guilt was still felt over how short of providing a land fit for heroes Britain had fallen in the 1920s and 1930s. There was a general determination not to fail a second time. By the end of 1940, despite the terror of the Blitz, the danger of an invasion of Britain had considerably lessened. Morale had risen and made planning for peacetime seem not wholly unrealistic. The presence in the government of a number of Labour Party leaders was a guarantee that social issues would be kept to the fore.

Indeed, planning was not a matter of political dispute at this stage; all the parties accepted the need to extend social welfare in the post-war world. In the words of Paul Addison, a modern authority, 'welfare took its place as the highest common denominator between the parties.' Significantly, the **Atlantic Charter** had, thanks to the insistence of Ernest Bevin, included in its peace aims a commitment to raise the level of social welfare.

It was in this atmosphere that Britain saw the preparation and presentation of one of the great social documents of the twentieth century – the Beveridge Report. Late in 1940 Arthur Greenwood, who had been a health minister in the Labour government of 1929–31 (see page 118), was instructed by Churchill to take the preliminary steps towards post-war reorganisation. In June 1941, Greenwood set up an interdepartmental committee to study the existing schemes of social insurance and make recommendations for their improvement. **William Beveridge** was appointed chairman of this committee of senior civil servants. He immersed himself totally in his work. Beveridge's role in the drafting of the report containing the committee's proposals was so central that it was considered appropriate that he alone should sign the document which bore his name and which was presented to the House of Commons in November 1942.

Source J (page 178) is a key passage expressing the vision that inspired Beveridge's proposals:

KEY TERM

Atlantic Charter
An agreement signed by Churchill and Franklin Roosevelt, the US president, laying out the principles on which a better world could be constructed once the Allies had won the war. It became the basis for the later United Nations (UN).

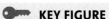

KEY FIGURE

William Beveridge (1879–1963)

Had a long experience as a civil servant, specialising in social security provision; he was an MP 1944–5.

SOURCE J

From the Beveridge Report, November 1942 (available from www.fordham.edu/halsall/mod/1942beveridge.html).

This is first and foremost a plan of insurance – of giving, in return for contributions, benefits up to a subsistence level, as of right and without means test, so that individuals may build freely upon it. Organisation of social insurance should be treated as one part only of a comprehensive policy of social progress. Social insurance fully developed may provide income security; it is an attack upon Want. But Want is only one of five giants on the road of reconstruction, and in some ways the easiest to attack. The others are Disease, Ignorance, Squalor and Idleness.

Beveridge's 'five giants'

- Want: to be ended by National Insurance.
- Disease: to be ended by a comprehensive health service.
- Ignorance: to be ended by an effective education system.
- Squalor: to be ended by slum clearance and rehousing.
- Idleness: to be ended by full employment.

Beveridge's aims

Beveridge aimed at the abolition of material want. He believed that it was possible to establish a national minimum level of welfare without recourse to extreme methods. He proposed a universal scheme of insurance which would provide protection against the distress that invariably accompanied sickness, injury and unemployment.

Insurance was to form the base, with welfare organisations providing the superstructure. Additionally, there would be grants to ease the financial hardships that came with maternity, parenthood and bereavement. The term 'protection from the cradle to the grave' although not Beveridge's own, was an appropriate description of the envisaged scale of welfare provision. The plan was to replace the current unsystematic pattern of welfare with a centrally funded and regulated system. Since it would be based on insurance, it would avoid being associated with the hated **means test** or the Poor Law.

Beveridge proposed to take the best aspects of the existing welfare systems and integrate them into a universal plan. It was no mere coincidence that as a younger man Beveridge had been directly involved in the introduction of the social service programme of the pre-1914 Liberal governments.

According to Beveridge in Source J, what is the social principle on which his plan is based?

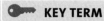 **KEY TERM**

Means test In the interwar period, to qualify for dole or relief, individuals or families had to give precise details of all the money they had coming in.

SOURCE K

Beveridge's 'five giants'. A cartoon by George Whitelaw published in the *Daily Herald*, 2 December 1942.

In his proposals Beveridge, true to his Liberal background, insisted on the principle of insurance. He specifically denied that his plan aimed at 'giving everybody something for nothing'. Freedom from want could not be 'forced on or given to a democracy'; it had to be wanted by the people. Beveridge stressed that a good society depended not on the State but on the individual. He spoke of the retention of 'personal responsibilities'. Individuals would be encouraged to save as private citizens. These ideas were very much in the Liberal tradition, as was his belief that his proposals would not involve an increase in government expenditure.

As a good Liberal, Beveridge at every point assumed the continuation of capitalism. The political movement called socialism can be defined in various ways, but one attitude common to all its forms is a conviction that the capitalist system is exploitative and unjust and, therefore, ultimately indefensible. Throughout the Beveridge Report there is an essential understanding that ⌐welfare reconstruction will take place within the framework of continuing capitalism⌐. It is for that reason that historically the Report has to be seen as belonging to the mainstream of liberal rather than socialist thinking and planning.

Beveridge's scheme pointed towards the 'Welfare State', a term which pre-dated the Report by some ten years but which began to be widely used during the

Study Source K. What was the cartoonist's view of the problems facing Beveridge?

war years. Hardly any of Beveridge's proposals were new. What made them significant in 1942 was their integration into a comprehensive scheme. Beveridge had laid the theoretical foundations for all subsequent developments in the field of social welfare provision.

William Beveridge stood as a Liberal candidate in the 1945 election, hoping to retain the seat he had won a year earlier. But his defeat meant that he was unable to oversee the progress of his plan through Parliament. Nevertheless, he had provided the essential basis on which Clement Attlee's government between 1945 and 1951 (see page 191) would build the Welfare State, both a fulfilment of the Beveridge plan and a fitting tribute to its creator.

The extremist parties in wartime

The war destroyed such credibility as Oswald Mosley had in his claims to speak for Britain (see page 139). His argument before 1939 had been that he was an honest politician defending Britain's interests in the face of the incompetence and ignorance of the established political class represented by the National Government. This became impossible to maintain when his natural sympathy for Britain's enemies, German and Italy, made him appear a traitor to the land he supposedly loved. For national security reasons Mosley, his wife Diana and a number of other fascists were interned in May 1940, and the BUF was declared an illegal organisation. Three years later, believing that the war was going well enough to render him no longer a danger, Herbert Morrison, as home secretary, authorised the release of Mosley and his wife on humanitarian grounds. It was around this time that many of the other internees were also set free.

If ever Mosley's brand of fascism had been a threat to Britain, the war and its outcome finally removed the danger. Mosley would try to resurrect the Fascist Party in the post-war period but the war had brought his loyalty into question and ended any hopes he may still have harboured of making fascism part of the mainstream of British politics.

The CPGB and the war

The Communists in Britain had an odd war. For the first two years of the struggle the CPGB under its secretary, Harry Pollitt, spent its time protesting against the war and seeking to slow down Britain's war effort. This was not from love of Germany but from devotion to the Soviet Union. Of all the Communist parties in Europe, the British one was the most subservient to the demands of Moscow and the Comintern. Between 1939 and 1941 Hitler's Germany and Stalin's Soviet Union were not the deadly enemies they were soon to become. Having signed the Nazi–Soviet Pact in August 1939; they were allies (see page 127). Soviet instructions to the CPGB, therefore, were for it to obstruct the war effort where possible. This had been the reason why the government had closed down the party's newspaper, the *Daily Worker*, and interned some of the more outspoken Communists.

But this all changed on 22 June 1941 when Hitler launched the invasion of the USSR. Germany was now the deadly enemy and British Communists, doing a U-turn, now rushed to support the war. As poachers turned gamekeepers, they now used their influence to prevent strikes and industrial disruption. This gave an immediate lift to the CPGB. Its opposition to the war had seen it lose 12,000 of its 17,000 members by the end of 1939. Its commitment to the war after June 1941 saw its membership rise to over 30,000.

However, the party's twists and turns did it considerable damage in the longer term. Workers in Britain could clearly see that they came no more than second in the CPGB's order of priorities. It was its subordination to the orders of the Soviet Union that determined the policy and behaviour of British Communists. This became increasingly apparent when the party directed all its energies into a 'start a second front now' campaign. To take the pressure off the Soviet forces in their desperate struggle on the Eastern Front between 1941 and 1943, Stalin continually appealed to Britain and the USA to open a second front by a major invasion of some part of German-occupied Western Europe. To Stalin's disgust, the Allies claimed that they could not do this successfully until they were fully ready, which in the event was not until the **D-Day landings** of June 1944.

The Communists obviously rejoiced in the final victory over Germany in 1945, but their assertion that from the beginning they had taken part in a great anti-fascist crusade on Britain's behalf conveniently overlooked the fact that they had taken up the fight only after Nazi Germany had ceased to be an ally of the Soviet Union and become its enemy. The CPGB had compromised itself by its changes of policy during the war. It would continue with its efforts to infiltrate the Labour Party and influence its policies, but its support of the Soviet Union in the **Cold War**, which began as the German war closed, put its loyalty to Britain in doubt. Unlike the Labour Party, which grew in strength and confidence because of its contribution to the war effort, the CPGB condemned itself by its wartime behaviour to remain a fringe party.

🔑 KEY TERMS

D-Day landings A massive Anglo-American invasion of occupied western France.

Cold War The period of tension between the USSR and its allies and the USA and its allies 1945–91.

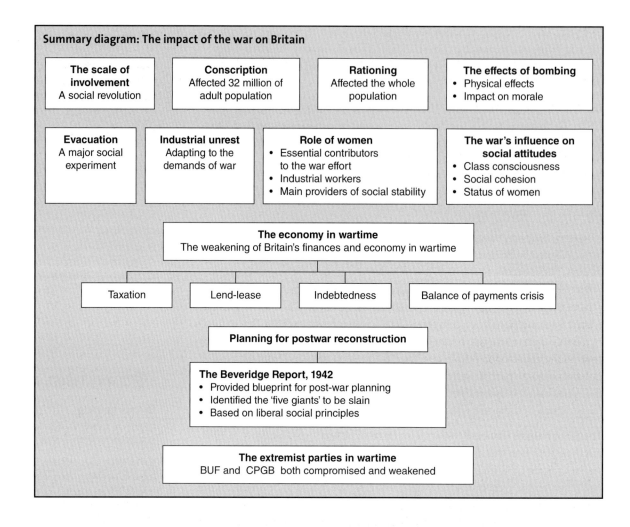

Summary diagram: The impact of the war on Britain

The scale of involvement
A social revolution

Conscription
Affected 32 million of adult population

Rationing
Affected the whole population

The effects of bombing
- Physical effects
- Impact on morale

Evacuation
A major social experiment

Industrial unrest
Adapting to the demands of war

Role of women
- Essential contributors to the war effort
- Industrial workers
- Main providers of social stability

The war's influence on social attitudes
- Class consciousness
- Social cohesion
- Status of women

The economy in wartime
The weakening of Britain's finances and economy in wartime

Taxation

Lend-lease

Indebtedness

Balance of payments crisis

Planning for postwar reconstruction

The Beveridge Report, 1942
- Provided blueprint for post-war planning
- Identified the 'five giants' to be slain
- Based on liberal social principles

The extremist parties in wartime
BUF and CPGB both compromised and weakened

3 The growth in the power of the State

▶ *How did government control increase in wartime?*

A striking feature of war in the twentieth century was the encouragement it gave to centralist tendencies in government. Faced with the strains of total war, nations without exception showed a readiness to accept extension of State control as a means of creating the maximum war effort. This was as evident in democratic countries as in totalitarian regimes. Britain's coalition government moved so far towards regulation that the post-war Labour government inherited an established pattern of centralised control (see page 195).

Extension of State power in Britain during the war

Britain, in effect, became a **collectivist** state during the Second World War. The major examples of government control were as follows:

- food and fuel rationing
- restrictions on press freedom
- suspension of legal rights
- conscription of men and women into the armed services
- direction of workers to undertake specific work in nominated areas
- control of rates of pay and hours of employment
- subjection of employers to ministerial control
- control over exchange rates and import–export dealings
- right to arrest and detain citizens without trial.

New government departments were established covering such areas as:

- food supply
- information
- economic warfare
- civilian aviation
- town and country planning.

The Emergency Powers Act, passed through Parliament in 1939 soon after the start of the war, granted an extraordinary degree of authority to the home secretary and the minister of labour. It is instructive to quote the terms of the Act (Source L):

SOURCE L

The Emergency Powers Act, 3 September 1939, *Hansard*, volume 54, p. 343.

Such persons may be detained whose detention appears to the Secretary of State [the home secretary] to be expedient in the interests of public safety or the defence of the realm. The Secretary of State, the Minister of Labour, has the authority to oblige any person in the United Kingdom to perform any service required in any place. He may prescribe the remuneration of such services and the hours of work. He may require such persons to register particulars of themselves; he might order employers to keep and produce any records and books.

These were unprecedented powers for British ministers, and the fact that they were exercised with discretion and moderation did not lessen their significance or, in the opinion of some, their danger.

Internment

The State's power was seen at its most direct in regard to internment. On the grounds that they represented a potential threat to the war effort, many

KEY TERM

Collectivist The notion that, in times of crisis, individual rights must be subordinated to the greater good of the group.

According to Source L, what powers are the home secretary and the minister granted under the Act?

thousands of aliens were interned in special camps. A popular newspaper, the *Daily Mirror*, described the process, particularly as it affected women (Source M).

? What evidence is there in Source M to suggest that the *Daily Mirror* is being ironic?

SOURCE M

From the *Daily Mirror*, 28 May 1940.

Three thousand five hundred women enemy aliens were interned yesterday. Police acted swiftly on a sudden order from the Home Office and many of the women were still in bed when the police walked in.

Most of them will be sent to comfortable billets on the Isle of Man. They will have a great deal of freedom, except that they will not be allowed out of the town in which they are interned.

The women are Germans and Austrians between the ages of sixteen and sixty. Those who have children under sixteen will be allowed to take them along.

More than 1,500 of them lived in London; usually domestic servants and housemaids.

The total number of aliens now interned in Britain is 10,000.

The internees even included Jewish refugees who had fled to Britain to escape Nazi persecution. While the camps were often surrounded by barbed wire and patrolled by armed guards, conditions inside were not notably severe; it was deprivation of liberty and livelihood that was the hardest thing for the innocent to bear. Some 1800 British subjects were also interned; 763 of these were members of the BUF (see page 140). However, by the end of the war nearly all internees had been released.

Libertarians were unhappy about the legal and economic powers that the government exercised. Nevertheless, as had happened during the First World War, when a similar extension of government authority had occurred, the argument of national security carried the day. Necessity was regarded as justifying the increase in government power. Legal niceties took second place to the struggle for survival. As its title was meant to convey, the Emergency Powers Act was a temporary measure, not a permanent enlargement of State power. To survive the war, the nation had to be organised at its most effective. If this required a massive spread of government power, that was the price that had to be paid. This, in essence, was the case put forward by government and Parliament and was accepted by the mass of the people.

A far-reaching consequence of the 1939–45 war was that it made the idea of government direction of the economy seem practical and reasonable. The six-year struggle was a national effort led by a coalition government, which introduced a range of measures that would have been unacceptable in peacetime. For example, thousands of farmers were dispossessed of their land during the war for failing to conform to the production levels laid down by the government.

Propaganda

Throughout the war, the government remained determined to put the best construction on events. Despite Churchill's claim that he would always tell the British people the truth, his government was careful to highlight the good news and play down the bad. There is little doubt that the news was manipulated in regard to timing and presentation, if not to fact. During the first two years of the war, when the USSR was an ally of Nazi Germany, the pro-Soviet Communist *Daily Worker* was closed down (see page 181). While there was little direct censorship of the newspapers that did publish, the press were expected not to endanger security or morale. That was why Herbert Morrison and Winston Churchill reacted angrily over the supposedly unpatriotic *Daily Mirror* cartoon in March 1942 (see page 161). Although it was not subject to direct control, the BBC was similarly expected in its news broadcasts and the content of its programmes to conform to government wishes, a requirement that the broadcasters consistently honoured. The cinema industry also conformed, British directors producing a string of films on the theme of Britons gallantly fighting on the war front or patiently enduring on the Home Front.

The Ministry of Information became in effect a ministry of propaganda. Its 3000 staff spent their days producing leaflets, posters and instructive films intended to convince the people of such duties as accepting rationing (see page 166), 'doing their bit' and adopting a positive attitude. Colourful posters, bearing such slogans as 'Careless Talk Costs Lives', 'Make Do and Mend', 'Waste Not Want Not' were among the thousands of exhortations from the ministry which became part of everyday speech. Angus Calder, an authority on Britain during the war, suggests the advertising industry became nationalised during this period. His description of the impact of government propaganda makes instructive reading (*The People's War*, Pimlico, 2006, p. 502):

> The Ministry of 'Information', and Government departments in general had three broad methods of imposing their ideas on the public through the mass media. One was to suppress news and views which should not be known, a second was to release, or to invent, news which should be known. A third was to give writers special facilities to report what was happening, on paper or on screen; with concomitant restrictions on the liberty both of the chosen few, and those who were not given special privileges.

Keynesianism

The concept of necessity in a national crisis helped to create an atmosphere in which it was accepted that government knew best. In 1944, the government formally announced that it was now responsible for the 'maintenance of a high and stable level of employment'. A.J.P. Taylor, a provocative English historian, wrote that the war 'produced a revolution in British economic life, until in the end direction and control turned Great Britain into a country more fully socialist than anything achieved by the conscious planners of Soviet Russia'.

By an interesting coincidence, it so happened that a powerful theory was available to justify the government's intrusion into the running of economic affairs. Every so often a particular financial or economic theory arrives to dominate its time and oblige governments to structure their policies in accordance with it. For most of the period between the late 1930s and the late 1970s, the ideas of **John Maynard Keynes** provided the basic frame of reference. The National Government had chosen to ignore Keynes' ideas but they began to appear increasingly relevant in wartime.

Dismayed by the Depression in the 1930s, Keynes had written a number of works suggesting ways of tackling unemployment. He believed that economic depressions were avoidable if particular steps were taken. His starting point was demand. He calculated that it was a fall in demand for manufactured products that caused industrial economies to slip into recession. If demand could be sustained, decline could be prevented and jobs preserved. Keynes maintained that the only agency with sufficient power and influence to keep demand high enough was the government itself. He urged, therefore, that:

- The government should use its budgets and its revenue-raising powers to acquire capital, which it could then reinvest in the economy to keep it at a high level of activity.
- This artificial boost to the economy would lead to genuine recovery and growth. Companies and firms would have full order books and the workers would have jobs and earnings.
- Those earnings would be spent on goods and services, with the result that the forces of supply and demand would be stimulated.
- The government should abandon the practice of always trying to balance the budget between income and expenditure. It should be willing to run **deficit budgets** in the short term, even if this meant borrowing to do so. The government would eventually be able to repay its debts by taxing the companies and workers, whose profits and wages would rise in a flourishing economy.

The six years of government-directed war effort, during which Keynes was an influential figure at the Treasury, helped to give strength to his arguments. What is interesting is that, although Keynes thought in terms of limited government action, it was the notion of government being an *essential* part of economic planning that become widely accepted. The Labour governments under Clement Attlee after 1945 were to benefit from this new conviction (see page 201).

KEY FIGURE

John Maynard Keynes (1883–1946)

A Cambridge don, a director of the Bank of England during the war and the government's chief economic adviser.

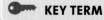

KEY TERM

Deficit budgets Allowing the government's annual planned expenditure to exceed the amount raised in revenue.

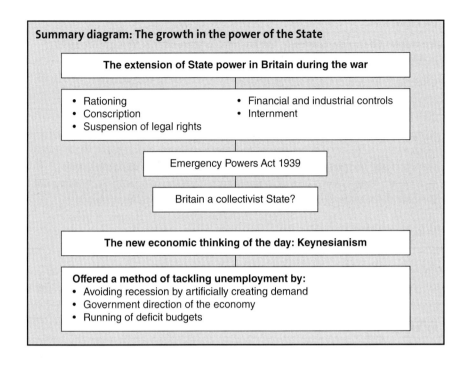

Summary diagram: The growth in the power of the State

The extension of State power in Britain during the war

- Rationing
- Conscription
- Suspension of legal rights

- Financial and industrial controls
- Internment

Emergency Powers Act 1939

Britain a collectivist State?

The new economic thinking of the day: Keynesianism

Offered a method of tackling unemployment by:
- Avoiding recession by artificially creating demand
- Government direction of the economy
- Running of deficit budgets

 # Key debate

▶ *Did Churchill's wartime leadership strengthen or weaken Britain's position as an international power?*

The traditional view of Churchill as war leader

Such was his personal contribution to Britain's survival during the darkest days of war that A.J.P. Taylor described him as 'the saviour of his country'. This is very much the traditional picture of Churchill in wartime. His chief biographer, Martin Gilbert, paints him as an inspiring leader guiding a united nation through peril to victory over a deadly enemy and, in so doing, establishing himself as an outstanding world figure.

Revisionist challenges

But there have been challenges to that view. Interestingly these have come not from the left but from the right. Revisionist historians, such as Alan Clark and John Charmley, have advanced interesting alternative interpretations. Charmley's weightiest charge is that Churchill as war leader clung to the notion of victory when he had the opportunity to make a reasonable peace with Germany and thereby prevent the destruction brought by five years of war.

EXTRACT 1

From John Charmley, *Churchill: The End of Glory*, Hodder & Stoughton, 1993, p. 403.

Churchill's vision of what might happen in the event of Britain failing to win can be seen from the terms of reference that he gave to his Chiefs of Staff on 26 May, when he asked them to say what situation would arise in the event of terms being offered to Britain which would place her entirely at the mercy of Germany … The very act of posing the alternatives in such a stark form helped predetermine the answer; but what grounds were there for supposing that Germany's terms would be so Carthaginian [excessively harsh]. Were there not grounds for supposing that Hitler might be disposed to pay handsomely to avoid the perilous task of a sea and air-borne invasion? Viscount Halifax thought so.

John Lukacs, the Hungarian-American authority on Hitler, will have none of that. He stresses that in the circumstances of May 1940 peace talks were simply not a realistic option.

EXTRACT 2

From John Lukacs, *Five Days in London: May 1940*, Yale University Press, 2001, pp. 187–9.

Had Hitler won the Second World War we would be living in a different world. That is not arguable. What is arguable is the crucial importance of 24–28 May 1940, those five days in London … My argument is that Hitler was never closer to his ultimate victory than during those five days … [However], the man in Hitler's way was Churchill. In May 1940 neither the US nor Soviet Russia was at war with Germany. At that time there were reasons for a British government to at least ascertain whether a temporary compromise with Hitler was at all possible. Churchill thought and said no, that even the first cautious moves would mean stepping on a slippery slope; he was right, and not only morally speaking. Had Britain stopped fighting in May 1940, Hitler would have won his war.

Another gloss on Churchill's record has been provided by British historian David Carlton, who has argued that what motivated Churchill during the later war years was the same thing that had consistently inspired him since 1917: hatred and fear of Soviet Communism. Carlton's argument is that, despite being Stalin's ally, Churchill, as his private correspondence has revealed, believed that by 1944 the Soviet Union was as great a threat to British interests as ever Nazi Germany had been.

EXTRACT 3

From David Carlton, 'Churchill's Secret War with Stalin', *Daily Telegraph*, 11 February 2000.

Churchill became obsessed with the Communist threat and thereafter saw the struggle to defeat Germany as no more than a second-order crusade. Increasingly he devoted attention to frustrating Soviet expansionist aims. Accordingly he struck a brutal but realistic bargain with Stalin in 1944 with respect to Bulgaria, Romania and anti-communist POWs [prisoners of war], but Britain was able to intervene in Greece to prevent communists seizing power.

> In what ways do the arguments in Extracts 1–3 concur or differ in their interpretation of Churchill's wartime role?

The 'brutal bargain' between Stalin and Churchill to which Carlton refers was the agreement by which the Soviet Union was given a free hand in Bulgaria and Romania and allowed to deal as it chose with any Soviet citizens who, after being captured by the Germans, had fought against the USSR. In return, the Soviet Union would not enforce a Communist takeover in Greece. This is an aspect of what may be called Churchill's appeasement of Stalin at the end of the war. In order to limit Soviet ambitions, Churchill at the **Yalta Conference** in February 1945 joined with the USA in accepting the USSR's right to remain in control of the territories in Eastern Europe that it had taken in its push westwards against Germany. By a bitter irony this included Poland, the country whose independence Britain had gone to war in 1939 to defend.

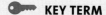 **KEY TERM**

Yalta Conference Attended by the USSR, Britain and the USA to consider the post-war settlement. The discussions were continued at the Potsdam Conference in July and August 1945.

Chapter summary

Becoming prime minister at a low point in the war, Winston Churchill refused to consider negotiated peace terms with Germany and went on, over the next five years, to be an inspiring national leader. Although opposed in the Commons at times, his position as leader was never seriously challenged. This was in large part because his cabinet colleagues, whose chief figures were Labour Party members, showed both consistent loyalty and great competence as ministers.

The war had a profound effect on the British people. The Blitz which was its most concentrated in 1940–1 continued intermittently until 1944 when Hitler's V weapons brought terror. However, the rocket attacks never reached the scale Hitler had intended and British morale was sustained. Such developments in the total war as conscription, evacuation and rationing had a marked influence on ordinary people, changing their perceptions of social class and status. Not everybody pulled together, as the black market illustrated, but, with the extremist parties being either suppressed or supportive, a collective spirit did largely prevail. An aspect of this was the Beveridge Report which established a blueprint for post-war reconstruction. The demands of war and severe economic disruption led to greatly increased State power and the acceptance of Keynesian economic planning.

Refresher questions

Use these questions to remind yourself of the key material covered in this chapter.

1 What circumstances led to Chamberlain's replacement by Churchill as prime minister in May 1940?

2 Why did the cabinet decline to pursue the idea of peace talks in May 1940?

3 What personal characteristics enabled Churchill to become an effective wartime leader?

4 How was civilian morale affected by the war?

5 Did rationing have a cohesive or disruptive influence on wartime Britain?

6 How was conscription organised in wartime Britain?

7 How did evacuation help to alter social perceptions?

8 How extensive was the role of women in the war effort?

9 How did the British economy adjust to the demands of war?

10 Why was the Beveridge Report such a significant social document?

11 What were the Beveridge Report's basic social principles?

12 How did government control increase in wartime?

13 How was the growth in State power justified?

14 According to Keynes, what role should government play in the economy?

15 What was the impact of the war on the BUF and the CPGB?

 Question practice

ESSAY QUESTIONS

1 Assess the reasons why Churchill displaced Chamberlain as prime minister in May 1940.

2 How far were social attitudes in Britain changed by the experience of the Second World War?

3 How successful were the wartime measures taken by the British government to ensure that the burdens of war were equally distributed among the people?

4 'The Second World War produced a revolution in British economic life.' Assess the validity of this view.

SOURCE ANALYSIS QUESTIONS

1 With reference to Sources A (page 155), B (page 157) and C (page 158), and your understanding of the historical context, assess the value of these sources to a historian studying Churchill's attitude towards the role of prime minister in 1940.

2 With reference to Sources G (page 171), H (page 172) and I (page 173), and your understanding of the historical context, assess the value of these sources to a historian studying the impact of the Second World War on the civilian population in Britain.

CHAPTER 6

From Labour to Conservative 1945–57

In 1945, Labour came into power with a large majority, following an impressive victory in the first general election after the Second World War. During the next six years it introduced the Welfare State and nationalised a significant part of the industrial economy. That it had set a pattern was evident in the policies followed by the succeeding Conservative governments between 1951 and 1957. This chapter covers these developments under the following headings:

★ Labour's victory in 1945

★ Labour's creation of the Welfare State

★ Labour's economic policy 1941–51

★ Foreign affairs

★ Labour's defeat 1951

★ The legacy of the Labour governments 1945–51

★ Churchill and Eden 1951–7

★ Macmillan's government 1957

The key debate on *page 242* of this chapter asks the question: How unpopular was Eden's Suez venture in 1956?

Key dates

1945	Overwhelming election victory for Labour		1949	Government forced to devalue the pound
1946	National Insurance Act		1950	Start of Korean War
	Nationalisation programme began			Election reduced Labour majority to five MPs
1947	Government undertook to develop independent nuclear deterrent		1951	Narrow election success for Conservatives
	Independence of India		1955	Eden succeeded Churchill
1948	National Health Service began		1956	Suez War
1949	Nationalisation of iron and steel		1957	Macmillan became prime minister

1 Labour's victory in 1945

▶ *Why was Labour's election victory in 1945 on such a large scale?*

The scale of Labour's victory in 1945 surprised even the Labour Party itself. It had gained a huge majority of 180 over the Conservatives and one of 148 overall.

Table 6.1 The July 1945 general election result

Party	Votes	Seats	Percentage of vote
Conservative	9,988,306	213	39.8
Liberal	2,248,226	12	9.0
Labour	11,995,152	393	47.8
Communist	102,780	2	0.4
Others	751,514	20	3.0

In proportional terms, the victory was less overwhelming; Labour was two per cent short of winning half the total vote, and the opposition parties collectively had polled more votes and had a greater percentage of popular support. Despite its very large majority in terms of seats, Labour was a minority government. The disparity that the 'first past the post' electoral system had produced is evident in the following figures:

- for each seat the Labour Party won, it had polled 30,522 votes
- for each seat the Conservative Party won, it had polled 46,893 votes
- for each seat the Liberal Party won, it had polled 187,352 votes.

However, the observations made above apply to all the governments elected up to 2015; none of them came to power with the majority of the electorate having voted for them. In all their future election victories, the Conservatives would similarly gain from the inbuilt imbalance of the system, which does not operate according to the principle of **proportional representation (PR)**. It was only the Liberals who missed out because they could not convert their popular following into seats in Parliament.

That said, the fact remained that Labour had performed extraordinarily well. In the previous general election in 1935, it had gained 37.9 per cent of the overall vote but had won only 154 seats. In 1945 it gained ten per cent more of the vote, increased its popular support by 3.5 million and won 393 seats. This remarkable result is best explained by describing Conservative Party handicaps and Labour Party advantages in the election campaign.

Conservatives' handicaps

- Churchill's great popularity as a wartime leader did not carry over into peacetime. In the minds of many of the electorate, his Conservative Party was associated with the Depression of the 1930s and with appeasement (see pages 130 and 147).

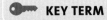 **KEY TERM**

Proportional representation (PR)
The allocation of seats to parties according to the number of votes they gain overall.

Clement Attlee

1883	Born in London into a comfortable middle-class family
1901–4	Read law at Oxford
1922	Elected Labour MP for Limehouse
1930–1	Served in second Labour government
1935–55	Leader of the Labour Party
1940–5	Deputy prime minister in Churchill's coalition government
1945–51	Prime minister
1955	Retired to House of Lords
1967	Died

Despite his comfortable social background, Clement Attlee was moved by the poverty he witnessed in London in the early 1900s, when he ran a centre for disadvantaged young people. He concluded that destitution could be cured only by political action.

In his own time and for years afterwards, Attlee tended to be underrated. He suffered by comparison with Winston Churchill. Attlee's unprepossessing physical presence and limited skills as a public speaker did not create a grand image. However, in the 1970s, historians began to reassess Attlee, emphasising his skill in surviving as prime minister six years of one of the most difficult periods of twentieth-century government. His record as prime minister was truly remarkable. Nationalisation, the Welfare State, **NATO**, Indian independence: these were the striking successes of this unassuming man. His ordinariness was, indeed, a positive virtue in that he came to typify the very people whose well-being he did so much to advance. Attlee's achievements would have been impressive at any time, but when it is appreciated that they were accomplished in a post-war period, dominated by demanding domestic and international crises, they appear even more striking.

In an interview in 1960, Attlee summed up his own practical, down-to-earth style of conducting government business: 'The job of the prime minister is to get the general feeling – collect the voices. And then, when everything reasonable has been said, to get on with the job.' Stories are often told of Churchill's withering comments on Attlee's lack of personality. The stories are apocryphal and Churchill always denied them. Despite their party differences, Churchill had the deepest respect for the talent and integrity of the man who had been his loyal wartime deputy.

- In 1945 there was also a widespread feeling in Britain that effective post-war social and economic reconstruction was both vital and deserved, and that the tired old Conservative-dominated establishment that had dominated the interwar years would be incapable of providing it.
- The Conservatives ran a poor election campaign. Confident of victory, Churchill, prime minister since 1940, misread the mood of the nation. On one notorious occasion he suggested that the Labour Party's proposed reform programme would require 'a **Gestapo**' to enforce it. It was a slur he later regretted since it seemed to suggest that he doubted the loyalty of the Labour figures who had faithfully served under him in his own wartime coalition government.

Labour's advantages

- Even the Conservatives had accepted the need for post-war construction, but the general view was that Labour was better fitted to carry it out.
- In 1945, the Labour Party fitted the progressive *zeitgeist* that encouraged reform and reconstruction.

🔑 KEY TERMS

NATO The North Atlantic Treaty Organisation, a defensive alliance formed in 1949 by Britain, France and the Benelux counties (Belgium, the Netherlands and Luxembourg) as a safeguard against Soviet expansion into Western Europe. The USA became a member by invitation.

Gestapo The notorious Nazi secret police which had terrorised Germany under Adolf Hitler between 1933 and 1945.

Zeitgeist The spirit of the time, the dominant prevailing attitude in society.

- The leading Labour figures – Attlee, Cripps, Bevin, Morrison, Dalton – had gained invaluable experience as ministers in the wartime coalition and had gained the respect of the electorate.
- Aside from personalities and policies, a critical factor was that in 1945 the imbalance in the electoral system worked heavily in Labour's favour.

It used to be claimed that the size of Labour's victory was due to the pro-Labour teaching in the education services of the armed forces. The argument was that the teachers conscripted into the education corps during the war were predominantly left wing and gave pro-Labour talks and instruction in the classes they put on for the troops. When the servicemen cast their vote in the election, therefore, they had already been indoctrinated into supporting Labour.

The claim is difficult to sustain. The personnel in education may indeed have leaned to the left, but to ascribe Labour's victory to their efforts would be an exaggeration. What is more likely to have had an impact on voters' attitudes was the work of the government's wartime propaganda department. The documentary films that it put on regularly in the cinemas were not simply anti-German. A recurring theme was the need for the people to look beyond the war and think in terms of acting together to reconstruct a better nation. Such films were not overtly supportive of the Labour Party, and were probably not deliberately intended to be, but their message was much more in tune with the ideas of Labour than any of the other parties.

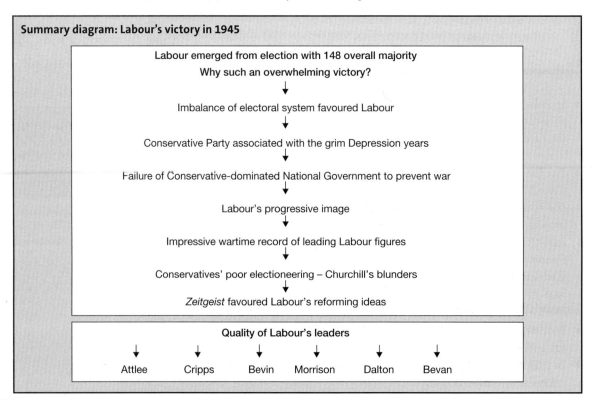

Summary diagram: Labour's victory in 1945

Labour emerged from election with 148 overall majority
Why such an overwhelming victory?
↓
Imbalance of electoral system favoured Labour
↓
Conservative Party associated with the grim Depression years
↓
Failure of Conservative-dominated National Government to prevent war
↓
Labour's progressive image
↓
Impressive wartime record of leading Labour figures
↓
Conservatives' poor electioneering – Churchill's blunders
↓
Zeitgeist favoured Labour's reforming ideas

Quality of Labour's leaders
↓   ↓   ↓   ↓   ↓   ↓
Attlee   Cripps   Bevin   Morrison   Dalton   Bevan

Labour's creation of the Welfare State

▶ *What steps did the Labour government take to implement the Beveridge Report?*

When the Beveridge Report appeared in 1942 (see page 176), it had been welcomed by all the parties among whom there was broad agreement that **social reconstruction** would be a post-war necessity in Britain. This showed how much ground had been made in Britain by the principle of collectivism (see page 183), which in turn was evidence of the influence of the moderate socialism that the Labour Party espoused. Yet Churchill did not regard the Report as socialist; his reluctance to put it into practice was on the grounds of cost rather than principle. It was also the case that the Labour members of his wartime coalition had supported him in 1942 and 1943 in defeating House of Commons' motions calling for the immediate implementation of the Report.

However, in office after 1945 with a massive majority, the Labour government immediately took steps to put in place the main proposals in the Beveridge Report. Labour's election campaign had promoted the notion that after six years of war effort, the people were entitled to their just reward. It would also be a fitting recompense for the sufferings of the nation during the Depression of the interwar years. The Report had provided the new government with its blueprint for social reconstruction.

Labour's welfare programme

The Labour government's strategy for an integrated social welfare system was expressed in four major measures, which came into effect in the summer of 1948. In a prime ministerial broadcast on the eve of their introduction, Attlee explained that they were 'comprehensive and available to every citizen' and gave 'security to all members of the family.' The measures to which Attlee referred were:

- The National Insurance Act, which created a system of universal and compulsory government–employer–employee contributions to provide against unemployment, sickness, maternity expenses, widowhood and retirement.
- The National Assistance Act, which complemented National Insurance by establishing National Assistance Boards to deal directly and financially with cases of hardship and poverty.
- The Industrial Injuries Act, which provided cover for accidents occurring in the workplace.
- The National Health Service Act, which brought the whole population, regardless of status or income, into a scheme of free medical and hospital

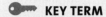 **KEY TERM**

Social reconstruction
Shaping society so as to provide protection and opportunity for all its citizens.

treatment. Drug prescriptions, dental and optical care were included. Under the Act, the existing voluntary and local authority hospitals were co-ordinated into a single, national system, to be operated at local level by appointed health boards. The National Health Service (NHS) would be funded through general taxation and National Insurance.

Two other measures need to be added to the four listed by Attlee: the Education Act of 1944 and the Family Allowances Act of 1945. These were introduced before Labour came into office but were put into practice by Attlee's government:

- The Education Act (or Butler Act), 1944, was introduced by R.A. Butler, a Conservative, and may be regarded as the first organised attack on one of Beveridge's 'five giants': ignorance (see page 178). It provided compulsory free education within a three-tier secondary school system. Pupils, at age eleven, in their last year at primary school, were to take the 'eleven plus', an examination to determine whether they were to attend a secondary-grammar (for the academically inclined), a secondary-technical (for the vocationally gifted) or a secondary-modern (for those not fitted for either of the former two categories).
- The Family Allowances Act (1945) provided a weekly payment of 5s. (25p) for every additional child after the first. The money was paid directly to the mother and did not require a means test (see page 178).

The Welfare State: a revolution?

The Labour government's implementation of the Welfare State has been described as a social revolution. It was certainly an event of major significance, but it is important to see it in context. It was not a revolution forced on an unwilling people and it was not a revolution that overthrew existing structures. It built on what was already there. It is true that Beveridge had described his plan as a revolution, but he had been keen to stress that it was a 'British revolution', by which he meant it was not destructive but constructive, built upon precedent. He said it was 'a natural development from the past'; the nation was ready for such a revolution.

Interestingly, Attlee's government, when introducing the welfare measures, was also careful to point out that, far from representing revolutionary socialism, the adoption of the Welfare State was a responsible act of social reconstruction. Ernest Bevin expressed the government's basic view in a speech in the Commons in June 1949: 'From the point of view of what is called the Welfare State and social services, I beg the House not to drag this business into a kind of partisan warfare. This so-called Welfare State has developed everywhere; the United States is as much a Welfare State as we are only in a different form.' In saying this, Bevin was responding to the criticism by the Conservative opposition who voted against nearly all the major clauses of the various welfare measures. He was hoping to take the question out of the political arena, arguing that the Welfare State was not peculiar to Britain.

The Welfare State: fulfilment of socialism or liberalism?

While Bevin's comparison could be faulted, since the American system at the time bore little relation to the one that Britain was adopting, his claim deserves attention. It showed that the Labour government was not hell-bent on pursuing revolutionary socialist policies. In the light of such views, it is perhaps best to see Labour's impressive achievement in the field of social services not as an entirely new departure but as the implementation of welfare policies that represented progressive thinking in all parties. It is particularly significant that, although Churchill and the Conservatives opposed the measures when they were first introduced, all the Conservative governments that were to follow between 1951 and 2015 committed themselves to the preservation and, indeed, the extension of the Welfare State in all its main aspects. It is true that the main parties would continually row about how it was funded and how efficiently it was managed, but there was no serious difference between them over the need to preserve the Welfare State.

Rather than being the advent of revolutionary socialism, Labour's moves towards a Welfare State marked the high point of progressive liberalism. It was very much in the tradition begun by the Liberal governments between 1906 and 1914 (see page 24). Although the Liberal Party had ceased to be a major political force by 1945, it could be argued that the coming of the Welfare State marked the final great triumph of liberalism as a set of ideas. It had set the agenda for the foreseeable future.

Yet when due note has been taken of Liberal influence and of the ultimate consensus between the parties over welfare, the clear historical fact remains that it was the Labour Party under Attlee that between 1945 and 1951 found the commitment and sense of purpose to turn good intentions into workable and permanent structures. This was often, moreover, achieved in the face of determined opposition.

Resistance to the National Health Service

One of the most controversial examples of opposition was the resistance of the British Medical Association (BMA) to the introduction of the NHS. The Act setting up the NHS was passed in 1946 and was intended to come into effect in 1947. However, the resistance of the medical profession meant its introduction was delayed until 1948. Professions are notoriously reluctant to accept changes that might threaten their interests. It was certainly the case that the majority of the medical consultants and general practitioners (GPs), fearing a loss of income, initially refused to co-operate with Aneurin Bevan, who, as minister of health, had the task of planning and implementing the NHS. A poll of doctors in March 1948 revealed that out of the 80 per cent of the profession who voted, only 4735 supported the NHS scheme while 40,814 were against it. Along with money worries, the doctors' basic objections were:

- They did not wish to become mere 'State-salaried civil servants'.

- They feared government interference in the doctor–patient relationship.
- They were concerned that the regional management boards which would run the NHS would take away their independence as practitioners.
- They regarded the proposed NHS as a form of nationalisation (see page 201) which treated the medical profession as if it were an industry.

Role of Aneurin Bevan

Although not formally stated, one of the doctors' grievances was Bevan himself. The BMA felt that Attlee had made a mistake in appointing as health minister a man renowned for his aggressive left-wing views, who would make negotiations very difficult. The doctors complained that Bevan looked on the NHS as a political crusade rather than a practical plan for improving healthcare. They were able to quote such statements of his as, 'a free health service is pure Socialism and as such it is opposed to the hedonism of capitalist society'. In fairness, however, it should be said that, despite his reputation as a bullying fanatic, Bevan could be charming when he chose. Many of those who opposed his views remarked that in his personal dealings with them he was invariably courteous and understanding.

In the end, Bevan had to buy off the BMA. It was only in return for a guarantee that they would not suffer financially and would be allowed to keep their private practices that the doctors eventually agreed to enter the NHS. Bevan remarked bitterly that to establish the NHS, with its ideal of medical care provided free to all at the point of treatment, he had won the doctors over only by 'stuffing their mouths with gold'.

When it finally came into effect in 1948 the NHS had the following main features:

- Primary care would be provided by GPs who would work as independent contractors and be paid for each patient on their books.
- Dentists and opticians, while providing NHS treatment, would continue to operate as private practitioners.
- Hospitals would be run by fourteen regional boards which would appoint local management committees to oversee matters at local level.
- Community health provision, such as maternity care, vaccinations and the ambulance service, were to be provided by the local authorities.
- Medical prescriptions would be provided free of charge.

Further concessions that Bevan had to make to the BMA's demands included:

- Private practices and hospitals in which doctors charged their patients fees were to be allowed to continue, thus enabling GPs to be both NHS and private doctors.
- 'Pay beds' for private fee-paying patients were to be reserved in NHS hospitals.
- Teaching hospitals were to be run by independent governors outside government control.

SOURCE A

DOTHEBOYS HALL

"It still tastes awful."

How accurately does the cartoon in Source A depict the relationship between Bevan and the BMA?

'It still tastes awful.' 'Matron' Bevan (AB) forcing doctors to take the 'nasty' medicine of the NHS. A cartoon published in the British satirical magazine *Punch* in 1948.

Regardless of his long and often bitter struggle with the medical profession, Bevan still believed that the NHS would not only solve the nation's major social problems, but also pay for itself. A healthy society would mean far fewer workers being absent. Efficiency and wages would rise. Higher wages would produce higher tax yields. From that increased revenue the State would be able to finance its welfare provision. This proved an unrealistic forecast. Bevan declined to listen when he was told that the demand for treatment would outstrip supply and that the cost of drugs and medical appliances would spiral beyond the capacity of the government to match it from revenue. This had already begun to happen by the mid-1950s.

Bevan was less culpable in regard to another development that undermined the NHS. He could not know that there would be a major population shift in the second half of the century, caused by people living longer, and, in old age, making demands on a service that could be financed only by a dwindling proportion of tax-paying workers. Nor could Bevan know just how expensive drugs and medical machinery would become. The growth is clear from these figures showing the costs of the health and social security budget:

- in 1949: £597 million (equivalent to 4.7 per cent of gross domestic product)
- in 1990: £91 billion (equivalent to 14 per cent of gross domestic product).

However, to dwell overmuch on cost would be to detract from the scale of Bevan's achievement. The NHS, which he had brought into being against formidable resistance, had created the essential feature of the Welfare State. He had put into practical form the principle that the safeguarding of the health of the people, individually and collectively, was a prime duty of government. In doing this, Bevan had taken a major step towards the development of what would later be called 'the caring society'.

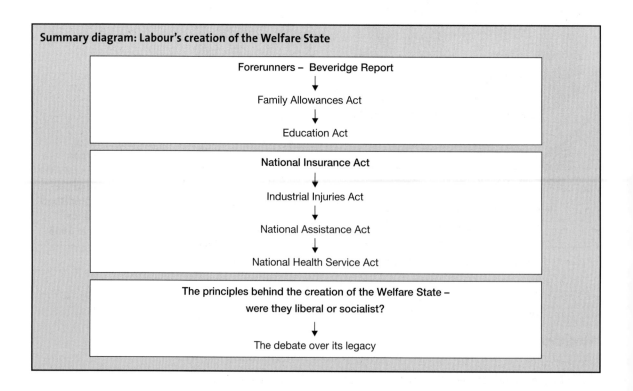

Summary diagram: Labour's creation of the Welfare State

Forerunners – Beveridge Report
↓
Family Allowances Act
↓
Education Act

National Insurance Act
↓
Industrial Injuries Act
↓
National Assistance Act
↓
National Health Service Act

The principles behind the creation of the Welfare State –
were they liberal or socialist?
↓
The debate over its legacy

Labour's economic policy 1945–51

> ▶ *How extensive was the Labour government's restructuring of the economy?*

Nationalisation

From its earliest days, the Labour Party had advanced the principle that government had the right to direct the key aspects of economy in order to create efficiency and social justice. Clause IV of the party's constitution committed it to nationalisation, which it defined as 'the common ownership of the means of production, distribution and exchange'.

In practice, common ownership or public control meant government control. In its 1945 election manifesto, *Let Us Face the Future*, Labour promised to implement an ambitious programme for the nationalisation of Britain's major industries. These were specified as fuel and power, iron and steel, and inland transport. In office over the next six years, Attlee's government endeavoured to honour that pledge. In support of this extension of State control over the economy, it claimed that its policies were in keeping with those Keynesian principles, which advocated the involvement of government in economic planning (see page 186).

The nationalisation programme

> ## Main industries and institutions nationalised
> - 1946: coal, civil aviation, Cable & Wireless, the Bank of England
> - 1947: road transport, electricity services
> - 1948: gas
> - 1949: iron and steel.

Fuel and power

Coal, which was Britain's most vital industry, had for decades suffered from disruption and underproduction. It was the first to be selected for public ownership. The government considered that the modernisation that this would bring would, in turn, have positive effects on the gas and electricity industries. Nationalisation would create greater safety, productivity and efficiency, with the result that all the other industries associated with fuel and power production would benefit.

Transport

It was also reckoned that the ending of private ownership in transport, which would be the prelude to the co-ordination of the road, rail and canal system, would similarly improve the quality of the nation's essential services.

Iron and steel

The odd-one-out in the list of enterprises scheduled for nationalisation was the iron and steel industry. It had been included only because of a Labour conference decision in 1944, which had imposed it on the unwilling Labour leaders. Since steel was the only profit-making industry at the time, it had stout defenders, willing to fight against nationalisation. This made the legislation relating to its takeover a fierce battleground.

The key factor here was that nationalisation involved compensating the former owners of the concerns that were taken into public ownership. In a declining industry, such as coal, nationalisation might well be a welcome relief to the owners since it bought them out at a price that cut their losses. However, in the case of an industry that was still profit-making, compensation was a much more difficult issue to resolve. It raised the question of what was a fair settlement, but, more significantly, it opened up the larger issue of whether the State had the right to overrule the declared objections of the owners and shareholders. It broadened into an argument over justice in a free society.

Opponents of the nationalisation of iron and steel protested on four main grounds:

- It was not a public utility but a privately owned manufacturing industry.
- It was an efficiently run and profit-making concern.
- Large investments had recently been made into it.
- It had an impressive record of co-operation between managers and workers.

Conservative resistance

The dispute over iron and steel proved a blessing to the Conservatives. Their heavy election defeat in 1945 has damaged their morale and reputation. Now, in 1948, the proposal to nationalise iron and steel created a rallying ground for them. Up to that point, the Conservative opposition had offered only token resistance to nationalisation. There was a sense in which the war seemed to have won the Keynesian argument for State direction. The principle of public ownership itself had been rarely discussed; most of the debates were taken up with the dry detail of the methods for making the change and with the levels of compensation. The Iron and Steel Bill changed all that. The Conservatives now had a cause to defend. In Parliament, their guns began to fire again as they launched their salvoes against the government's nationalisation programme as an abuse of government power.

Despite this resistance, the government was able to push the Iron and Steel Bill through in 1950. The path to success was greatly eased by the passing of the **Parliamentary Reform Act of 1949**, a measure which effectively prevented the Conservatives from using their majority in the House of Lords to block the steel nationalisation Bill. This allowed it to become law before the scheduled end of the Labour government's term in office in 1950.

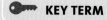 **KEY TERM**

Parliamentary Reform Act of 1949 Reduced the delaying power of the House of Lords over a Commons Bill from two years to one.

Financial problems

The idealism that inspired the government's welfare and nationalisation programmes came at a heavy cost which added to the financial burdens it had inherited in 1945. By the end of the war, Britain faced the following problems:

- Debts of £4198 million.
- A balance of payments deficit (see page 176) of nearly £870 million.
- Exports of manufactures had dropped by 60 per cent in wartime.
- **Invisible exports** had shrunk from £248 million in 1938 to £120 million in 1946.
- Costs of maintaining overseas military commitments had quintupled between 1938 and 1946.
- In the year 1945–6 Britain spent £750 million more abroad than it received.

Defence costs

A factor that increased Britain's difficulties was that it had agreed with the USA, its Cold War ally, to increase its spending on defence from £2.3 billion to £4.7 billion. Despite demobilisation in 1945, Britain, as one of the occupying forces in Europe and as a member of the **UN Security Council**, continued to maintain a large peacetime army. In 1950 this stood at nearly a million men. In addition to the expense entailed by this was the extra financial burden the nation had shouldered when Attlee's government in 1947 committed Britain to the development of its own independent nuclear deterrent (see page 213). Such developments meant that by the late 1940s Britain was spending fourteen per cent of its gross national product on defence.

Austerity

Faced with these burdens, Hugh Dalton, chancellor of the exchequer (1945–7), and his successor, Stafford Cripps (1947–50), embarked on a policy of national **austerity**, whose main features were:

- the continuation of rationing of food and fuel
- tight financial controls to prevent **inflation**
- controls on wages and salaries
- increased taxation on incomes and goods
- restrictions on imports to keep dollar spending to a minimum.

As was to be expected, the government's austerity measures were unpopular. The section most offended were the trade unions, which were asked to show restraint during Britain's difficult times and accept a **wage freeze**. There were thinly veiled threats from the government that if the unions did not do this voluntarily, wage restrictions would have to be legally imposed. Despite being the government's natural supporters and its chief provider of funds, the unions were not prepared to be docile. As they saw it, a Labour government was in power to provide for the needs of the workers first, not involve itself in

 **KEY TERMS**

Invisible exports The sale of financial and insurance services to foreign buyers, traditionally one of Britain's major sources of income from abroad.

UN Security Council The United Nations' body responsible for maintaining international peace, using military force where necessary.

Austerity A programme of cuts in government expenditure, control of private spending and rationing of goods.

Inflation A decline in the value of money, which leads to rising prices.

Wage freeze An undertaking not to press for higher wages.

financial deals which kept the USA happy but left British workers vulnerable. Arthur Deakin, general secretary of the large and influential Transport and General Workers' Union (TGWU), had warned the government in its first year in office that the unions would resist any moves to weaken their members' interests: 'We shall go forward building up our wage claims in conformity with our understanding of the people we are representing. Any attempt to interfere with that position would have disastrous consequences.' The warning proved well grounded. During the period of Attlee's governments there were a number of serious strikes among such key workers as miners, dockers and transport workers.

Devaluation

Knowing that austerity alone could not meet the demands on Britain's economy, Dalton had negotiated a loan of $6000 million from the USA and Canada. The government's hope was that, in accordance with Keynesian theory, the loan would provide the basis of an industrial recovery. But such recovery as did occur was never enough to meet expectations. A large part of the problem arose from one of the conditions attaching to the loan, which required that the British pound sterling had to be made convertible with the dollar in international trade. However, since the post-war American dollar was much stronger than the pound, the consequence was that Britain began to suffer from what was known as the '**dollar gap**'. American and other international traders could insist that Britain paid for its purchases from them in dollars. This drained Britain of a substantial part of the loan it had negotiated, while at the same time making it harder to meet the repayments.

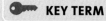

KEY TERM

Dollar gap Since sterling was weaker than the dollar, the goods that Britain bought from North America had to be paid for in dollars.

The consequence of the financial imbalance led to what were known as sterling crises, the two most serious occurring in 1947 and 1949. In both cases the crises took the form of 'a run on the pound', foreign investors withdrawing their money from Britain in large amounts. The crisis in 1947 was deepened by the fact that the year witnessed the worst winter weather yet experienced in Britain in the twentieth century. The crisis had these features:

- Coal mines and power stations could not meet increased demand.
- Two million workers were laid off as lack of fuel forced factories to close.
- Decreased production caused export losses of £200 million in value.
- Britain's trade deficit rose to £380 million.
- The monthly dollar gap widened to $150 million between January and April 1947.

Britain eventually survived the 1947 crisis but the drain on its finances continued over the next two years. In 1949, Attlee's government reluctantly took the step that all its deflationary and austerity measures had been intended to avoid: it devalued the pound. The exchange rate of sterling was reduced from $4.03 to $2.80, a fall of some 30 per cent. While this certainly made British exports cheaper and boosted overseas sales in the short term, the devaluation was a sure sign that the government's previous policies had not prevented the weakening of the economy.

Marshall Aid

It was something of a paradox that Britain, having been put under severe strain by its indebtedness to the USA, should find that it was the USA that offered it financial salvation. Britain's economic difficulties would have been even greater had it not been for the relief provided by the Marshall Plan, which began to operate in 1948. After 1945, the world's trading nations all experienced severe balance of payments problems. Worried that this would destroy international commerce, the USA, the only economy with sufficient resources, adopted a programme in 1947 to provide dollars to any country willing to receive them in return for granting trade concessions to the USA. Whatever America's self-interest may have been, it is difficult to see how Europe could have recovered without a massive inflow of US capital. Under the plan, which bore the name of the US Secretary of State **George Marshall**, Europe received $15 billion, Britain's share being ten per cent of that.

The Marshall Plan ranks as one the major achievements of Ernest Bevin as foreign secretary. It was he who did so much to convince the USA of the necessity of such a plan both for shoring up Europe against the threat from the USSR and for sustaining the international economy, without which the USA itself could not maintain its strength as the world's greatest industrial power.

🔑 KEY FIGURE

George Marshall (1880–1959)
One of the USA's most distinguished soldier–statesmen of the twentieth century; although he did not originate the aid plan named after him, he was its great advocate.

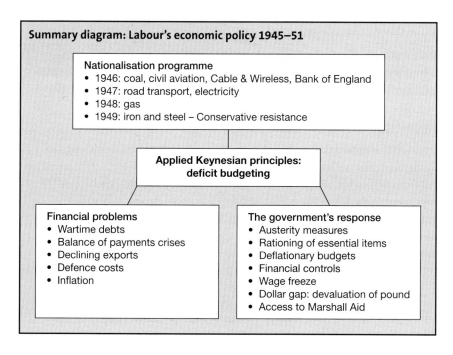

Summary diagram: Labour's economic policy 1945–51

Nationalisation programme
- 1946: coal, civil aviation, Cable & Wireless, Bank of England
- 1947: road transport, electricity
- 1948: gas
- 1949: iron and steel – Conservative resistance

Applied Keynesian principles: deficit budgeting

Financial problems
- Wartime debts
- Balance of payments crises
- Declining exports
- Defence costs
- Inflation

The government's response
- Austerity measures
- Rationing of essential items
- Deflationary budgets
- Financial controls
- Wage freeze
- Dollar gap: devaluation of pound
- Access to Marshall Aid

Foreign affairs

▶ *What issues in foreign affairs confronted the Labour government?*
▶ *Why was foreign policy a divisive issue within the Labour Party?*

The question that confronted Britain after 1945 was what role it should play in the post-war international order. The Labour government's answer came in the form of a range of momentous decisions:

- Britain became one of the **'big five'** members of the UN Security Council.
- Britain chose to side with the USA in the Cold War divide.
- Britain declined to become formally involved in Europe.
- Britain granted India independence.
- Britain became a nuclear power.

These decisions indicated that Britain, led by a Labour government, had opted to remain a world power. By taking on such heavy burdens, Britain, at a time when it was implementing the Welfare State at home, subjected itself to chronic economic strain.

Labour and the Cold War

It was as British statesmen rather than socialists that Attlee and Ernest Bevin, his foreign secretary, approached the problem of Britain's policies in the post-war world. Their intention was to protect British interests, which in the nature of things after 1945 also meant Western interests, in the face of what they regarded as the threat to Europe presented by the Soviet Union.

Josef Stalin, the Soviet leader, had refused to withdraw his forces from the territories of Eastern Europe which they had occupied during the course of the war. Bevin often said that his natural desire was to be neither anti-Soviet nor pro-American, but that Stalin's stubbornness in occupying half of Europe, and threatening the other half, obliged him to be so.

It was in this regard that early in his government Attlee faced a challenge in Parliament over his foreign policy. Interestingly, it came not from the opposition but from within his own party. In 1946, a group of 60 **backbench** Labour MPs, representing the left of the party, introduced an amendment criticising the government for its pro-American stance. Moved by **Richard Crossman**, the amendment called on Attlee's government to co-operate less with the USA and more with the Soviet Union.

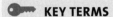 **KEY TERMS**

Big five USA, USSR, Britain, France and, at the time, Nationalist China.

Backbench The area in the Commons where MPs sit who hold no official position in the government or opposition.

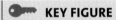 **KEY FIGURE**

Richard Crossman (1907–74)

An influential leading left-wing Labour intellectual; a strong Bevanite, his tendency to quarrel with party colleagues was a factor in his never gaining high office in the government.

SOURCE B

From a speech by Richard Crossman in the House of Commons, 18 November 1946, *Hansard*, volume 430, cc. 525–39.

We hope that the Government will so review its conduct of International Affairs as to afford the utmost encouragement to, and collaboration with, all Nations striving to secure full Socialist planning and control of the world's resources and thus provide a democratic and constructive Socialist alternative to an otherwise inevitable conflict between American Capitalism and Soviet Communism in which all hope of World Government would be destroyed … We get the impression that not only is there a complete and exclusive Anglo-American tie-up, but a tie-up between the two front benches …

We realise the difficulties with which the Government are faced, especially the economic problem which limits freedom of action. We believe that a Socialist Britain which puts into effect an independent British policy and refuses to join any ideological bloc is the only power which can break the present deadlock and save this country and the world.

According to Source B, what is Crossman's complaint concerning the government's conduct of foreign policy?

Attlee replied by repeating Bevin's claim that the government was not anti-Soviet through prejudice, but simply because the USSR under Stalin was continuing the aggressive, anti-Western approach that had characterised Russian policy since the days of the tsars (Source C). This made genuine co-operation with the Soviet Union extremely difficult.

SOURCE C

From Clement Attlee's reply to Crossman's amendment, 18 November 1946, *Hansard*, volume 430, c. 583.

I think if our critics examined the question carefully, they would find that when we have voted against Soviet Russia, although we may have been wrong on one or two occasions, we were generally in the right … I notice there has been a great deal of complaint about our collaboration with the United States of America in economic matters. Large parts of the world are in great distress, including the whole of Europe. Who are the people who can help and who are helping Europe; the people who have the wherewithal to help us as we try to set the world and especially Europe on its feet? It is the United States, and is it not natural, therefore, that we should collaborate with the United States? Europe has been overrun, and indeed almost every supply has been stopped. Large areas of Russia have been made waste and that prevents her helping. Help comes from the country that can give it, and yet this help is called American imperialism.

How, in Source C, does Attlee defend the government's record over its dealings with the USSR and the USA?

Behind this disagreement between Attlee and the left wing of his party lay a fundamental and lasting difference of opinion as to the real character and purpose of the Labour Party. The mainstream members, typified by Attlee, saw Labour as a radical but non-revolutionary force that was prepared to work within the existing political system to achieve its aim of social reform. In contrast, those on the Marxist left believed that Labour's essential role was to work for the replacement of the prevailing capitalist system in Britain with a truly socialist one. They had hoped that with a Labour Party in power, Anglo-Soviet relations would vastly improve: 'left would understand left'. However, the rapid development of the Cold War after 1945 shattered this hope. Britain found itself siding with the USA against the Soviet Union. The Labour left argued that this was not inevitable; they asserted that, in leaning so heavily on the USA for financial aid, the government was destroying the chance of genuine British independence in international affairs. Desperate though Britain was for Marshall Aid, the left of the Labour Party was dismayed by the government's acceptance of it. For many Labour MPs, the financial arrangement tied Britain to the USA in the relationship of beggar and master and so denied the government any chance of acting independently in the post-war world.

Bevin's angry reaction to this was to accuse the left of a total lack of political realism: without American dollars from the Marshall Aid programme and military support, Britain and Europe could not be sustained. Bevin also angered the left of the party by his contribution to the creation of the NATO alliance. Bevin, having played a major role in forming the alliance, then invited the USA to be a member. The USA, which had declared its attitude two years earlier in the **Truman Doctrine**, eagerly accepted the invitation. America's great industrial strength and nuclear power made it the dominant force in the alliance. Throughout the Cold War, NATO remained the West's first line of defence.

It is notable that, powerfully held though the ideas of the left were, they had little impact on the shaping of Labour policy. Bevin's policies were a victory for the centre and right of the Labour Party. The importance of Ernest Bevin as foreign secretary at this critical period was that he established the tradition of post-war British foreign policy: pro-American and anti-Soviet. This was an approach that was to be followed by all the British governments, Labour and Conservative, throughout the Cold War between 1945 and the early 1990s.

Two particular developments indicated the willingness of the Labour government to support the USA in the growing Cold War: the Berlin Airlift and the Korean War.

The Berlin Airlift 1948–9

At the end of the war the four Allied powers divided defeated Germany into four separately occupied zones (see Figure 6.1). The eastern zone, which was under Soviet control, included Berlin, which itself was divided into four sectors. The descent of the **Iron Curtain** left West Berlin in a very vulnerable position. A hundred miles within East Germany, it was accessible from the West only by the most limited routes. When the Western powers in June 1948 introduced the new German currency, already operative in West Germany, into West Berlin, the

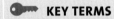

KEY TERMS

Truman Doctrine In 1947 President Truman pledged the USA 'to support free peoples who are resisting attempted subjugation by armed minorities or by outside pressure'. Although he did not mention the Soviet Union by name he clearly had it in mind as the aggressor.

Iron Curtain An imaginary line that divided Western Europe from Soviet-controlled Eastern Europe.

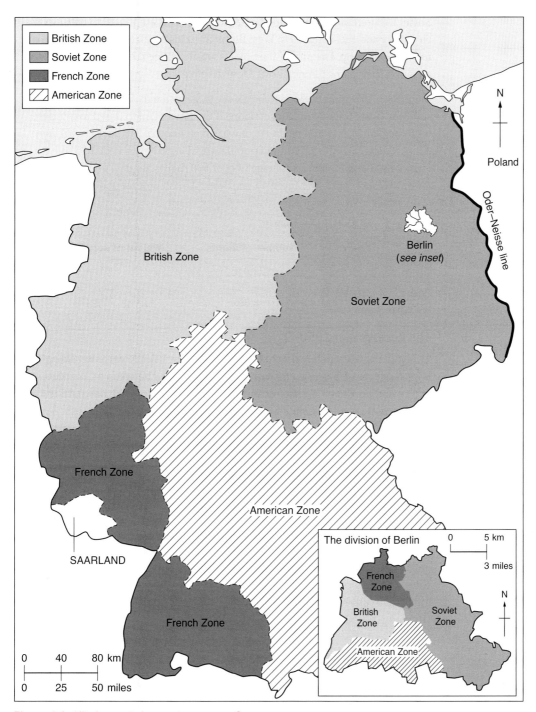

Figure 6.1 Allied occupied zones in post-war Germany.

Soviet Union retaliated by imposing a blockade. This amounted to cutting off all electricity and fuel supplies to West Berlin and closing all road and canal links to West Germany. The aim of the Soviets was to oblige the Western Allies to abandon their plans for a separate German state.

The USA and Britain decided to break the siege by a massive airlift of essential supplies, using the narrow air corridors; if the Soviet Union dared to interfere with the planes, it would be an act of war. In a period of 318 days the Western Allies maintained the 2.5 million population of West Berlin with 1.25 million tons of food and fuel by an average of over 600 flights per day. The prodigious effort was successful. In May 1949, the Soviet Union ordered the siege to be abandoned.

Table 6.2 The Berlin Airlift 1948–9

Carrier	Number of flights	Weight of supplies (tons)
USAF	131,918	1,101,405
RAF	49,733	255,526
British charter	13,897	79,470

The Korean War 1950–3

This was the first open conflict of the Cold War. In 1945, Korea, after being liberated from Japanese occupation, had been divided between a Communist-dominated north and an American-dominated south. In 1950, northern troops, strongly supported by Chinese forces from the **PRC**, invaded the south. South Korea appealed to the UN Security Council for assistance. The USA immediately proposed that a UN force be sent to aid the South Koreans. The Soviet Union had temporarily withdrawn from the Security Council in protest against its refusal to recognise the PRC. This enabled the American resolution to be pushed through without the USSR being present to exercise its usual **veto**. Large numbers of American troops under the UN flag were dispatched to Korea, where bitter fighting causing heavy casualties, particularly on the Chinese side, ensued before a stalemate truce ended the war in 1953. From the first, Britain gave the USA substantial diplomatic and military support. British casualties were 1788 servicemen killed or missing and 2498 wounded. The USA lost 36,000 men and South Korea 139,000. Western calculations suggest that North Korea suffered 300,000 fatalities and the PRC 250,000.

Labour and Europe

After 1945 there was a significant movement among the war-weary Western European nations to avoid future conflict by agreeing on mutual co-operation and the establishing of some form of economic and political organisation to link them. This led to the acceptance in 1951 of the Schuman Plan. First introduced by **Robert Schuman** in 1950, this was a scheme for the European nations to pool their most productive resources – coal and steel – in a European Coal and Steel Community (ECSC). Britain deliberately refrained from being involved.

Not having experienced hostile occupation in wartime and now a nuclear power (see page 213), it was not convinced of the need for a formal European union as a means of preserving peace. Ernest Bevin, believing that Britain's future could best be guaranteed by developing its ties with the USA and the Commonwealth, chose not to attend the preliminary talks and so did not join **the Six** in the signing of the Treaty of Paris in April 1951 which formally set up the ECSC.

Bevin had also been deterred by the willingness of the Six to accept the loss of individual national sovereignty entailed in granting the ECSC **supranational** authority. Bevin said pointedly, 'Britain was not a Luxembourg'. **Manny Shinwell** added, 'I've nothing against the other European governments; I simply don't want to have anything to do with them'. Furthermore, given Labour's achievements over nationalisation, in particular its bitter struggle to bring iron and steel into public ownership, it was understandable that it was not prepared to hand over control of these economic areas to a foreign body. A further explanation for Labour's reluctance was the attitude of the trade unions, the Labour Party's principal financial backers and political supporters. The trade unions were concerned that joining a European organisation that was outside British control would put at risk the hard-won gains that they had achieved for their workers. Having read a document which attempted to explain the workings of the ECSC, Herbert Morrison dismissed it with the comment: 'It's no good. We can't do it. The Durham miners wouldn't like it.'

When Clement Attlee was asked in the House of Commons in 1950 why his government was not considering joining the Schuman Plan, he replied unequivocally: 'We are not prepared to accept the principle that the most vital economic forces of this country should be handed over to an authority that is utterly undemocratic and is responsible to nobody.' Interestingly, the Conservatives at this time fully shared the Labour government's view on Europe. Harold Macmillan directly echoed Attlee and the trade unions when he declared, also in 1950, that Britain was not prepared to take risks with the British economy by subjecting it to the control of a foreign organisation. 'We will allow no supra-national authority to put large masses of our people out of work in Durham, in the Midlands, in South Wales and in Scotland.'

Labour and Indian independence 1947

It was during the Second World War that Britain had begun to accept that its possession and retention of colonies involved unbearable burdens. The early defeats suffered by British forces at the hands of the Japanese revealed Britain's weakness **east of Suez**. Seizing the moment, the Indian nationalists intensified their efforts to force Britain to relinquish its colonial authority over India. In 1942, Mohandas Gandhi inaugurated the 'Quit India' movement, which openly agitated against British rule. The native police and army remained largely loyal and British control was maintained, though only through increased political repression.

KEY TERMS

The Six France, Germany, Italy, Belgium, the Netherlands and Luxembourg.

Supranational An organisation having power over its individual member states.

East of Suez A traditional shorthand way of referring to Britain's military and naval bases and commitments in the Middle East and Asia.

KEY FIGURE

Emanuel ('Manny') Shinwell (1884–1986) Fuel and power minister 1945–7, war minister 1947–50; a consistent opponent of Britain's entering Europe.

At the close of the Japanese war in 1945, it was clear that to retain India against the wish of its peoples would stretch Britain's resources to breaking point. Moreover, the will to do so had largely gone. The Labour Party, which from its beginnings had condemned colonialism as immoral, came to power in 1945 fully committed to independence for India. The problem was when and how this could be best arranged. The Muslim League, led by Mohammed Jinnah, was increasingly suspicious of the Hindus, represented by the Congress Party and its leader Pandit Nehru. A sizeable Sikh minority was equally apprehensive of being swamped in an independent India.

Religious divisions in India

The three great faiths of the people of India – Hinduism, Islam and Sikhism – were a source of profound social and political division and prevented a peaceful transition to independence. To such groups, federation within a single sovereign state was not acceptable, although it had been proposed a number of times previously and was again suggested by the Labour government's representative, Stafford Cripps (see page 160).

Eager now to settle 'the Indian problem', the government dispatched Earl Mountbatten as special envoy to negotiate Britain's final withdrawal. The reluctance of the parties concerned to consider federation made partition the only feasible solution. After much haggling, the Hindu Congress and Muslim League agreed to the Mountbatten proposals:

- The subcontinent was to be divided into two distinct states: India, predominantly Hindu, and Pakistan and East Pakistan, predominantly Muslim.
- The previously independent Indian princes would give up their local rule in return for the freedom to retain their wealth.
- The date for the formal end of British rule was brought forward from 1948 to 1947.

Independence and its aftermath

Given the scale of the problem, this compromise was doubtless the best solution that could be arrived at, but how far it was from being a lasting one was soon revealed by the tragedy that ensued. Jinnah and the League resented having had to settle for a 'moth-eaten' Pakistan; Congress was dismayed at seeing India broken up; while the Sikhs, not being in a majority in any single region, were resolved to resist subjection in whichever of the new states they found themselves. In the same week in which the transfer of power from Britain took place, civil war broke out. Muslim–Hindu–Sikh passions spilled over into desperate acts of communal violence.

The independence of India had thus come at a terrible price. The creation of the separate states of India and Pakistan led to a massive cross-migration of refugees: Muslims from India into Pakistan, Hindus and Sikhs from Pakistan into India. The communal riots and massacres that accompanied all this resulted in the killing of over 3 million men women and children, 1 million dying in the Punjab alone.

Britain's independent nuclear deterrent

As with economics, so with foreign policy, Attlee and Bevin were traditionalists at heart. Given this, a dispute with the left of the party was bound to be a feature of internal Labour politics. An interesting example was the dispute over the development and retention of the atomic bomb, Britain's independent nuclear deterrent. Ernest Bevin claimed that his experience of dealing with American diplomats and officials had convinced him that, if Britain wished to maintain parity with the USA as a world power, it had to have its own nuclear weapon. Referring to the atom bomb, Bevin declared: 'We've got to have it here, whatever it costs, and it's got to have a bloody Union Jack on it.' Attlee fully accepted his foreign secretary's reasoning. In January 1947, he told a secret cabinet sub-committee that Britain could not allow the USA to have a nuclear monopoly and was, therefore, embarking on a programme for the construction of its own bomb. The research programme was begun in 1947, although this information was not revealed to Parliament or the people at the time of the decision. Britain's first atomic bomb was detonated in 1952 and its hydrogen bomb in 1957.

The adoption of a nuclear-weapon programme outraged the Labour left, who were offended both by the decision itself and by the way it had been arrived at, in secret with no opportunity given to Labour MPs or party members to discuss the issue. The question of whether the possession of an independent nuclear deterrent was morally defensible or strategically necessary, quite apart from whether Britain could afford it, caused deep dissension in the Labour Party for generations. Anti-nuclear resolutions were frequently passed at party conferences, but in government Labour remained committed to the retention and development of the British deterrent.

```
┌─────────────────────────────────────────────────────────────────┐
│ Summary diagram: Foreign affairs                                  │
│                                                                   │
│   ┌───────────────────────────────────────────────────────────┐  │
│   │ Britain one of the 'big five' members of the UN Security  │  │
│   │ Council. Bevin sided with USA against USSR in Cold War    │  │
│   └───────────────────────────────────────────────────────────┘  │
│                                                                   │
│   ┌───────────────────────────────────────────────────────────┐  │
│   │ Left–right internal party rivalry over government's:      │  │
│   │ • Pro-Americanism                                         │  │
│   │ • Decision to develop atomic weapons                      │  │
│   │ • Support of Truman Doctrine                              │  │
│   └───────────────────────────────────────────────────────────┘  │
│                                                                   │
│   ┌───────────────────────────────────────────────────────────┐  │
│   │ Government proactive in                                   │  │
│   │ • Berlin Airlift 1948–9: RAF joined USAF in supplying     │  │
│   │   Berlin                                                  │  │
│   │ • Korean War 1950–3: British troops fought as part of UN  │  │
│   │   forces                                                  │  │
│   └───────────────────────────────────────────────────────────┘  │
│                                                                   │
│   ┌───────────────────────────────────────────────────────────┐  │
│   │ Europe                                                    │  │
│   │ Government uninterested in joining European supranational │  │
│   │ body                                                      │  │
│   └───────────────────────────────────────────────────────────┘  │
│                                                                   │
│   ┌───────────────────────────────────────────────────────────┐  │
│   │ India                                                     │  │
│   │ Labour fulfilled its pledge to grant Indian independence  │  │
│   └───────────────────────────────────────────────────────────┘  │
│                                                                   │
│   ┌───────────────────────────────────────────────────────────┐  │
│   │ Independent deterrent                                     │  │
│   │ Britain became a nuclear power                            │  │
│   └───────────────────────────────────────────────────────────┘  │
└─────────────────────────────────────────────────────────────────┘
```

5 Labour's defeat 1951

▶ *Why did Labour eventually lose office in 1951?*

The defeat of Labour in the general election of 1951 was the result of the cumulative result of six wearying years in office.

The 1950 general election

There is little doubt that, however idealistic and courageous the Labour government had been since 1945 in reforming the economy and laying the basis of the Welfare State, the austerity measures to which it had resorted to sustain its programme had damaged it politically. This was evident from the results of the 1950 election, which saw Labour's majority over the Conservatives cut from 180 to 17.

Table 6.3 The 1950 general election result

Party	Votes	Seats	Percentage of vote
Conservative	12,502,567	298	43.5
Labour	13,266,592	315	46.1
Liberal	2,621,548	9	9.1
Others	381,964	3	1.3

However, the degree of damage must not be overstated. Labour had increased its popular vote by 1.25 million. The reason for the drop in its majority was principally that the Conservatives had recovered from 1945 and had gained over 2.5 million votes, leaving Labour with an overall majority of only five. Despite this, Attlee decided to struggle on, but the tiny majority proved so tight that, when there was a close vote in the Commons, sick Labour MPs had to be brought from their hospital beds and assisted through the division lobby. Governing in this fashion proved too great a strain. After twenty months, Attlee called another election.

What had also pushed him towards this decision was open rebellion within the government. In 1951, forced by its financial difficulties to make savings in public expenditure, the government had imposed charges on medical prescriptions. Aneurin Bevan, the designer of the NHS (see page 198), led a number of ministers in resigning from the cabinet in protest. Those who followed him in this became known as Bevanites; they protested that the charges contravened the founding principle that the NHS should be free to all at the point of treatment. The Bevanite rebellion encouraged other Labour MPs and members of the party to voice their doubts over the direction the government had taken over economic and foreign policy. Such divisions stimulated the Conservatives and gave them ammunition for the 1951 election campaign. In the election itself they gained a narrow but working majority. It was doubtless with some relief that a weary and beleaguered Labour government left office.

Table 6.4 The 1951 general election result

Party	Votes	Seats	Percentage of vote
Conservative	13,717,538	321	48.0
Labour	13,948,605	295	48.8
Liberal	730,556	6	2.5
Others	198,969	3	0.7

Reasons for Labour's 1951 defeat

While the Bevanite revolt certainly contributed to Labour's problems in 1951, there were other factors that together explain the election defeat:

- Attlee's government was worn down by heavy economic and financial difficulties.
- Collectively and individually, the government was exhausted after six troubled years in office.
- A number of its ministers, for example, Attlee himself and Bevin, had been working continuously in office since 1940.
- Serious divisions had developed between the right and left of the party over economic, welfare and foreign policies.
- There was resentment among some trade unions at Labour's slowness in responding to workers' demands.

- The shrinking in the 1950 election of its previously large majority made governing difficult and damaged party morale.
- Labour found it hard to shake off its image as a party of rationing and high taxation.
- In their call for the austerity that they claimed the times demanded, leading ministers such as the ascetic Stafford Cripps as chancellor of the exchequer did not present an attractive picture to the electorate.
- Britain's entry into the Korean War in 1950 made Labour's left wing unhappy; they argued that although technically British units fought as part of a UN force, in reality the Labour government was sheepishly following the USA in a Cold War engagement.

The mixed response to Labour's record in government was captured by the answers in a 1951 opinion poll to the question 'What do you think the Labour Party stands for?'

SOURCE D

From an opinion poll, 1951, quoted in David Kynaston, *Family Britain 1951–57*, Bloomsbury, 2009, p. 44.

'*What do you think the Labour party stands for?*'

More money for less work. (Headmaster's wife)

Giving the working classes power they are not fitted to use. (Commercial traveller)

They say social security but I think class warfare. (Solicitor's wife)

Pampering the working man. (Dentist)

Class hatred, revenge and grab. (Engineering technician)

To keep down the people with money. (Butcher's wife)

Fair shares for all – if they are working people. (Managing director)

The sense of dissatisfaction was also felt by some members of the Labour Party. In answer to an opinion poll in August 1949, a Labour-voting housewife made the following comments (Source E).

SOURCE E

From a Labour supporter's answer to an opinion poll in August 1949, quoted in Martin Francis, *British Journal of Sociology*, September 1962, p. 240.

Like many 'upper class' socialists, I thought with security of employment and adequate pay, as well as a government of their own, workers would act as we should act in similar circumstances, i.e., work with a will, and enjoy doing so. In the event it seems that we have been wrong and that removing the threats of unemployment, starvation, etc. has only made the worker more discontented

What is the value of Source D as an indicator of the public's attitude towards the Labour Party?

In what respects has the respondent in Source E become disappointed with the Labour government?

which also seems to apply to nationalisation which is certainly a failure up to now.

It is a matter of atmosphere. Somehow, a Labour Government has managed to take a lot of the joy and the interest out of the atmosphere. It is not so much 'austerity', but the general discontent.

Conservative strengths

There were, of course, more positive aspects to the victory of the Conservatives. Their heavy and unexpected defeat in 1945 had left them shell-shocked. However, by the late 1940s their fortunes had begun to improve. Much of this was due to the reorganisation of the party undertaken by **Lord Woolton**, the Conservative Party chairman. It was also at this time that younger Tory MPs, such as **R.A. Butler**, began to bring new ideas and confidence to the party. The nationalisation issue gave them a cause round which they could rally and on which they could attack the government. Conservative advantages in 1951 can be listed as:

- The Conservatives had begun to recover from the shock of their defeat in 1945.
- The 1950 election saw an influx of bright young Conservative MPs eager for battle against a tiring government.
- The attack on the government's nationalisation of iron and steel provided a strong platform for opposition attacks.
- Some of the electorate were impressed by the Conservatives' projection of themselves as upholders of liberty and individualism against the deadening hand of State centralisation and collectivism.
- Under the direction of the dynamic Lord Woolton, 'a cheerful cove', as a colleague put it, the Conservative Party had reformed its finances and constituency organisation and was much better positioned to fight an election than in 1945.

Woolton, in his later reflections (Source F), recalled that his essential aim had been to revive the party by asking it to embrace a new, progressive form of Conservatism.

SOURCE F

From Frederick James Marquis (Earl of Woolton), *The Memoirs of the Rt Hon. the Earl of Woolton*, Cassell, 1959, p. 347.

It is always dangerous in politics to be committed to detail in any programme. But I concluded that it was at least as dangerous to be so vague that the nation could think that the Conservatism that we were expounding would be no different from the Conservatism of the 'thirties. We therefore decided to take the risk of defining it in terms of policies we would encourage the nation to undertake.

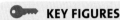

KEY FIGURES

Lord Woolton (1883–1964)

Minister of food in Churchill's wartime government, minister of reconstruction 1943–45, Conservative Party chairman 1946–55; capable of arousing enthusiasm and optimism among Conservatives.

R.A. Butler (1902–82)

MP 1929–65, minister of education 1941–5; respected by colleagues and opponents as one of the most progressive Conservatives.

In Source F, why is Woolton eager to distinguish between two types of Conservatism?

Among the progressive Conservatives who responded enthusiastically to Woolton's call was R.A. Butler. He was the main influence behind the party's producing *The Industrial Charter*, which argued that forward-thinking economic policies were perfectly in keeping with traditional Conservative values of freedom and social justice.

SOURCE G

From *The Industrial Charter*, May 1947, quoted in Stuart Ball, *The Conservative Party and British Politics*, Longman, 1995, p. 140.

The desire for increased rewards, whether it be expressed in terms of profit motive or higher wages, animates the great bulk of mankind. We hold that there should be healthy rewards for work done. We shall propose methods to curb monopolies and unfair privileges. We are determined to restore by all reasonable means that great stimulus to personal endeavour – fair incentive. A restoration of freedom and incentives would not mean, as has been falsely held, an end to security in our social and industrial system.

Justice demands that the aim of national policy should be to provide a basic standard of living and security of outlook for all our people.

? What form of industrial policy is being advocated in Source G?

Yet, not all Conservatives were progressives. Some were concerned that the party was leaning too far to the left in its attempt to recover and make itself electable. An example was the backbench MP, Sir Cuthbert Headlam, who cautioned the Conservatives against becoming too like the Labour government in its wish to move towards a planned economy.

SOURCE H

The comments of Sir Cuthbert Headlam, October 1948, quoted in David Kynaston, *Austerity Britain 1945–51*, Bloomsbury, 2008, p. 240.

I find this pinkish portion of our party are more prominent but less popular with the rank and file than they used to be. People instinctively dislike their economic planning and plotting and yet can see no alternative to some policy of the kind in present conditions. In this I fancy they are right – the great thing, however, is not to emphasise the necessity for controls so much – if and when we get back into power, it will be time enough to decide how much Government intervention in the conduct of industry is required.

? What is meant in Source H by 'the pinkish portion of our party'?

The explanation for Attlee's losing office in 1951 is not so much Labour's decline as the Conservatives' recovery. Yet they only just squeezed into power. What benefited them was the Liberal Party's decision to put up only 109 candidates, a drop of 366 compared with 1950. The nearly 2 million ex-Liberal votes that became available went largely to the Conservatives.

The election figures for 1951 reveal one of the oddest aspects of British electoral politics. It is possible for a party to poll more votes than its opponents yet still be defeated. After six years of government Labour had in fact more than held its share of the vote. Remarkably, the 1951 election saw Labour gain the highest aggregate vote ever achieved by any party up to that point. It outnumbered the Conservatives by a quarter of a million and had nearly one per cent more of the vote. The ratio of votes to seats was:

- Labour: 47,283:1
- Conservatives: 42,733:1
- Liberals: 121,759:1.

It was clearly not the case that Labour had been thrown out of office by a disillusioned electorate. It was more that on this occasion the Labour Party was the victim, not the beneficiary, of the imbalance in the British electoral system.

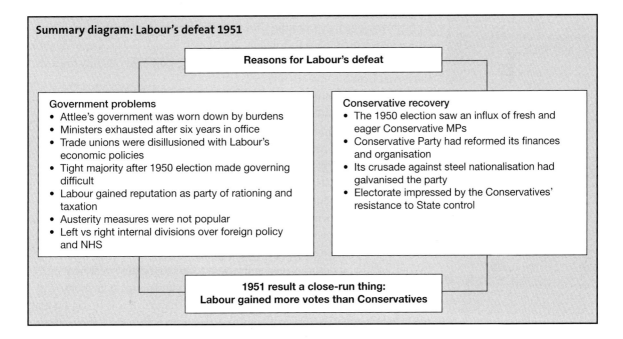

Summary diagram: Labour's defeat 1951

Reasons for Labour's defeat

Government problems
- Attlee's government was worn down by burdens
- Ministers exhausted after six years in office
- Trade unions were disillusioned with Labour's economic policies
- Tight majority after 1950 election made governing difficult
- Labour gained reputation as party of rationing and taxation
- Austerity measures were not popular
- Left vs right internal divisions over foreign policy and NHS

Conservative recovery
- The 1950 election saw an influx of fresh and eager Conservative MPs
- Conservative Party had reformed its finances and organisation
- Its crusade against steel nationalisation had galvanised the party
- Electorate impressed by the Conservatives' resistance to State control

1951 result a close-run thing: Labour gained more votes than Conservatives

6 The legacy of the Labour governments 1945–51

▶ *How successfully did Attlee's governments tackle the problems that faced them in the period 1945–51?*

▶ *What was the legacy of the Attlee governments?*

Criticism from the left

So large had Labour's majority been in the 1945 election that its opponents feared it would leave Attlee's government free to usher in sweeping socialist changes into Britain. It is true that during the next six years many significant and lasting reforms were introduced, but the Labour governments made no attempt either to disrupt the capitalist system in Britain or to destroy the social structure. That indeed was the complaint of the Labour left, who argued that Attlee's government, with its unassailable majority, was in a position to bring about a genuine transformation of British society, but by 1951 had thrown away the opportunity to be truly radical. The following are some of the main complaints of the left:

- The government's nationalisation programme was not really an attempt to take central control of the economy. With the exception of steel, it was restricted to non-profit-making concerns and made no effort to take over the private banks or insurance companies.
- By borrowing heavily from the USA in order to meet its financial difficulties, Attlee's government lost its freedom of action in foreign policy. Dependent on America, Britain found itself locked into a lasting Cold War hostility towards the Soviet Union.
- Britain's class structure remained largely unaltered.
- Social reforms had not greatly improved the conditions and status of such groups as workers and women.
- The NHS, Labour's proudest creation and the one which best defined its character as a party of the working class, failed to fulfil expectations. It was not the poorer and disadvantaged sections of the population who benefited most from the introduction of the NHS, but the already privileged middle classes. It was they who no longer had to pay for medical treatment, but who could now call on the services of the best-qualified GPs, whose practices tended to be in the more prosperous areas where the middle classes lived. In contrast, the underprivileged still lacked access to the best treatment and were worst hit when the Labour government, backtracking on its promise to maintain a free service, introduced prescription charges. It was this issue that produced the most serious challenge to Attlee from within the Labour Party.

Criticism from the right

A powerful argument from an opposite political viewpoint was that the Labour government had indeed thrown away a historic opportunity to reform Britain – not, however, by doing too little but by doing too much. A representative voice here is historian Corelli Barnett who, writing over a twenty-year period from the late 1980s, argued that what Britain needed after the war was the reconstruction of its industrial base. Priority should have been given to financial recovery and investment in the nation's **infrastructure**. This would have provided the means for Britain to re-establish itself as a major manufacturing economy, able to respond to the post-war international demand for commodity goods. Instead, Barnett asserted, Britain made a priority not of industrial recovery but of social welfare. However, welfare was costly and Britain, being practically bankrupt at

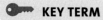 **KEY TERM**

Infrastructure
The interlocking systems which enable a nation's industrial economy to operate, for example, transport, power supply, communications.

the end of the war, had to borrow heavily to fund it. Saddled with large debts, Britain was able to sustain only low economic growth. To strengthen his case, Barnett quoted the example of West Germany, which, by delaying the adoption of a welfare state until it had achieved industrial recovery, put itself on the path to an economic miracle.

Labour's broader significance

Whatever the weight of the criticisms of the Labour government regarding particular policy failures, there is a broader significance to the period 1945–51. In its years of government the Labour Party laid down the policies that were followed in all essentials by successive Labour and Conservative governments during the next 35 years. Until Margaret Thatcher came into power in 1979 and challenged this consensus, there was a broad level of agreement on what the major domestic and foreign issues were and how they were to be handled.

Labour and Conservative strategies were both founded on:

- economic policies based on Keynesian principles of public expenditure and state direction
- welfare policies based on the implementation of the Beveridge Report
- foreign policies based on a pro-American, anti-Soviet stance
- imperial policies based on the principle of decolonisation and independence for Britain's former colonies.

This common area of agreement did not prevent serious political rivalry and constant accusations by each party that its opponents were failing to pursue the correct policies. However, when in government, the Labour and Conservative parties followed fundamentally similar policies.

Notwithstanding the later questions concerning the Labour governments' performance, there was little doubt among contemporaries that something momentous had occurred between 1945 and 1951:

- Labour had created the Welfare State.
- Labour had carried into peacetime the notion of State-directed planning, which had always been one of its objectives.
- In so doing, Labour had established Keynesianism as the basic British approach to economic planning.
- By withdrawing from India, Labour had set a precedent for **British decolonisation**.

R.A. Butler, a leading Conservative, put the Labour reforms into historical perspective by describing them as 'the greatest social revolution in our history'. What gives particular significance to Butler's words is that the Conservative Party came in all major respects to accept that revolution. The distinctive characteristic of the policies followed by Conservative governments from 1951 was how closely they coincided with those introduced by the Attlee

 **KEY TERM**

British decolonisation
The granting of independence by Britain to the majority of its colonies and dependencies.

governments. In the words of a modern historian, Dilwyn Porter (1997), 'Attlee's patriotic socialists gave way to Churchill's social patriots.'

Just as Labour had moved to the right by accepting capitalism and the mixed economy, so the Conservatives moved to the left by accepting Keynesianism and the managed economy. In opposition the Conservatives had opposed every nationalisation measure and many of the welfare proposals. Yet, in government themselves after 1951, they fully denationalised only one industry, steel, and built on the welfare programme which they had inherited. Labour could justly claim that it had converted the Conservative Party to welfarism. This was perhaps one of Attlee's most enduring legacies.

The Festival of Britain 1951

A notable achievement before Labour went out of office was its creation in 1951 of the Festival of Britain. Overseen by Herbert Morrison as home secretary, the Festival commemorated the Great Exhibition of 1851 by an ambitious programme intended to showcase to the world British talents and achievements in the fields of technology, science and culture. The centrepiece was the construction on a derelict site on the south bank of the Thames in London of a range of buildings housing exhibitions and displays mounted by Britain's leading artists, sculptors, engineers and craftsmen. The buildings themselves, designed by the architect Hugh Casson, were intended to achieve an embracing of the traditional and the modern. An outstanding example was the Festival Hall, a giant concert and exhibition centre. Physically dominating the Festival site were 'The Dome of Discovery', which housed multiple exhibits showing British advances in technology and engineering, and the 'Skylon', a huge obelisk suspended on barely visible wires.

The Festival had its critics, the mischievous orchestral conductor, Sir Thomas Beecham, describing it as 'a celebration of six years of incompetence funded by the American tax-payer'. However, such sceptics were in the minority; general opinion in Britain was that the ambitious project had been successful. It had provided a refreshing challenge to the notion that Britain was sunk in drab austerity. The Festival certainly attracted worldwide attention and approval and boosted Britain's tourist industry by attracting millions of foreign visitors.

Main achievements of the Attlee governments 1945–51

- Implemented a large-scale nationalisation programme.
- Created the Welfare State.
- Helped to convince the USA of the need for the Marshall Plan.
- Granted India independence.

- Played a key role in the formation of NATO.
- Committed Britain to the Berlin Airlift and the Korean War.
- Started the programme that turned Britain into a nuclear power.
- Organised the 1951 Festival of Britain.

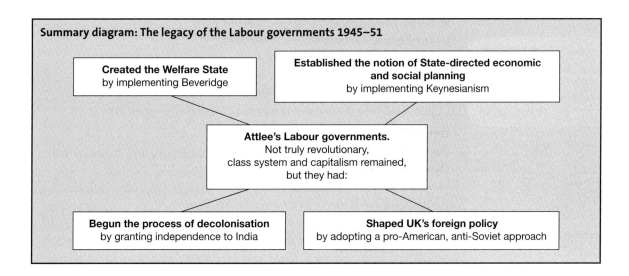

Summary diagram: The legacy of the Labour governments 1945–51

Created the Welfare State
by implementing Beveridge

Established the notion of State-directed economic and social planning
by implementing Keynesianism

Attlee's Labour governments.
Not truly revolutionary,
class system and capitalism remained,
but they had:

Begun the process of decolonisation
by granting independence to India

Shaped UK's foreign policy
by adopting a pro-American, anti-Soviet approach

 # Churchill and Eden 1951–7

▶ *What key developments took place under the Conservatives 1951–7?*

Churchill's government 1951–5

Winston Churchill was 77 years old when he became prime minister for the second time. He regarded his return to office in 1951 as a belated thank you from the British people for his wartime leadership. He was now too old and frail to be much more than a figurehead. Indeed, for some months in 1953 he was out of action altogether following a stroke, although this did not become public knowledge. Emma Soames, his granddaughter, remarked later that during this period the government was, in effect, run by her father, Christopher Soames. She explained that there was so little intrusion from the media in those days it was possible to get away with it. The fact was that Churchill did not need to do much; he was sustained by his past reputation as a statesman. Yet his period in government between 1951 and 1955 witnessed a number of important developments.

Developments 1951–5

- Rationing was ended.
- The steel industry was denationalised
- The Conservative Party committed itself to building 300,00 houses a year.
- The government continued with Keynesian policies.
- The accession of Queen Elizabeth II (aged 25) in 1952 ushered in a new 'Elizabethan age'.

- Britain detonated its first atomic bomb in 1952.
- The Korean War ended in 1953 (see page 210)

'Butskellism' and consensus

With hindsight, it can be seen that the key figure in Churchill's government of 1951–5 was not the prime minister but R.A. Butler, his chancellor of the exchequer.

Although Butler never became prime minister or Conservative leader, he held all the other major offices of state (chancellor of the exchequer 1951–5, home secretary 1957–62, foreign secretary 1962–4), and was a formative influence in the development of modern Conservatism, pushing the party in a progressive direction. As minister of education in Churchill's wartime coalition, Butler had been responsible for the Education Act of 1944 (see page 196). Arguably, this was to remain his greatest achievement; it indicated his concern for social issues, something that the Conservatives were to adopt as one of the planks in their political platform.

After his party's heavy defeat in 1945, Butler went on to play a central role in restoring Conservative morale during the Attlee years. He was a leading light among a group of Conservatives who had begun to study ways in which they could modernise their party's attitude and policies so as to prevent the Labour Party, claiming a monopoly of progressive thinking. An interesting product of this was the presentation in 1947 of a document known as the Industrial Charter in which Butler and his colleagues accepted that Britain should operate a **mixed economy** in which the trade unions would have a legitimate and respected role. It was Butler who set the pattern of economic policy that was followed throughout the period of Conservative government to 1964. His policies between 1951 and 1955 showed that he had accepted the new form of Keynesian economics adopted by the preceding Labour government (see page 201). He continued Labour's main aims of:

- trying to maintain full employment while at the same time achieving 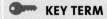economic growth
- expanding the Welfare State
- keeping to Britain's heavily committed military defence programme (which included the costly Korean War 1950–3)
- developing a nuclear weapon programme.

Butler acknowledged that the deflationary policies of the Labour government before 1951 had had beneficial effects in the short term (see page 203). The cost of British goods had dropped and exports had picked up. There was also a major uplift in the international economy in the early 1950s, largely as a result of the Marshall Plan (see page 205), which led to increased demand for British products. Yet Butler was faced, as Labour had been, with the hard fact that Britain was heavily in debt, a consequence of its wartime borrowing

🔑 KEY TERM

Mixed economy A system in which the private and public sectors of the economy both operate.

and continuing defence commitments. All this had produced a severe and continuous balance of payments deficit. A strong criticism made at the time and voiced by later observers was that Butler continued Labour's impossible policy of trying to achieve economic growth while at the same time continuing to incur the huge costs of running a Welfare State and maintaining an extensive defence programme.

Butler's ideas were seen to be so close to those of the Labour Party that his name was used to coin a particular term: 'Butskellism'. The word, first used in 1954 by the journal, *The Economist*, joined together the names of Butler, seen as representing the Conservative left, and **Hugh Gaitskell**, regarded as a key figure on the Labour right. It suggested that the left and right wings of the two parties met in the middle to form a consensus on matters such as finance, the economy and the Welfare State.

There have been suggestions that there was insufficient common ground between Butler and Gaitskell for the word to be more than a clever but inaccurate piece of terminology. However, although it is true that there were differences between Butler and Gaitskell over detail, particularly in financial matters (Gaitskell favoured high direct taxation, while Butler believed in economic control through the use of **interest rates**), the two men did share a noticeably similar approach in a number of key areas. Kenneth Morgan, a leading authority on British political history, defined 'Butskellism' as 'a state of mind'. Writing in the 1990s, he suggested: 'It implied a coherent attempt to maintain a social consensus and to try to "set the people free" through greater liberalization, lower [indirect] taxation and decontrol, without dismantling the popular welfare and industrial fabric of the Attlee years.' What is clear is that all the succeeding administrations, Labour and Conservative, tried to govern from the centre, believing that that was the position the bulk of the electorate would support.

Eden's government 1955–7

Anthony Eden had long been regarded as the heir-apparent to Churchill as Conservative leader. However, he had to wait far longer than he had expected since Churchill did not finally retire until 1955. The election that Eden called soon after becoming prime minister in 1955 produced an increased Conservative majority. This was to prove the only real success of his short administration.

It was Eden's fate to have lived the greater part of his political life in the shadow of Winston Churchill, the man he admired and whom he was destined to succeed, but not until 1955 when he himself was ageing and past his best. It is true that Eden had held the prestigious office of foreign secretary for ten years under Churchill. However, given that throughout that time Churchill had made foreign affairs his particular area of interest, Eden's role as foreign secretary was reduced to that of the ever-present loyal confidant and background figure.

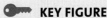

KEY FIGURE

Hugh Gaitskell (1906–63)
MP 1945–63, minister of fuel 1947–50, chancellor of the exchequer 1950–1, leader of the Labour Party 1955–63.

KEY TERM

Interest rates
A mechanism for raising or lowering the cost of borrowing money by adjusting the amount of interest charged on financial loans.

KEY TERMS

'Smack of firm government' Eden had a habit, when emphasising a point, of smacking the palm of one hand with the back of the other. It was this image the press used to mock his indecision.

Aswan Dam Eventually constructed between 1960 and 1970, it was intended to modernise Egypt by providing a huge supply of hydro-electric power.

Soviet bloc The countries of Eastern Europe under the domination of the USSR, for example, Poland, Hungary and Czechoslovakia.

French Algeria A French colony, the majority of whose indigenous Arab population supported the Algerian independence movement. French forces became involved in a bitter struggle (1954–62) against Algerian nationalists.

Having had to wait so long, Eden by the time he reached the highest office in 1955 was a man in a hurry. Irritated by criticism in the Tory press that his uninspiring domestic policies lacked the **'smack of firm government'**, he was determined to silence criticism by achieving success in foreign affairs, in which he felt he had a special expertise. This drew him into the ill-fated Suez Affair, the event which overshadowed his years as prime minister and destroyed his reputation as a statesman.

The Suez Affair 1956

Colonel Nasser, Egypt's president since 1952, had at first been on good terms with the West. He had been promised American and British loans for the construction of the **Aswan Dam** on the upper Nile, a project on which he had staked his own and his country's future. However, when the USA learned that Nasser had also approached the **Soviet bloc** countries for aid, it withdrew its original offer. In July 1956, Nasser, in desperation, announced the nationalisation of the Suez Canal as a means of raising the necessary finance. Foreign ships would have to pay to pass through what was now an Egyptian waterway.

Eden declared that such a man as Nasser could not be allowed 'to leave his thumb on Britain's windpipe', a reference to the threat to the essential oil supplies that came to Britain from the Middle East through the Canal. He began to plan ways to bring Nasser down. The French, long resentful of Egypt's support of Arab nationalists in **French Algeria**, were very willing to join the British in anti-Nasser moves. Eden also hoped that the Americans would favour such a policy; he had been led to believe that the USA would give at least moral backing to Anglo-French attempts to free the Canal. The Americans did, indeed, join Britain and France in seeking to apply pressure to Egypt by the creation of a Canal Users' Association.

Nasser, however, despite the international line-up against him, refused to budge. Britain and France then referred the issue to the UN Security Council. This proved fruitless, since the Soviet Union used its veto to block proposals in the Council to have Egypt condemned internationally. All this confirmed Eden in his belief that only force could shift Nasser. He began secret discussions with the French and the Israelis, who were eager to launch a major strike against Egypt, which had become a major base for terror attacks on Israel. Anglo-French-Israeli plans were prepared for a combined military invasion of Egypt. The strategy, finalised in mid-October 1956, was that the Israelis would attack Egypt across Sinai. Britain and France, after allowing sufficient time for the Israelis to reach the Canal, would then mount a joint assault on the Canal region from the north, under the pretence of forcing Egypt and Israel to observe a ceasefire. The plan was accepted by Eden's cabinet. On 29 October, the Israelis duly attacked across the Gaza Strip; on 30 October the Anglo-French ultimatum

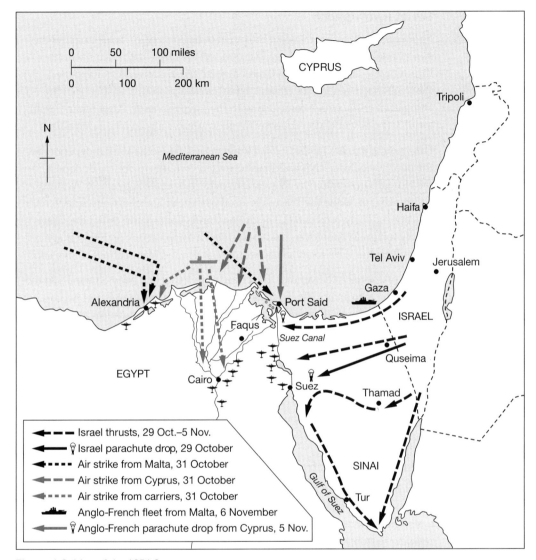

Figure 6.2 Map of the 1956 Suez invasion.

was delivered, and on the following day the two European allies began their invasion of Egypt.

The UN immediately entered into an emergency debate in which the Americans, infuriated by Eden's having totally ignored them, led the condemnation of Israel and its two allies. Over the special telephone hotline that linked the US president and British prime minister, Eisenhower swore at Eden in four-letter expletives. In a particular irony, Britain, deprived of US backing, used its veto for the first time to defeat a UN resolution demanding an immediate ceasefire.

Soviet involvement

Besides resentment at not being informed of Britain's plans, what angered the Americans was that in the Cold War atmosphere of the day, Eden's actions threatened to allow the Soviet Union to seize the initiative. As it happened, the USSR had been initially distracted by its own problems arising from the Hungarian crisis, which coincided with the Egyptian issue. After Stalin's death in 1953, the Soviet Union appeared to allow greater freedom to its **satellites**.

However, when, in October 1956, Hungary pushed too hard for independence, the new Soviet leader Nikita Khrushchev sent in tanks to occupy Budapest, the Hungarian capital. The Hungarians made desperate appeals for Western assistance, but, while the West expressed outrage at Soviet actions, intervention was not seriously considered. The military and geographical difficulties were simply too great. Moreover, the Anglo-French-Israeli attack on Egypt made it difficult for the West to adopt the moral high ground over matters of invasion.

By the first week of November, the Hungarian rising had been crushed and the USA's refusal to accept the legitimacy of the allied invasion of Egypt had become clear beyond doubt. This encouraged the Soviet Union to make its biggest move yet over Egypt. On 5 November, it issued a formal Note to Britain. Condemning the Anglo-French invasion of Egypt as the bullying of the weaker by the stronger, the Note warned that the USSR was prepared to use rockets against the Western invaders: 'We are fully determined to crush the aggressors and restore peace in the Middle East through the use of force. We hope at this critical moment you will display due prudence and draw the corresponding conclusions from this.'

British withdrawal from Suez

The day after the receipt of the Soviet Note, Eden gave way and Britain accepted the UN demand for disengagement. But while the possibility of Soviet intervention undoubtedly helped to concentrate Eden's mind, the still more pressing reasons for his ordering a withdrawal from Suez were:

- the strength of opposition among the British people; Gaitskell and Bevan made withering attacks on what they described as Eden's 'mad venture'
- the fury of Eisenhower and the Americans at not being consulted
- Britain's failure to gain international backing
- condemnation of Britain at the UN
- the reluctance of all but a few of the Commonwealth countries to support Britain
- a catastrophic fall in Britain's currency reserves caused by large withdrawals of deposits by international investors. Britain faced the threat of economic collapse.

Eden's personal role

Historians, reflecting on the Suez Affair, have made much of the role played personally by Anthony Eden. It has been suggested that the crisis took the form it did largely because of his particular perception of the problem and how it might be solved. Eden had a deep distaste for Nasser, whom he saw in the mould of the **European dictators** of the 1930s, with whom he had dealt as foreign secretary between 1935 and 1938. This led him to put the worst construction on the Egyptian leader's actions. Anxious for the maintenance of essential oil supplies, Eden suspected that beneath Nasser's campaign to modernise Egypt lay an essentially anti-British motive. He concluded that in the end it might be that Nasser would have to be stopped by military force. Mistaking the initial Western disapproval of the Egyptian seizure of the Canal as implying support for any moves he might initiate, Eden had colluded with France and Israel for a pretext to invade Egypt and topple Nasser.

Already on dangerous ground, Eden did not help his cause by the manner in which he acted. Tetchy and short-tempered, he did not try to hide his distaste for those who disagreed with him. This mattered especially in his dealings with the USA, the ally that Britain most needed at this critical juncture. Eden's undisguised annoyance with Eisenhower was hardly likely to win the Americans over to his point of view. A particular blindness was Eden's failure to appreciate that with a presidential election imminent in the USA, the American government was simply not prepared to become embroiled in a costly military venture that recalled old-style imperialism.

It was also likely that Eden's chronic poor health, which deteriorated further during the crisis, weakened his judgement. The strain of Suez wore him out. J.P. Mallalieu, a Labour MP, gave a striking description (Source I) of the physical and mental state to which the Eden had been reduced:

KEY TERM

European dictators
Chiefly Adolf Hitler (German leader, 1933–45) and Benito Mussolini (Italian leader, 1922–43).

SOURCE I

From J.P. Mallalieu, a Labour MP, quoted in Paul Johnson, *The Suez War*, MacGibbon & Kee, 1957, p. 126.

The Prime Minister sprawled on the front bench, head thrown back and mouth agape. His eyes, inflamed with sleeplessness, stared into vacancies beyond the roof except when they switched with meaningless intensity to the face of the clock, probed it for a few seconds, then rose again in vacancy. His hands twitched at his horn-rimmed spectacles or mopped themselves in a handkerchief, but were never still. The face was grey except where black-ringed caverns surrounded the dying embers of his eyes. The whole personality, if not prostrated seemed completely withdrawn … the overwhelming burden of taking on his own account, decisions which have come near to breaking the Anglo-American alliance and the Commonwealth have now made him incapable of distinguishing between success or failure as it has made him incapable of distinguishing between truth and lies.

What image of the strain Eden was under is presented in Source I?

Eden's wife, Clarissa, recorded that during the weeks of the crisis it felt as if the Suez Canal was flowing through her drawing room. Within weeks of the crisis, Eden stepped down as prime minister. The official reason was ill-health and it was certainly true that he was seriously unwell but the Suez disaster had shattered his standing at home and abroad. Even had he been fully fit, he could not have carried on as head of government.

Significance of the Suez Affair for Britain

It is important to note that Britain was not defeated militarily in Egypt. Indeed, British forces were withdrawn from Suez when they were on the verge of success. That was why the Israelis were so bitter with the British for leaving the job half done. Britain's withdrawal was a failure not of military resolve but of political will. Fearing the consequences of being internationally isolated, Eden's nerve broke and he accepted that Britain could no longer continue with a policy that the world condemned. It was an admission that in the post-war world Britain could not act alone. The realisation of this led a number of people in both major political parties to consider whether Britain should consider closer union with Europe.

The Suez Affair was a landmark in Britain's foreign policy. In attacking Egypt, Britain had attempted to act independently of NATO and the USA, without consulting the Commonwealth, and in disregard of the UN. The international and domestic protests that the Suez venture aroused meant that it was the last time Britain would attempt such independent action. While there would be occasions in the future when Britain would use armed force unilaterally, as for example over the Falklands in 1982, this would only be when it considered its own sovereign territory had been occupied by a hostile power.

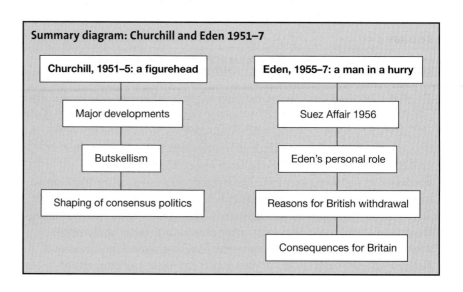

Summary diagram: Churchill and Eden 1951–7

Macmillan's government 1957

▶ *What were the characteristics of Conservative government under Macmillan?*

Despite his outwardly relaxed demeanour, Harold Macmillan had a sharp political sense. Although he had firmly supported Eden over Suez, he came out of the escapade relatively unscathed. As chancellor of the exchequer, he made a rallying call to the cabinet on 3 January 1957. Admitting that the military operation had swollen Britain's debts by £564 million, he told his colleagues that they must learn lessons from Suez but not be overwhelmed by it: 'The Suez operation has been a tactical defeat. It is our task to ensure that it should prove the prelude to strategic victory.' His rousing speech undoubtedly helped his bid for leadership. A week later he became prime minister.

Macmillan's 'middle-way' Conservatism

In forming his first cabinet in 1957, Macmillan made Butler his home secretary. This proved an important move towards a 'middle-way' Conservatism, one that avoided extremes and embraced progress. At the Home Office, Butler took a basically liberal approach towards legal and social issues, placing the emphasis in penal matters on reform rather than punishment. A significant example was the introduction of the Homicide Act in 1957, which effectively abolished the death penalty. Butler's liberal stance as home secretary hinted strongly that the Conservative Party under Macmillan was prepared to modify its traditional social attitudes. Its opponents would find it harder to dismiss it simply as a party of reactionaries. Butler's liberal attitude was one on which subsequent home secretaries, such as Labour's Roy Jenkins, would build, providing another example of the consensus that applied to so many areas of British politics and government in the second half of the twentieth century.

'Never had it so good' Britain: consumerism

In July 1957, Harold Macmillan memorably stated that the British people had 'never had it so good'. Although the assertion was challenged by his opponents, it has come to be regarded as a representative description of the achievements of the Conservative governments between 1951 and 1957. What has sometimes been overlooked is that in that speech Macmillan also sounded a note of warning:

SOURCE J

> According to Source J, what are Macmillan's main concerns about the British economy?

From Macmillan's speech in July 1957, quoted in D. Kavanagh and P. Morris, *Consensus Politics from Attlee to Thatcher*, Oxford University Press, 1989, p. 40.

Let's be frank about it: most of our people have never had it so good. Go around the country, go to the industrial towns, go to the farms, and you will see a state of prosperity, such as we have never seen in my lifetime – nor indeed in the history of the country. [However] what is beginning to worry some of us is 'Is it too good to be true?' or perhaps I should say 'Is it too good to last?' For midst all this prosperity, there is one problem that has troubled us – in one way or another since the war. It's the problem of rising prices. Our constant concern today is – can prices be steadied while at the same time we maintain full employment in the expanding economy? Can we control inflation? This is the problem of our time.

Living standards

Despite periods of serious hardship for some of the population in Britain under the Conservatives, the broad picture was one of a continuous rise in living standards. The various financial problems that confronted the nation did not prevent the great majority of the population from gaining in material prosperity. This is an area where figures speak loudest.

Wages

Wages rose ahead of prices. One example of the overall improvement in working people's income is that the average weekly wage of the adult male worker increased from £8-6s. (£8.30) in 1951 to £18-7s. (£18.35) in 1964. It was not simply that wages increased in overall amount. The key fact was a growth in real wages; income kept ahead of prices. People were able to buy more with their money. This meant that although inflation continued to climb throughout the period it never overtook the increase in real wages.

Table 6.5 Growth in real wages 1951–64 (calculated as an average hourly rate percentage increase for each individual worker)

Period	Percentage increase
1951–5	2.2%
1955–60	2.9%
1960–4	4.0%

Credit

Another vital factor in the raising of living standards was the greater availability of credit, a facility provided by finance companies that enabled people to borrow much larger sums of money than they could obtain by saving. With loan repayment spread out over a number of years on 'easy terms', usually a relatively small amount each month, people were able to buy items they previously could not have afforded.

Access to credit (also known as hire purchase) enabled consumers to buy an unprecedented range of manufactured goods. A consumer boom began. In the period 1950–65 the sales of private cars nearly quadrupled from 1.5 million to 5.5 million. In addition, foreign holidays, clothing and mod cons came within the reach of ordinary people in ways that would have been impossible without the existence of credit.

Housing

Perhaps the most impressive feature of the consumer boom was the growth in house buying. Housing had been a proud claim of Attlee's government, which had built over 600,000 homes by 1951. The Conservatives tried to better the Labour record. To great acclaim at the 1950 Conservative conference, the party leaders had responded to emotional pleas from the floor by committing themselves to build 300,000 houses annually. Macmillan was instrumental in the fulfilling of that pledge. As housing minister between 1951 and 1954, he achieved the target of 300,000 new homes each year. Although the pace slowed considerably after that, when the Conservatives went out of office in 1964 they could claim to have built 1.7 million homes, 60 per cent of those being private dwellings.

Rent Act 1957

It was during his own administration that Macmillan in 1957 presided over the introduction of the Rent Act which, by abolishing rent control, put 6 million properties on the market. The downside of this was that rents rose considerably, making it difficult for tenants at the lower end of the scale to afford leases. But that was the trade-off Macmillan felt had to be made in order to stimulate the rented property market.

A 'property-owning democracy'

What made this housing explosion possible was the relative ease with which money could be borrowed and repaid over long periods of time. Encouraged by the government, banks and building societies advanced the necessary capital in the form of mortgages that allowed increasing numbers to own their own homes, thus creating the conditions for what the Conservatives called a **'property-owning democracy'**. It was such developments that Harold Macmillan had in mind when he declared in 1957 that the British people had 'never had it so good'.

Unemployment

Macmillan was well aware that, despite the evident improvement in the material well-being of so many in the population, problems remained. Although the Conservatives willingly inherited the Labour Party's commitment to full

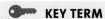

KEY TERM

Property-owning democracy A society in which as many people as possible are encouraged to become homeowners, an extension of the principle that the ownership of property is an essential component of democracy.

employment as a basic economic aim, achieving this proved much more difficult. Table 6.6 shows that the lowest annual figure for joblessness was well over a quarter of a million in the mid-1950s, rose rapidly in the late 1950s, and, after falling in the early 1960s, reached an embarrassingly high figure in Macmillan's last year in government. The persistence of high unemployment cast doubt on just how realistic it was to claim that the people had 'never had it so good'.

Table 6.6 Number of workers unemployed in Britain 1951–64

1951	367,000	1958	536,000
1952	468,000	1959	621,000
1953	452,000	1960	461,000
1954	387,000	1961	419,000
1955	298,000	1962	566,000
1956	297,000	1963	878,000
1957	383,000	1964	501,000

Class and affluence

By the late 1950s significant shifts in British social attitudes and behaviour had occurred. These were intimately bound up with the changing attitudes towards class, and the fact that class mobility became particularly evident in the Macmillan years.

In 1960, R.A. Butler claimed that, since 1951, modern Conservatism, far from perpetuating class differences in Britain, had actually begun to end them: 'We have developed instead an *affluent*, open and democratic *society*, in which the class escalators are continually moving and in which people are divided not so much between "haves" and "have-nots" as between "haves" and "have-mores".' Butler's words clearly complemented Macmillan's 'never had it so good' speech three years earlier. Between them, the two speakers had defined the aim of the Conservative government as being the development of a socially mobile society which left its individual members free through their own efforts to enjoy the fruits of the nation's increasing wealth.

The key to the social shift and the blurring of class divisions was the availability of financial credit. In a pre-credit age, only the rich had been able afford to buy ostentatiously. But, now that borrowing and purchasing on credit were possible for nearly everybody, having possessions was no longer a clear guide to social status. Since people on a regular wage could buy things on hire purchase, there was an increase in the number of consumers and a consequent increase in production to meet their demands. Such consumerism was the great equaliser in class terms. Indeed, a process developed in which working-class incomes often exceeded lower middle-class ones. Yet it was still possible for lower middle-class people living in genteel poverty to regard themselves as in some way socially superior to and more respectable than car workers or plumbers who were earning much more than they were. This suggests that in Britain class was as much an attitude of mind as of possessions and wealth.

Responses to the Conservatives' social and economic policies

Critics of the Conservative economic record stressed that, although Britain had indeed become more affluent by the late 1950s, the gap between rich and poor had widened in that same period. Supporters of Macmillan's policies accepted the truth of this, but argued that wealth and poverty were relative terms. The material quality of life was improving for nearly everybody. The reality was that the great majority of those designated poor in Britain now had access to resources that their forebears could not even have imagined.

Those unimpressed by this argument faulted the Conservatives on the following points:

- The Conservative governments had not developed coherent economic policies but had simply employed 'stop-go' tactics to prevent the economy swinging too wildly between deflation and inflation.
- Apart from a wish to keep the value of the pound sterling, they had no structured financial strategy. They had used budgets and tax adjustments not in a responsible way but as a technique for buying votes at election time.

There were also moralists who argued that Macmillan's pursuit of a property-owning democracy was based not on genuine national prosperity but on heavy borrowing by government and consumers. The scale of debt which this created was economically dangerous and socially harmful since it encouraged materialism, consumerism and irresponsibility. A particular charge related to Britain's development of nuclear weapons.

Nuclear weapons

In 1947, the Labour government had taken the momentous decision to make Britain a nuclear power (see page 213), a commitment that was fully supported by the Conservatives when they came to power. This resulted in Britain's detonating its first atomic bomb in 1952 and its first hydrogen bomb in 1957. Having adopted nuclear power as a means of military defence, the decision was taken to develop it for civilian means. In 1954, the United Kingdom Atomic Energy Authority (UKAEA) was established; its role was to oversee policies for the civilian and defence use of atomic energy. By 1958, UKAEA had carried out over twenty nuclear weapon tests in selected areas of the Pacific. It was this aspect of UKAEA's work that raised one of the great moral issues of the twentieth century and led to protests in which **CND** was the major voice.

Unilateralism

Although CND never formally attached itself to a political party, its strong bias against the USA, which it blamed for nuclear weapon proliferation, made it attractive to left-wingers in the Labour Party and the trade unions. These groups were strongly represented in its ranks. Initially, CND's aim was radical but not revolutionary. Its strategy was to persuade the Labour Party to adopt

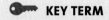 **KEY TERM**

CND The Campaign for Nuclear Disarmament, established in 1957, to agitate for Britain's unilateral abandonment of its nuclear weapons.

unilateralism as official party policy which any future Labour government would be bound to implement. The Labour Party leaders, judging that CND, no matter how strong its moral convictions, was in national terms only a minority movement, calculated that for the party to embrace unilateralism would be a huge vote loser. The struggle over this was to cause the Labour Party great problems in the 1960s.

Technology

As nuclear weaponry illustrated, the post-war decades witnessed remarkable technological advances, which began to change the living and working lives of the population. These were not exclusive to Britain; indeed many were initiated elsewhere, but they contributed notably to the development of British society, particularly in the areas of work and leisure.

Motor cars

A particularly striking feature of technology was the phenomenal growth in the number of cars on British roads. Having a car was one of the most liberating features for ordinary people in the 1950s, giving individuals and families a sense of independence and opening access to a wide range of leisure pursuits.

Table 6.7 Number of privately owned cars

Year	Number of cars
1950	2.3 million
1955	5.6 million
1957	8.1 million

This growth intensified the need for more and better roads which in turn raised the issue of how Britain's transport structure was to be organised. The first stretch of the M1 motorway was opened in 1959. This was an impressive step in itself but it was clear that what was needed was an integrated transport plan, something that has yet to be achieved in Britain.

Unsuccessful though the transport schemes may have proved, the attempts at road building in nearly every local authority invariably involved reconstruction and change. It was this that aroused the fears of those who came later to form an environmentalist movement in the later years of Macmillan's administration.

Leisure

By the late 1950s, three out of four homes had a television set. Nightly viewing joined the weekly cinema visit as the defining character of family leisure.

Table 6.8 Percentage of homes with domestic appliances

Year	Refrigerators	Televisions	Washing machines	Telephones
1955	8%	40%	20%	16%
1958	30%	75%	50%	35%

Workers

By 1957, 94 per cent of British workers took an annual two-week paid holiday. This was a sign both of greater workers' rights and workers' incomes, which on average rose by a third in purchasing power. The seaside was the main venue for working-class families and holiday camps, such as Butlins, which had opened its first site in Skegness in the 1930s, grew in number and popularity. As earnings rose and disposable incomes grew, holidays abroad became possible. Travel companies offering package holidays brought travel within the range of ordinary families. Activities that before 1950 had been the preserve of the well-to-do were now available to most British people, another feature of the 'never had it so good' years.

Status of women

Significant progress for women was largely a response to the development of the feminist movement in the 1950s. It is hard to give a precise date to the start of this movement, but what was certainly important was the growth in the formal education of women at secondary and higher level. From this group came a literate, articulate demand for the recognition of the legal, social and economic equality of women. At the forefront of the demand was an insistence that the law be changed in those areas where women suffered particular discrimination. It is in relation to such pressure that a number of critical legal changes were made. These did not appear until the 1960s and 1970s, but the groundwork had been laid in the 1950s.

Table 6.9 Women as a percentage of those in higher education in the UK

Year	Percentage
1950	20%
1959	25%
1965	35%

Table 6.10 Women as percentage of the workforce in the UK

Year	Percentage
1951	31%
1959	39%
1990	43%

Although there is a natural emphasis on the success of feminism in eventually bringing about legal change, equally important was the movement's insistence that there were many social injustices afflicting women which were beyond the scope of legislation since they belonged to the world of ingrained prejudice among women as well as men. What was needed, therefore, was a fundamental change of attitude in society at large. This is why feminism, in turn, has to be understood as part of a broad movement of thought that became particularly influential by the late 1950s. This was made up of many strands but essentially what motivated it was the wish to remove traditional social and moral restraints. The 1960s saw changes that merited the term 'sexual revolution', whose basis had been set down in the 1950s.

Youth

One of the fruits of technology was that it provided young people with spending power and leisure time. This gave them a place in society that no young generation had ever before possessed. Teenagers and people in their twenties became a new type of social being. This meant they were wooed by advertisers eager in an age of intensifying consumerism to create a **niche market**. By the late 1950s young people were spending over 50 per cent of their disposable income on clothes.

Few of those in what the media referred to imprecisely as the 'youth culture' had specific political aims, which was why the existing political parties were unappealing to them. The young did not have a single attitude of mind, of course, but their clothing and music could be interpreted as a broad protest against the system and the **Establishment** that operated in Britain.

Literary responses

The growth of Britain under the 1950s' Conservative government attracted a striking literary reaction. In 1956, C.P. Snow, both a distinguished physicist and novelist, had written what proved to be a highly influential and divisive article. His argument was that post-war Britain was divided into 'Two Cultures'. One was a dated, self-regarding, coterie of intellectuals and writers, drawn from the humanities and arts in the universities, who made up the Establishment and who were wholly ignorant of science. The other was a progressive body of scientists who understood the absolute necessity of Britain's adapting to the modern world of technology, but who were denied influence by the literary Establishment. Snow met many challenges from those who accused him of selectivity and exaggeration. However, what he had done was supply a provocative analysis of the times to which others could respond with their own assessment.

A much more directly critical book was *The Age of Affluence* by American economist J.K. Galbraith, published in 1958. His analysis became the reference point for all other writers concerned with the growth of materialism and the decline of social values that consumerism represented. Galbraith's main target was the USA, but by clear implication it applied to Britain as well. His main argument was that Western governments, by making economic growth into a god to be worshipped, were deliberately encouraging consumerism, a process that allowed the rich to grow richer and the poor to become poorer. Galbraith, as a socialist, was also open to the charge of exaggeration and selectivity in his use

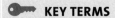

KEY TERMS

Niche market A particular section of society targeted by advertisers and manufacturers.

Establishment Individuals or groups, whose political connections or intellectual status, gave them the means to influence government policy and shape public opinion and attitudes – sometimes called the 'old boy network'.

of evidence. Opponents in the USA and Britain suggested that, as an intellectual, he had ignored the fact that consumerism was an expansive economic system that created employment, increased wages, and stimulated social mobility, the very argument that Butler and Macmillan had used to describe and justify the economic improvements under 1950s' Conservatism.

In Britain, in the 1950s a group of anti-Establishment novelists and playwrights appeared who were dubbed 'Angry Young Men'. They never formed a school of writers; their works were individual, but what appeared to unite them was their distaste for the Establishment. Arguably, the most representative among them was John Osborne, whose play 'Look Back in Anger' (1956), largely consisted of its self-centred central character, Jimmy Porter railing about the stultifying conformity of comfortable, middle-class Britain in the 1950s. Sceptical theatre critics said the anger was contrived and that Jimmy Porter, the work-shy anti-hero of the play, gave the game away in the line 'There aren't any good causes left.' In other words, years of peace and rising living standards had helped to remove the fear and uncertainties of preceding decades, leaving only literary intellectuals to complain about their times.

Immigration and racial tension

One of the most notable features of Britain in the second half of the twentieth century was its development as a multiracial society. A key stage in this occurred in 1948 with the sailing of a converted troopship, the *Empire Windrush*, from Kingston, Jamaica, to Britain. The ship carried hundreds of West Indian workers; the majority were young males, but there were also families and a number of older men, most of whom were Second World War veterans. They were coming to find work. The official welcome they received was a warm one. Cinema newsreels enthusiastically recorded the event and assured the newcomers that they would soon find homes and jobs.

New Commonwealth immigrants

Under the British Nationality Act of 1948, the newcomers, classified as **New Commonwealth** immigrants (see Table 6.11 on page 240), had full rights of British citizenship. This encouraged further emigration from the West Indies. The government encouraged this with organised appeals for Caribbean workers to fill the vacancies, principally in hospitals and transport services that Britain's acute post-war labour shortage had left. By the mid-1950s employers in Britain had extended their recruitment to the Asian subcontinent. Textile firms in London and the north of England eagerly took on workers from India and Pakistan.

 **KEY TERM**

New Commonwealth
Official immigration statistics distinguished between the Old Commonwealth, referring broadly to the people of the dominions, and the New Commonwealth, referring broadly to the people of the newly independent ex-colonies.

Table 6.11 Commonwealth immigrants living in the UK

Year	Old Commonwealth (Australia, New Zealand, Canada and South Africa)	New Commonwealth (West Indies, India, Pakistan and Bangladesh*)	Total
1961	307,697	289,058	596,755
1971	528,810	765,095	1,293,905

* Formerly East Pakistan. Bangladesh gained independence in 1971.

Table 6.12 UK emigration and immigration (to nearest 100,000)

Decade	Outflow	Inflow
1900–9	4,404,000	2,287,000
1910–19	3,526,000	2,224,000
1920–9	3,960,000	2,590,000
1930–9	2,273,000	2,361,000
1940–9	590,000	240,000
1950–9	1,327,000	676,000
1960–9	1,916,000	1,243,000

However, by the late 1950s, disturbing reactions had begun to occur among some of the white host population. 'No coloured' notices appeared in boarding house windows and on factory gates; mutterings were heard to the effect that the newcomers were attracted to Britain as much by the generous welfare benefits as by the prospect of work. The actual number of white residents who believed such slanders may have been small, but troublemakers were able to exploit the housing shortage, which was a major problem in the poorer areas, by suggesting that it was all the fault of the immigrants. However, race relations problems have never been simply about numbers. Those who spoke of Britain being 'swamped by waves of immigrants' were grossly exaggerating. In 1960, the proportion of people of non-European origins was only six per cent of the overall population of Britain. Moreover, as Table 6.12 shows, in every decade of the century up to the 1970s net emigration exceeded net immigration.

The main difficulties arose over accommodation. When immigrants first arrived in Britain they tended to live in the poorer areas of cities and urban areas where the cheaper properties for buying or renting were to be found. This was unavoidable given their limited resources. But since Britain's inner cities suffered from a severe shortage of affordable housing, there was bound to be competition between residents on low incomes and newcomers. The same problems arose in the job market. Where work was scarce, those who could not get a job tended to blame immigrants for squeezing them out of employment by taking work at lower pay rates than whites were prepared to accept. The issues with which Macmillan's administration began to grapple would confront all succeeding governments.

Britain's role in the world in 1957

Strengths

- Britain was one of a small group of nations with the resources to use nuclear power for domestic and military purposes.
- The City of London was a major hub of international finance and commercial exchange. The flow of money through the City and the sale of financial services helped to keep the UK solvent.
- Although committed to decolonisation, Britain, because of its imperial past, had a knowledge and experience of other countries that could be highly valuable when called on to play a peacekeeping role.
- It was Britain's military prowess and reputation that made it a leading member of NATO.
- As a permanent member of the UN Security Council, Britain was a major player in international peacekeeping affairs.

Limitations

- The Suez Affair had shown that Britain could no longer act unilaterally in foreign affairs.
- Britain was no longer an imperial power.
- Britain's strength as a nuclear power was dependent on essential supplies and support from the USA.
- This dependence on the USA limited its diplomatic freedom.
- The demands of the Cold War meant it always had to act within the terms of alliance with the USA.
- Despite the prowess of its armed forces, they were always in danger of being overstretched.
- Britain's uncertainty about joining Europe meant it was not in a position to influence continental affairs.

```
┌─────────────────────────────────────────────────────────────────────┐
│ Summary diagram: Macmillan's government 1957                          │
│                                                                       │
│  ┌─────────────────────────────────────────────────────────────────┐ │
│  │          Macmillan's middle-way Conservatism                     │ │
│  │                 Avoidance of extremes                            │ │
│  └─────────────────────────────────────────────────────────────────┘ │
│                                                                       │
│  ┌─────────────────────────────────────────────────────────────────┐ │
│  │              Conservative economic policy                        │ │
│  │      • Mild Keynesianism retained                                │ │
│  │      • Maintaining the mixed economy                             │ │
│  └─────────────────────────────────────────────────────────────────┘ │
│                                                                       │
│  ┌─────────────────────────────────────────────────────────────────┐ │
│  │           Macmillan's 'never had it so good' Britain             │ │
│  │  • Rise in real wages          • Credit availability             │ │
│  │  • Workers' greater spending   • Property-owning democracy       │ │
│  │    power                       • Recognition of class shift      │ │
│  │  • Consumer boom               • Growing affluence               │ │
│  │  • Housing boom                                                  │ │
│  │                         But                                      │ │
│  │               Growing unemployment                               │ │
│  └─────────────────────────────────────────────────────────────────┘ │
│                                                                       │
│  ┌─────────────────────────────────────────────────────────────────┐ │
│  │ Culture                                                          │ │
│  │  • Distinctive youth subculture   • Rise in status of women      │ │
│  └─────────────────────────────────────────────────────────────────┘ │
│                                                                       │
│  ┌─────────────────────────────────────────────────────────────────┐ │
│  │ Technology assisted growth of:                                   │ │
│  │  • Leisure                     • Motor cars                      │ │
│  │  • Television                  • Holidays                        │ │
│  └─────────────────────────────────────────────────────────────────┘ │
│                                                                       │
│  ┌─────────────────────────────────────────────────────────────────┐ │
│  │ Nuclear energy                                                   │ │
│  │  • Independent deterrent retained  • Resistance from CND         │ │
│  └─────────────────────────────────────────────────────────────────┘ │
│                                                                       │
│  ┌─────────────────────────────────────────────────────────────────┐ │
│  │        Critical literary responses to consumerist Britain        │ │
│  └─────────────────────────────────────────────────────────────────┘ │
│                                                                       │
│  ┌─────────────────────────────────────────────────────────────────┐ │
│  │                Britain's role in the world                       │ │
│  │          Still significant but considerably lessened             │ │
│  └─────────────────────────────────────────────────────────────────┘ │
└─────────────────────────────────────────────────────────────────────┘
```

9   Key debate

▶ *How unpopular was Eden's Suez venture in 1956?*

So vociferous was the anti-war campaign in 1956 that it is easy to forget that Eden may well have had majority support among the British people. This has led writers then and since to debate the key question, 'How unpopular was Eden's Suez venture?'

The tone was set in a sense by the Trafalgar Square anti-war rally of 4 November 1956, at which the principal speaker was Aneurin Bevan. Addressing the 30,000 protesters in passionate terms, Bevan accused the government of blackening the name of Britain: 'They have offended against every principle of decency and there is only one way in which they can even begin to restore their tarnished reputation and that is to get out! Get out! Get out!' Powerful rhetoric though this was, it did not necessarily reflect public opinion. British historian Barry Turner later wrote that:

EXTRACT 1

From Barry Turner, *Suez 1956*, Hodder & Stoughton, 2006, p. 354.

The public reaction to press comment highlighted the divisions within the country. But there was no doubt that Eden still commanded strong support from a sizable minority, maybe even a majority, of voters who thought that it was about time that the upset Arabs should be taught a lesson. The Observer *and* Guardian *lost readers; so too did the* News Chronicle, *a liberal newspaper that was soon to fold as a result of falling circulation.*

The Conservative novelist and essayist, A.N. Wilson, suggested that those who remained silent at the time may have been for Eden rather than against him:

EXTRACT 2

From A.N. Wilson, *Our Times*, Hutchinson, 2008, p. 66.

The bulk of the press, the Labour Party and that equally influential left-learning party, the London dinner party, were all against Suez together with the rent-a-mob of poets, dons, clergy and ankle-socked female graduates who deplored British action, but they did not necessarily constitute the majority of unexpressed public opinion.

It was certainly true that the left-wing press assumed that the British people were overwhelmingly against Britain's attack. Yet Eden himself was able to claim that the correspondence he received swung from eight to one against his Egyptian intervention to four to one in favour of it by the time of the ceasefire. However, Robert Blake, the leading analyst of the Conservative Party, while accepting that it was possible to exaggerate the degree of opposition to Eden, cautioned that neither should the degree of support be overstated:

EXTRACT 3

From Robert Blake, *The Conservative Party from Peel to Major*, Arrow Books, 1998, p. 279.

The 'nation' as far as judgement can be made about that intangible quality, felt bewildered rather than humiliated. It is not true, as sometimes said, that public opinion was strongly pro-Suez, but it was not against. Polls on 11 November and 2 December 1956 recorded slightly over 50 per cent in favour of Eden's policy. The moral issue cut little ice. Gaitskell, Attlee's successor, did himself harm by pressing it.

A balanced perspective of the question was offered by the left-leaning historian Dilwyn Porter:

EXTRACT 4

From Dilwyn Porter, *From Blitz to Blair*, Phoenix, 1997, p. 115.

For some British people [Suez] was a traumatic experience, mercifully short lived, which challenged widely held assumptions about the nation to which they belonged. Public opinion, though confused, had rallied to Eden at the height of the crisis, responding not just to headlines of the 'EDEN GETS TOUGH' and 'IT'S GREAT BRITAIN AGAIN!' variety, but to deeply rooted patriotic instincts and a sense of Britain's rightful place in the world.

? How convincing in their assessment of Eden's popularity are Extracts 1–4?

Chapter summary

Enjoying a huge majority after 1945, Attlee's government set about establishing the Welfare State and introducing nationalisation. However, heavily in debt at the war's end and burdened with a costly defence programme which included Britain's developing its own atomic bombs, Attlee's administration resorted to austerity at home and heavy borrowing from abroad. The result was two major sterling crises. The crisis of 1949 was so severe that it caused the government to devalue the pound.

Bevin followed an essentially pro-American, anti-Soviet policy which included the creation of NATO, the Berlin Airlift and the Korean War.

Elsewhere, Britain gained credit for granting Indian independence but showed a less progressive attitude by declining to join Europe in the ECSC. The Labour government's financial and political problems collectively led to its defeat in the 1951 election, but not before it had established the main lines of domestic and foreign policy that all subsequent governments were to follow.

The Conservative governments of Churchill and Eden, in a form of consensus politics known as Butskellism, continued essentially the same economic, welfare and foreign affairs programme as Labour's before 1951. The outstanding episode in Eden's term of office was the Suez War of 1956, which ended in failure for Eden and brought Macmillan into office. It was Macmillan who adopted a middle way for 'never had it so good' Britain.

Refresher questions

Use these questions to remind yourself of the key material covered in this chapter.

1 Why did the Labour Party win a large-scale victory in the 1945 election?

2 How had the Beveridge Report prepared the ground for Labour's introduction of the Welfare State?

3 How far was the Attlee government's introduction of the Welfare State the implementation of socialist principles?

4 What did Labour achieve during its six years of office 1945–51?

5 How radical were the policies of Attlee's governments?

6 Why did Labour lose office in 1951?

7 Why did the Labour government commit Britain to the support of the USA in the Berlin Airlift and the Korean War?

8 Why was foreign policy a divisive issue within the Labour Party?

9 How well had the Conservatives recovered by 1951?

10 What were the consequences for Britain of the Suez venture?

11 What was Butskellism?

12 In what sense was Macmillan seeking a political 'middle way'?

13 What did Macmillan mean by saying Britain had never had it so good?

14 What evidence is there to suggest that consumerism had become a defining characteristic of British society by 1957?

15 How accurate is it to claim that Britain was still a world power in 1957?

 # Question practice

ESSAY QUESTIONS

1 Assess the reasons for the Labour Party's landslide election victory in 1945.

2 To what extent was Labour's creation of the Welfare State between 1945 and 1951 the putting into practice of the Beveridge Report?

3 'The years 1945–57 were a period of consensus politics.' Assess the validity of this view.

4 To what extent do you agree that by 1957 the British people under the Conservatives had 'never had it so good'?

SOURCE ANALYSIS QUESTIONS

1 With reference to Sources B (page 207), C (page 207) and I (page 229), and your understanding of the historical context, assess the value of these sources to a historian studying British foreign policy between 1946 and 1956.

2 With references to Sources D (page 216), E (page 216), and F (page 217), and your understanding of the historical context, assess the value of these sources to a historian studying the recovery of the Conservatives between 1945 and 1951.

AQA A level History

Essay guidance

At both AS and A level for AQA Component 2: Depth Study: Wars and Welfare: Britain in Transition, 1906–1957, you will need to answer an essay question in the exam. Each essay question is marked out of 25:

- for the AS exam, Section B: answer **one** essay (from a choice of two)
- for the A level exam, Section B: answer **two** essays (from a choice of three).

There are several question stems which all have the same basic requirement: to analyse and reach a conclusion, based on the evidence you provide.

The AS questions often give a quotation and then ask whether you agree or disagree with this view. Almost inevitably, your answer will be a mixture of both. It is the same task as for A level – just phrased differently in the question. Detailed essays are more likely to do well than vague or generalised essays, especially in the Depth Studies of Paper 2.

The AQA mark scheme is essentially the same for AS and the full A level (see the AQA website, www.aqa.org.uk). Both emphasise the need to analyse and evaluate the key features related to the periods studied. The key feature of the highest level is sustained analysis: analysis that unites the whole of the essay.

Writing an essay: general skills

- *Focus and structure.* Be sure what the question is asking and plan what the paragraphs should be about.
- *Focused introduction to the essay.* Be sure that the introductory sentence relates directly to the focus of the question and that each paragraph highlights the structure of the answer.

- *Use detail.* Make sure that you show detailed knowledge, but only as part of an explanation being made in relation to the question. No knowledge should be standalone; it should be used in context.
- *Explanatory analysis and evaluation.* Consider what words and phrases to use in an answer to strengthen the explanation.
- *Argument and counter-argument.* Think of how arguments can be juxtaposed as part of a balancing act to give contrasting views.
- *Resolution.* Think how best to 'resolve' contradictory arguments.
- *Relative significance and evaluation.* Think how best to reach a judgement when trying to assess the relative importance of various factors, and their possible interrelationship.

Planning an essay

Practice question 1

To what extent was Labour's creation of the Welfare State between 1945 and 1951 the putting into practice of the Beveridge Report?

This question requires you to analyse the relationship between the Labour government's welfare programme and the Beveridge Report. You must discuss:

- The character of the Labour welfare programme (your primary focus).
- The proposals in the Beveridge Report (your secondary focus).

A clear structure makes for a much more effective essay and is crucial for achieving the highest marks. You need three or four paragraphs to structure this question effectively. In each paragraph you will deal with one factor. One of these *must* be the factor in the question.

A very basic plan for this question might look like this:

- Paragraph 1: the main features of the Labour welfare programme.
- Paragraph 2: the key proposals in the Beveridge Report.
- Paragraph 3: the links between Labour's programme and the Beveridge Report.

It is a good idea to cover the factor named in the question first, so that you don't run out of time and forget to do it. Then cover the other factors in what you think is their order of importance, or in the order that appears logical in terms of the sequence of paragraphs.

The introduction

Maintaining focus is vital. One way to do this from the beginning of your essay is to use the words in the question to help write your argument. The first sentence of question 1 (see page 246), for example, could look like this:

Labour came to power in 1945 committed to the introduction of a wide range of welfare reforms, which were to be largely based on the proposals contained in the Beveridge Report of 1942.

This opening sentence provides a clear focus on the demands of the question.

Focus throughout the essay

Structuring your essay well will help with keeping the focus of your essay on the question. To maintain a focus on the wording in question 1, you could include the words 'Beveridge Report' in your first main paragraph:

The basis for the welfare programme to which Labour was committed already existed in the form of the Beveridge Report.

- This sentence begins with a clear point that refers to the primary focus of the question (Labour's welfare reform programme) while linking it to a factor (the Beveridge proposals).

- You could then have a set of paragraphs showing how the key welfare measures related to specific proposals in the Beveridge Report.
- It will be important to make sure that each paragraph focuses on analysis and includes relevant details that are used as part of the argument. Inserting a reference to Attlee's 1948 broadcast announcement listing the major reforms would be appropriate.
- You may wish to number your factors. This helps to make your structure clear and helps you to maintain focus.

Deploying detail

As well as focus and structure, your essay will be judged on the extent to which it includes accurate detail. There are several different kinds of evidence you could use that might be described as detailed. These include correct dates, names of relevant people, statistics and events. In question 1 (see page 246), for example, you could use terms such as reconstruction, the 'Five Giants' and the NHS. You can also make your essays more detailed by using the correct technical vocabulary.

Analysis and explanation

'Analysis' covers a variety of high-level skills including explanation and evaluation; in essence, it means breaking down something complex into smaller parts. A clear structure which breaks down a complex question into a series of paragraphs is the first step towards writing an analytical essay.

The purpose of explanation is provide evidence of why something happened, or why something is true or false. An explanatory statement requires two parts: a *claim* and a *justification*.

In question 1, for example, you might want to argue that Labour's programme went beyond the Beveridge Report in some respects. Once you have made your point, and supported it with relevant detail, you can then explain how this answers the question. For example, you could conclude your paragraph like this:

The Labour government's measures clearly drew from the Beveridge Report in their reconstruction of post-war British welfare provision[1]. This was because[2] the chief measures such as the introduction of National Insurance and the NHS were intended as an implementation of Beveridge's attack on the 'Five Giants'[3].

1 The first part of this sentence is the claim while the second part justifies the claim.
2 'Because' is a very important word to use when writing an explanation, as it shows the relationship between the claim and the justification.
3 The justification of the claim.

Evaluation

Evaluation means considering the importance of two or more different factors, weighing them against each other, and reaching a judgement. This is a good skill to use at the end of an essay because the conclusion should reach a judgement which answers the question. Your conclusion to question 1 might read as follows:

Clearly, the Labour welfare programme coincided at many key points with the proposal in the Beveridge Report. However, the Labour Party had been committed to welfare reform since its formation in 1906. Therefore, although influenced by the Beveridge Report, the Labour government was not entirely dependent on the Report for its programme.

Words like 'clearly', 'however' and 'therefore' are helpful to contrast the importance of the different factors.

Complex essay writing: argument and counter-argument

Essays that develop a good argument are more likely to reach the highest levels. This is because argumentative essays are much more likely to develop sustained analysis. As you know, your essays are judged on the extent to which they analyse.

After setting up an argument in your introduction, you should develop it throughout the essay. One

way of doing this is to adopt an argument–counter-argument structure. A counter-argument is one that disagrees with the main argument of the essay. This is a good way of evaluating the importance of the different factors that you discuss. Essays of this type will develop an argument in one paragraph and then set out an opposing argument in another paragraph. Sometimes this will include juxtaposing the differing views of historians on a topic.

Good essays will analyse the key issues. They will probably have a clear piece of analysis at the end of each paragraph. While this analysis might be good, it will generally relate only to the issue discussed in that paragraph.

Excellent essays will be analytical throughout. As well as the analysis of each factor discussed above, there will be an overall analysis. This will run throughout the essay and can be achieved through developing a clear, relevant and coherent argument.

A good way of achieving sustained analysis is to consider which factor is most important.

Here is an example of an introduction that sets out an argument for question 1 (see page 246):

When Attlee's government came into office in 1945, intent on introducing welfare reform, it had at its disposal the Beveridge Report, published in 1942[1]. This provided a very convenient blueprint on which the government could formulate its practical programme[2]. However, the Labour Party's constitution and basic sense of purpose meant that it would have embarked on reform regardless of whether the Report existed. So, although the Report markedly influenced the shaping of the government's welfare programme in practical terms, the government was not wholly dependent on it for its social principles since Labour's commitment to welfare reform long pre-dated the Report[3].

1 The introduction begins with a claim.
2 The introduction continues with another reason.
3 Concludes with an outline of the argument of the most important reason.

- This introduction focuses on the question and sets out the key factors that the essay will develop.
- It introduces an argument about which factor was most significant.
- However, it also sets out an argument that can then be developed throughout each paragraph, and is rounded off with an overall judgement in the conclusion.

Complex essay writing: resolution and relative significance

Having written an essay that explains argument and counter-argument, you should then resolve the tension between the argument and the counter-argument in your conclusion. It is important that the writing is precise and summarises the arguments made in the main body of the essay. You need to reach a supported overall judgement. One very appropriate way to do this is by evaluating the relative significance of different factors, in the light of valid criteria. Relative significance means how important one factor is compared to another.

The best essays will always make a judgement about which was most important based on valid criteria. These can be very simple, and will depend on the topic and the exact question. The following criteria are often useful:

- Duration: which factor was important for the longest amount of time?
- Scope: which factor affected the most people?
- Effectiveness: which factor achieved most?
- Impact: which factor led to the most fundamental change?

As an example, you could compare the factors in terms of their duration and their impact.

Having written an introduction and the main body of an essay for question 1 (see page 246), a concluding paragraph that aims to meet the exacting criteria for reaching a complex judgement could look like this:

Thus, in judging the extent to which the Labour government put the Beveridge Report into practice in creating the Welfare State, account has to be taken of a number of factors. There were, indeed, some notable instances where the welfare programme seemed a straight application of the Report, the outstanding example being the NHS, which could be regarded as a direct fulfilment of Beveridge's attack on Disease, one of the 'Five Giants'. Nevertheless, it was not simply a matter of Attlee's government implementing the Beveridge proposals wholesale. Circumstances and financial constraints required that the reform programme had to be selective. Yet, what is noteworthy is the close coincidence between the Report and the Labour government's own social principles. Therein lay the true measure of the Report's influence on the creation of the Welfare State.

Sources guidance

Whether you are taking the AS exam or the full A level exam for AQA Component 2: Depth Study: Wars and Welfare: Britain in Transition, 1906–1957, Section A presents you with sources and a question which involves evaluation of their utility or value.

AS exam	A level exam
Section A: answer question 1 based on two primary sources. (25 marks)	Section A: answer question 1 based on three primary sources. (30 marks)
Question focus: with reference to these sources, and your understanding of the historical context, which of these two sources is more valuable in explaining … ?	Question focus: with reference to these sources, and your understanding of the historical context, assess the value of these three sources to a historian studying …

Sources and sample questions

Study the sources. They are all concerned with New Liberalism in the early twentieth century.

SOURCE I

From Seebohm Rowntree, *Poverty: A Study of Town Life*, 1902.

The wages paid for unskilled work in York are insufficient to provide food, shelter, and clothing to maintain a family of moderate size in a state of merely physical efficiency. And let us clearly understand what 'merely physical efficiency' means. A family living on the scale allowed for in this estimate must never go into the country unless they walk … They must write no letters to absent children for they cannot afford the postage … They cannot save, nor can they join sick club or Trade union, because they cannot pay the necessary subscriptions. The children must have no pocket money … The father must smoke no tobacco, and must drink no beer. The mother must never buy any pretty clothes for herself or her children … If any of these conditions are broken, the extra expenditure involved can only be met by limiting the diet; or in other words, by sacrificing physical efficiency. In this land of abounding wealth, during a time of perhaps unexampled prosperity, probably more than one-fourth of the population are living in poverty.

SOURCE 2

The Taff Vale ruling delivered by Lord MacNaughten in 1901.

Has the Legislature authorized the creation of numerous bodies of men capable of owning great wealth and of acting by agents with absolutely no responsibility for the wrongs they may do to other persons by the use of that wealth and the employment of those agents? In my opinion, Parliament has done nothing of the kind. I cannot find anything to warrant or suggest such a notion. It was intended by the strongest advocates of trade unionism that persons should be liable for concerted as well as for individual action; and for this purpose it seems to me that it cannot matter in the least whether the persons acting in concert be combined together in a trade union, or collected and united under any other form of association. I have no doubt whatever that a trade union, whether registered or unregistered, may be sued in a representative action if the persons selected as defendants be persons who, from their position, may be taken fairly to represent the body.

SOURCE 3

From a speech by Lloyd George in October 1906.

If at the end of an average term of office it were found that a Liberal Parliament had done nothing to cope seriously with the social condition of the people, to remove the national degradation of slums and widespread poverty and destitution in a land glittering with wealth; nor provided an honourable sustenance for deserving old age; that they had tamely allowed the House of Lords to extract all the virtue out of their Bills; then would a real cry arise in this land for a new party. But if a Liberal Government tackle the landlords and the peers and try to deliver the nation from this pernicious control then the Labour Party will call in vain upon the working men of Britain to desert Liberalism.

AS-style question

With reference to Sources 1 and 2, and your understanding of the historical context, which of these two sources is more valuable in explaining why New Liberalism developed within the Liberal Party?

A level-style question

With reference to Sources 1, 2 and 3, and your understanding of the historical context, assess the value of these sources to a historian studying the problems facing the Liberals in the early twentieth century.

AS mark scheme

See the AQA website (www.aqa.org.uk) for the full mark schemes. This summary of the AS mark scheme shows how it rewards analysis and evaluation of the source material within the historical context.

Level 1	Describing the source content or offering generic phrases.
Level 2	Some relevant but limited comments on the value of one source *or* some limited comments on both.
Level 3	Some relevant comments on the value of the sources and some explicit reference to the issue identified in the question.
Level 4	Relevant well-supported comments on the value and a supported conclusion, but with limited judgement.
Level 5	Very good understanding of the value in relation to the issue identified. Sources evaluated thoroughly and with a well-substantiated conclusion related to which is more valuable.

A level mark scheme

The A level mark scheme is similar to the AS one, but, of course, covers three sources, not two. Also the wording of the question means that there is no explicit requirement to decide which of the three sources is the most valuable. Concentrate instead on a very thorough analysis of the content and evaluation of the provenance of each source.

Level 1	Some limited comment on the value of at least one source.
Level 2	Some limited comments on the value of the sources *or* on content and provenance *or* comments on all three sources but no reference to the value of the sources.
Level 3	Some understanding of all three sources in relation to both content and provenance, with some historical context; but analysis limited.
Level 4	Good understanding of all three sources in relation to content, provenance and historical context to give a balanced argument on their value for the purpose specified in the question.
Level 5	As Level 4, but with a substantiated judgement on each of the three sources.

Working towards an answer

It is important that knowledge is used to show an understanding of the relationship between the sources and the issue raised in the question. Answers should be concerned with the following:

- provenance
- arguments used (and you can agree/disagree)
- tone and emphasis of the sources.

The sources

The two or three sources used each time will be contemporary – probably of varying types (for example, diaries, newspaper accounts, government reports). The sources will all be on the same broad topic area. Each source will have value. Your task is to evaluate how much – in terms of its content and its provenance.

You will need to assess the *value of the content* by using your own knowledge. Is the information accurate? Is it giving only part of the evidence and ignoring other aspects? Is the tone of the writing significant?

You will need to evaluate the *provenance* of the source by considering who wrote it, and when, where and why. What was its purpose? Was it produced to express an opinion; to record facts; to influence the opinion of others? Even if it was intended to be accurate, the writer may have been biased – either deliberately or unconsciously. The writer, for example, might have only known part of the situation and reached a judgement solely based on that.

Here is a guide to analysing the provenance, content and tone for Sources 1, 2 and 3 (see pages 250–1).

Analysing the sources

To answer the question effectively, you need to read the sources carefully and pull out the relevant points as well as add your own knowledge. You must remember to keep the focus on the question at all times.

Source 1 (page 250)

Provenance:

- The source is from a study of poverty by a social analyst, Seebohm Rowntree. He will have a particular view on poverty in Britain.
- The study describes the scale of urban poverty to a wide national audience.

Content and argument:

- The source argues that poverty is a profound social problem.
- Wages are so low that they do not meet basic needs.
- Workers and their families are living desperate lives.

Tone and emphasis:

- The tone is angry. Seebohm Rowntree is anxious to emphasise the degradation that poverty brings.

Own knowledge:

- Use your own knowledge to agree/disagree with the source, for example: details about Britain's underlying economic strength; wealth exists but it is not evenly distributed; poverty and wealth exist side by side.

Source 2 (page 250)

Provenance:

- The source is from a legal ruling.
- It illustrates the prevailing attitude of the law towards trade unions.

Content and argument:

- The source asserts that trade unions are liable for damages caused by a strike in which they are involved.

Tone and emphasis:

- The tone is hostile and dismissive of trade union claims to legal protection.

Own knowledge:

- Use your own knowledge to agree/disagree with the source, for example: the law had been customarily opposed to the extension of trade union rights; Parliament's concession to trade unions had seldom resulted in extending their legal protection.

Source 3 (page 251)
Provenance:

- The source is from a speech by Lloyd George.
- It is written by a radical Liberal eager to bring about social change.

Content and argument:

- The source is a plea for the Liberals to recognise that they must attend to the needs of the workers.
- If the Liberals were to truly take up the cause of the dispossessed, the Labour Party would attract little support from the workers.

Tone and emphasis:

- The tone is one of anxiety; the speaker points to the danger of the Liberals losing touch with the workers and being superseded by Labour.

Own knowledge:

- Use your own knowledge to agree/disagree with the source, for example: detailed knowledge about the ideas behind New Liberalism, and the growth and potential strength of the Labour Party.

Answering AS questions

You have 45 minutes to answer the question. It is important that you spend at least one-quarter of the time reading and planning your answer. Generally, when writing an answer, you need to check that you are remaining focused on the issue identified in the question and that you are relating this to the sources and your knowledge.

- You might decide to write a paragraph on each 'strand' (that is, provenance, content and tone),

comparing the two sources, and then write a short concluding paragraph with an explained judgement on which source is more valuable.
- For writing about content, you may find it helpful to adopt a comparative approach, for example when the evidence in one source is contradicted or questioned by the evidence in another source.

At AS level you are asked to provide a judgement on which is more valuable. Make sure that this is based on clear arguments with strong evidence, and not on general assertions.

Planning and writing your answer

- Think how you can best plan an answer.
- Plan in terms of the headings above, perhaps combining 'provenance' with 'tone and emphasis', and compare the two sources.

As an example, here is a comparison of Sources 1 and 2 in terms of provenance, and tone and emphasis:

The two sources are clearly different in tone. Source 1 is a strongly committed attack on poverty while Source 2 is a formal legal ruling on trade union rights. In terms of their provenance, Source 1 is based on observed conditions in a particularly poor urban area; Source 2 is a cold, detached legal verdict. Source 1 is an angry comment on the way the lives of the poor are blighted by grasping employers. Source 2 is solely concerned with defining the law in such a way that it denies trade unions legal protection in the event of a strike.

Then compare the *content and argument* of each source, by using your knowledge. For example:

Source 1 is making by implication a strong case for measures to be taken to relieve the suffering of the unskilled workers whose low pay reduces them and their families to desperate poverty. Source 2, however, is an Establishment view which leaves the trade unions liable to a civil action for damages in the event of a strike. It takes no heed of the role of the unions as protective organisations for the workers.

Which is *more valuable*? This can be judged by assessing which is likely to be more valuable in terms of where the source came from; or in terms of the accuracy of its content. However, remember the focus of the question: in this case, why New Liberalism developed within the Liberal Party.

With these sources, you could argue that Source 1 is the more valuable because it was written from observation of the plight of the urban poor, exposing the type of social problem that New Liberalism was designed to tackle. In contrast, Source 2 is more limited since it is merely a legal decision. However, it is arguable that Source 2 is equally valuable in that it illustrates the legal barriers to workers' advancement, another major injustice which New Liberalism was concerned to redress.

Then check the following:

- Have you covered the 'provenance' and 'content' strands?
- Have you included sufficient knowledge to show understanding of the historical context?

Answering A level questions

The same general points for answering AS questions (see 'Answering AS questions', page 253) apply to A level questions, although of course here there are three sources and you need to assess the value of each of the three, rather than choose which is most valuable. Make sure that you remain focused on the question and that when you use your knowledge it is used to substantiate (add to) an argument relating to the content or provenance of the source.

If you are answering the A level question with Sources 1, 2 and 3 above (see pages 250–1):

- Keep the different 'strands' explained above in your mind when working out how best to plan an answer.
- Follow the guidance about 'provenance' and 'content' (see the AS guidance).
- Here you are *not* asked to explain which is the most valuable of the three sources. You can deal with each of the three sources in turn if you wish.
- However, you can build in comparisons if it is helpful, but it is not essential. It will depend to some extent on the three sources.
- You need to include sufficient knowledge to show understanding of the historical context. This might encourage cross-referencing of the content of the three sources, mixed with your own knowledge.
- Each paragraph needs to show clarity of argument in terms of the issue identified by the question.

OCR A level History

Essay guidance

The assessment of OCR Units Y112 and Y142: Britain 1900–1951 (Enquiry topic: England and a New Century *c*.1900–1918) depends on whether you are studying it for AS or A level:

- for the AS exam, you will answer one essay question and one two-part source question
- for the A level exam, you will answer one essay question and one source question.

The guidance below is for answering both AS and A level essay questions.

For both OCR AS and A level History, the types of essay questions set and the skills required to achieve a high grade for Unit Group 1 are the same. The skills are made very clear by both mark schemes, which emphasise that the answer must:

- focus on the demands of the question
- be supported by accurate and relevant factual knowledge
- be analytical and logical
- reach a supported judgement about the issue in the question.

There are a number of skills that you will need to develop to reach the higher levels in the marking bands:

- understand the wording of the question
- plan an answer to the question set
- write a focused opening paragraph
- avoid irrelevance and description
- write analytically
- write a conclusion which reaches a supported judgement based on the argument in the main body of the essay.

These skills will be developed in the section below, but are further developed in the 'Period Study' chapters of the *OCR A level History* series (British Period Studies and Enquiries).

Understanding the wording of the question

To stay focused on the question set, it is important to read the question carefully and focus on the key words and phrases. Unless you directly address the demands of the question you will not score highly. Remember that in questions where there is a named factor you must write a good analytical paragraph about the given factor, even if you argue that it was not the most important.

Types of AS and A level questions you might find in the exams	The factors and issues you would need to consider in answering them
1 Assess the reasons why the 1926 General Strike was a failure for the TUC.	Weigh up the relative importance of a range of factors as to why the TUC failed in the General Strike.
2 How far was the TUC's lack of preparation the most important cause of its defeat in the 1926 General Strike?	Weigh up the relative importance of a range of factors, including comparing the TUC's lack of preparation with other factors.
3 'The TUC's lack of preparation was the most important reason for its failure in the General Strike of 1926.' How far do you agree?	Weigh up the relative importance of a range of factors, including the TUC's lack of preparation, to reach a balanced judgement.

Planning an answer

Many plans simply list dates and events – this should be avoided as it encourages a descriptive or narrative answer, rather than an analytical answer. The plan should be an outline of your argument; this means you need to think carefully about the issues you intend to discuss and their relative importance before you start writing your answer. It should therefore be a list of the factors or issues you are going to discuss and a comment on their relative importance.

For question 1 in the table on page 255, your plan might look something like this:

1 TUC weaknesses:
   – Key factor: TUC never fully united or sufficiently committed.
   – Britain's economic difficulties lessened the trade unions as an industrial force
   – Miners' Federation took the initiative – pushed TUC into the strike
   – Key unions did not support the strike
   – TUC did not prepare adequately
   – Majority of public opinion not won over to the strikers
   – Morale low among strikers.
2 Government strengths:
   – Baldwin's calm leadership
   – Government firmness – it made preparations for the strike
   – Strike was never truly disruptive
   – Media largely opposed to the strike
   – Loyalty of police and army
   – Volunteers from the public helped break the strike.

The opening paragraph

Many students spend time 'setting the scene'; the opening paragraph becomes little more than an introduction to the topic – this should be avoided. Instead, make it clear what your argument is going to be. Offer your view about the issue in the question – what was the most important reason for the TUC's failure – and then introduce the other issues you intend to discuss. In the plan it is suggested that the government's determination to resist the strike was the most weakening factor for the TUC. This should be made clear in the opening paragraph, with a brief comment as to why – perhaps that the TUC was simply unwilling to offer a sustained challenge in the face of the resolve of Baldwin's government. This will give the examiner a clear overview of your essay, rather than it being a 'mystery tour' where the argument becomes clear only at the end. You should also refer to any important issues that the question raises. For example:

> There are a number of reasons why the TUC failed to win the strike in 1926: poor organisation, ineffective leadership and a lack of popular support[1]. However, the most important reason was that the government, having made effective contingency plans, was able to stand firm against the strikers, refusing to make concessions[2]. This was particularly important since it meant that, no matter what preparation the strikers might have made, they would not be able to defeat a government that was able to rely on the loyalty of the police and army[3].

1 The student is aware that there were a number of important reasons.
2 The answer offers a clear view as to what the student considers to be the most important reason – a thesis is offered.
3 There is a brief justification to support the thesis.

Avoid irrelevance and description

It is hoped that the plan will stop you from simply writing all you know about why the strike failed and force you to weigh up the role of a range of factors. Similarly, it should also help prevent you from simply writing about the mistakes made by the strikers. You will not lose marks if you do that, but neither will you gain any credit, and you will waste valuable time.

Write analytically

This is perhaps the hardest, but most important skill you need to develop. An analytical approach can be helped by ensuring that the opening sentence of each paragraph introduces an idea, which directly answers the question and is not just a piece of factual information. In a very strong answer it should be possible to simply read the opening sentences of all the paragraphs and know what argument is being put forward.

If we look at question 2, on how far the TUC's lack of preparation was the most important cause of its defeat in the 1926 General Strike (see page 255), the following are possible sentences with which to start paragraphs:

- The TUC called the strike at a time when Britain's economic difficulties lessened the trade unions as an industrial force which meant that, regardless of their preparations, they were not a serious threat to the government.
- The strike was not well led or organised by the TUC.
- It was pressure from the miners which pushed the TUC into action before it was fully prepared.
- The strike was essentially a strike over coal and key unions were unwilling to back it fully.

You would then go on to discuss both sides of the argument raised by the opening sentence, using relevant knowledge about the issues to support each side of the argument. The final sentence of the paragraph would reach a judgement on the role played by the factor you are discussing in regard to the TUC's failure. This approach would ensure that the final sentence of each paragraph links back to the actual question you are answering. If you can do this for each paragraph you will have a series of mini-essays, which discuss a factor and reach a conclusion or judgement about the importance of that factor or issue. For example:

The TUC's failure can be measured as a set of relevant factors, of which lack of preparation was one, but not the most important. Cumulatively, the factors undermined the TUC's chances of success and left the government in a strong position[1]. If the resistance of Baldwin's government to the TUC's demands was to be seriously challenged, it

required a trade union movement fully supportive of the miners. But this was never achieved. Having itself made preparations and been backed by the armed services and police, and by the population at large, Baldwin's government was throughout in a strong position to resist the TUC[2].

1 The sentence puts forward a clear view that TUC failure was a consequence of a number of collective factors.
2 The claim that it was the resolve of the government not to give in to the TUC that proved crucial is developed and some evidence is provided to support the argument.

The conclusion

The conclusion provides the opportunity to bring together all the interim judgements to reach an overall judgement about the question. Using the interim judgements will ensure that your conclusion is based on the argument in the main body of the essay and does not offer a different view. For the essay answering question 1 (see page 255), you can select what you regard as the most important reasons for the TUC's failure, but for questions 2 and 3 you will need to comment on the importance of the named factor – the TUC's lack of preparation – as well as explain why you think a different factor, such as Liberal recovery, is more important, if that has been your line of argument. Or, if you think the named factor is the most important, you would need to explain why that was more important than the other factors or issues you have discussed.

Consider the following conclusion to question 2 (see page 255): 'How far was the TUC's lack of preparation the most important cause of its defeat in the 1926 General Strike?'

Although the TUC had certainly had not prepared effectively for the strike, as was evident in the disunity among the unions, the unwillingness of key unions to give support, and the inability to agree on a clear strategy, such deficiencies were not the most important factors in their defeat[1]. Of greater importance was the determination of the government led by Baldwin, who successfully projected himself as the man of reason and responsibility, not to give ground to the strikers. With popular opinion on its side and with the forces of law and order wholly loyal to it, the government was able to portray the strike as being an unrealistic response to Britain's economic needs[2].

1 This is a strong conclusion because it considers the importance of the named factor – the TUC's lack of preparation – but weighs that up against a range of other factors to reach an overall judgement.
2 It is also able to show links between the other factors to reach a balanced judgement, which brings in a range of issues, showing the interplay between them.

Sources guidance

OCR Units Y112 and Y142: Britain 1900–1951 (Enquiry topic: England and a New Century *c.*1900–1918) are assessed through an essay and a source-based or enquiry question. There is no choice for the enquiry question. At AS level you will have to answer two source questions using three sources and for the A level you will answer one question using four sources.

AS question 1

The skills needed to answer this question are made very clear by the mark scheme, which emphasises that the answer must:

- focus on the question
- evaluate the source using *both* provenance and relevant contextual knowledge
- reach a supported analysis of its utility in relation to the issue in the question.

AS question 2 and A level question 1

The skills needed to answer this question are made very clear by the mark scheme, which emphasises that the answer must:

- focus on the question
- evaluate the sources using *both* provenance and relevant contextual knowledge
- uses detailed and accurate knowledge
- reach a supported analysis of the sources in relation to the question.

There are a number of skills that you need to develop if you are to reach the higher levels in the marking bands for both the AS and A level questions:

- You have to *interpret* the evidence. You need to link it to the issue in the question and decide what the evidence is saying about that issue.

- You need to consider *how useful* the evidence is. This involves thinking carefully about a range of issues concerning the provenance of the source: you might think about who wrote it, why it was written, whether the person who wrote it was in a position to know and how typical it might be.
- You need to apply relevant contextual knowledge to the source to judge the validity of the source and its view. You therefore need a good knowledge of the topic in the question.
- You need to link your material to the issue in the question and not write a general essay about the topic.

These skills are illustrated in the guidance to answering the questions below, but are further developed in the 'Enquiry Study' chapters of the *OCR A level History series* (British Period Studies and Enquiries).

Practice questions

AS level

1 Use your knowledge of the social problems in Britain in the early twentieth century to assess how useful Source A is as evidence of conditions in urban areas.

2 Using Sources A, B and C in their historical context, assess how far they support the view that the Liberals were obliged by their increasing knowledge of working-class problems to adopt social welfare as their main priority.

A level

Using all the sources in their historical context, assess how far they support the view that New Liberalism was a response to the difficulties facing the working classes in the early twentieth century.

SOURCE A

A social researcher into urban poverty describes the grim circumstances in which some families live in Britain.

The wages paid for unskilled work in York are insufficient to maintain a family in a state of merely physical efficiency. And let us clearly understand what 'merely physical efficiency' means. A family living on this scale must write no letters for they cannot afford the postage. They cannot save, nor can they join sick club or Trade union. The children must have no pocket money. The father must drink no beer. The mother must never buy clothes. If any of these conditions are broken, the extra expenditure involved can only be met by limiting the diet; or in other words, by sacrificing physical efficiency. In this land of abounding wealth, probably more than one-fourth of the population are living in poverty.

Seebohm Rowntree, Poverty: A Study of Town Life, *1902.*

SOURCE B

A senior judge gives the definitive ruling that the trade union the Amalgamated Society of Railway Servants is liable for damages in the Taff Vale case, 1901.

Has the Legislature authorized the creation of numerous bodies of men capable of owning great wealth and of acting by agents with absolutely no responsibility for the wrongs they may do? In my opinion, Parliament has done nothing of the kind. I cannot find anything to warrant such a notion. It was intended by the strongest advocates of trade unionism that persons should be liable for concerted as well as for individual action; I have no doubt whatever that a trade union, whether registered or unregistered, may be sued in a representative action if the persons selected as defendants be persons who, from their position, may be taken fairly to represent the body.

Lord MacNaughten in 1901.

SOURCE C

The radical Liberal David Lloyd George urges his party to thwart the Labour Party by embracing social reform.

If at the end of an average term of office it were found that a Liberal Parliament had done nothing to remove the widespread poverty in a land glittering with wealth; that they had shrunk from attacking boldly the main causes of this wretchedness; nor provided an honourable sustenance for deserving old age; then would a real cry arise in this land for a new party. But if a Liberal Government tackle the landlords and the peers and try to deliver the nation from this pernicious control then the Labour Party will call in vain upon the working men of Britain to desert Liberalism that is fighting to rid the land of the wrongs that have oppressed those who labour in it.

David Lloyd George, speech in October 1906.

SOURCE D

An influential Liberal thinker describes how New Liberalism is changing the attitude and political priorities of the party.

Liberalism is now formally committed to a task which certainly involves a new conception of the State in its relation to the individual life and to private enterprise. From the standpoint which best presents its continuity with earlier Liberalism, it appears as a fuller appreciation and realisation of individual liberty contained in the provision of

equal opportunities for self-development. But to this individual standpoint must be joined a just apprehension of the social, viz., the insistence that these claims or rights of self-development must be adjusted to the sovereignty of social welfare.

J.A. Hobson, The Crisis of Liberalism, *1909.*

The guidance for AS question 2 and A level question 1 (see page 259) is the same. The only difference is that for the A level question you have to use four sources, whereas for the AS question you must use three.

Answering AS question 1

The first question is worth ten marks and will ask you to:

1 Use your knowledge of the social problems in Britain in the early twentieth century to assess how useful Source A is as evidence of conditions in urban areas.

In order to do well answering this type of question, you should evaluate the source, using both its provenance (see page 259) and your own relevant knowledge of the historical context (see page 259) that is specified in the question. This will allow you to engage with the source and reach a supported analysis of its usefulness as evidence for the issue in the question. You should reach a judgement about its value. Remember it might be useful for some issues but not others.

First, it is important that you use the right source: it will not always be Source A, therefore double check before you start writing! To stay focused on the question set, it is important that you read the question carefully and remain focused on the key phrase 'as evidence of'. Unless you directly address the issue in the question you will not score highly. You can write separate paragraphs on the

provenance of the source and the historical context, but the strongest answers will integrate them, often using the context to explain the provenance.

You should use short and appropriate quotations from the source to support the points you are making.

Although the mark scheme does not require you to reach a judgement about the value of the source in relation to the question, it would be helpful to summarise the strengths and weaknesses of the source as evidence for the issue in the question.

In answering question 1, an answer might start as follows:

Source A is the expressed view of a committed social reformer who has made a detailed study of the conditions among working-class families in York[1]. Since it is a formal, measured study, based on first-hand observation and statistical analysis, it may be regarded as accurate and reliable evidence of the conditions it describes.

The source's provenance makes it a highly useful document. This study of poverty was undertaken by a social analyst concerned to discover and report the truth concerning the reality of conditions for working-class families in urban areas[2]. The writer powerfully describes the destructive impact of poverty on family life, which in the particular case cited, has reduced the family to the level of 'merely physical efficiency'. He does this by referring to ordinary pursuits which the family's lack of adequate income denies them. Moved by a strong sense of social justice, the writer claims that in Britain, a land of great wealth, 'more than one-fourth of the population are living in poverty'. That claim points to a possible limitation of the source in that the writer's sense of outrage may have distorted his findings[3].

1 The opening sentence explains the origin of the source and summarises it.
2 The answer considers the origin of the source and discusses the strengths of this in terms of its usefulness.
3 The answer considers the content of the source and whether it is useful as a description of the effects of poverty in Britain's urban areas.

The answer should be further developed by discussing issues such as how typical the details described in the source are of conditions for working-class families and how accurate the claim is that one-quarter of population live in similar poverty. Reference to your own knowledge of other reports being produced at this time would be appropriate, as would consideration of the source as an example of the growing awareness among politicians of all parties of the range of social problems confronting industrial Britain. In judgement, the answer might suggest that although it is partial view of a committed social critic offended by the existence of poverty side by side with wealth, it remains reliable as evidence of urban conditions since it is based on observed and carefully recorded facts.

Answering AS question 2 and the A level question

The question will be worded as follows:

Using these three sources/four sources in their historical context, assess how far they support the view that …

- Keep a good focus on the question and don't drift off into describing everything the sources say.
- Evaluate the sources – that is say, how valid the evidence they give is. You can do this by looking at their *provenance* – that is, what they are, who wrote them, under what circumstances and why. You can also do this by looking at what they say about the issue and testing it against your own knowledge.
- You have to keep a balance. You should not write an essay on the topic in the question just by using knowledge, but you should not just explain what the sources say about the issue either. You need to apply some knowledge to all the sources to answer the question.

In planning your answer to this question it might be helpful to construct a chart similar to the one below (this can be modified to A, B and C for AS):

Source	View about the issue in the question	Evidence from the source	Provenance	Knowledge that supports the source	Knowledge that challenges the source	Judgement
A						
B						
C						
D						

In the second column you decide whether the source supports or challenges the view in the question, and in third column you should enter evidence from the source which supports your view. The next column considers the provenance, which may affect the reliability of the source. The next two columns bring in your knowledge to support or challenge the view in the source. The final column brings all this together to make a judgement about the source in terms of supporting or challenging the view in the question.

If you complete this chart it should provide you with the material you need to answer the question. Although the mark scheme does not require you to group the sources, it might be more sensible to deal with all the sources that support the view in the question together, and those that challenge the view together, before reaching an overall judgement. However, remember some sources may have parts that both support and challenge the view in the question.

An opening paragraph to the question using all the sources could start as follows:

Sources A and B provide evidence of the social and legal difficulties confronting the working class, while Sources C and D provide examples of the Liberal response to these difficulties. Source A describes how in Britain, 'a land of abounding wealth', large numbers live in poverty. Source B defines the formal restrictions placed on trade union power that leave the workers unrepresented[1]. Sources C and D pick up on the details given in Sources A and B, Source C repeating the reference to the inequitable distribution of wealth in Britain, while Source D appeals for the Liberals to embrace 'the sovereignty of welfare'[2]. All four sources show a sense of commitment, with Sources A and C being an attack on the social justice that causes poverty, while Source B upholds the right of employers to use the law to restrict the trade unions.

1 The answer deals with the two sources, A and B, which provide evidence of the grim urban circumstances of the poor and of the anti-union bias of the law.
2 The answer now considers the view that the other two sources, C and D, are examples, of the response of the Liberal social conscience, illustrated by brief quotations, to the disadvantages suffered by the working class as depicted in Sources A and B. The opening paragraph could be developed further by providing quotations from Sources B and A.

Answers can deal with each source separately and, in considering Source C, an answer might take the following approach:

Source C's provenance is a strong one, since it is a public statement by Lloyd George, the chancellor of the exchequer, who, as a radical Liberal, is eager to commit his party to social reform[1]. In his speech he refers to the 'pernicious control' that the landlords still have over the disadvantaged classes, and to the House of Lords, which is concerned to obstruct measures for the improvement of the lives of the aged and the workers[2]. Lloyd George makes an emotionally charged reference to the 'widespread poverty' existing in 'a land glittering with wealth'. He then develops that reference into a plea for the Liberals to recognise that they must attend to the needs of the workers. Worried by the danger of the Liberals losing touch with the workers and being superseded by Labour, he urges that if his party could truly take up the cause of the dispossessed, the Labour Party would attract little support from the workers[3]. In this way, without specific mention of New Liberalism in the source, Lloyd George illustrates how that movement is an ideological and practical response to the social ills confronting Britain[4].

1 The opening sentence outlines the view of Source C about the issue in the question and there is a brief explanation as to why it takes that view.
2 The answer considers the purpose of the source.
3 The reliability of the source is not in doubt and 'own knowledge' bears out the success with which Lloyd George put his message across.
4 The answer concludes by linking the source back to the central question.

Answers should treat each source in a similar way and then use the judgements reached about each source individually to reach an overall judgement in a concluding paragraph. The conclusion should be based on the evaluation of the sources and not simply own knowledge, as is seen in the following example:

Since the four sources were all meant for a public audience they are all valuable in the context of New Liberalism[1]. Source A is vital in its relation to New Liberalism in that it provides the evidence of urban poverty as a profound social problem which must be addressed. Source B illustrates how that problem is compounded by the legal establishment defining the law in such a way that it denies trade unions legal protection when they attempt to improve their members' conditions. Sources A and B, therefore, in their different ways, explain the anger that infuses Lloyd George's appeal in Source C to the Liberals to bypass the Labour

Party and become the true representatives of the workers in struggling against the reactionary landlords, employers and peers who obstruct social reform and seek to deny pensions to the aged and tolerable conditions to the workers. Source D adds ideological weight to Lloyd George's appeal by a strongly reasoned argument that the State must, in effect, adopt the new Liberal ideas and make 'the sovereignty of social welfare' the prime purpose of government[2]. Thus, the four sources complement each other in illustrating that New Liberalism was a response to the difficulties facing the working classes in the early twentieth century[3].

1 The opening sentences survey the character and value of the separate sources in relation to the central question.
2 The middle sentences use own knowledge to give added context to the sources.
3 The concluding sentence reaches an overall judgement based on an evaluation of the sources.

Glossary of terms

Allies   Principally France, Russia, Britain and its empire, Italy (from 1915) and the USA (from 1917).

Anglican Church   The established English Protestant Church, the nation's official religion.

Anschluss   German for union or incorporation.

Appeasement   A conviction that the main duty of government is to avoid war. If that means granting aggressors some of their demands in order to satisfy them, that is preferable to armed conflict.

ARP   Air Raid Precautions.

Aswan Dam   Eventually constructed between 1960 and 1970, it was intended to modernise Egypt by providing a huge supply of hydro-electric power.

Atlantic Charter   An agreement signed by Churchill and Franklin Roosevelt, the US president, laying out the principles on which a better world could be constructed once the Allies had won the war. It became the basis for the later United Nations (UN).

Attitude of the British military   Throughout the 1930s, the chiefs of the British armed services consistently warned the government that their forces were too overstretched and underfunded to be able to engage successfully in a major European conflict.

Austerity   A programme of cuts in government expenditure, control of private spending and rationing of goods.

Axis powers   Germany and Italy, the main opponents of the Allies in the Second World War in Europe.

Backbench   The area in the Commons where MPs sit who hold no official position in the government or opposition.

Balance of payments   A measurement of the profit or loss on trade in a given period. When the price of imports outstrips the income from exports, financial crisis follows.

Balanced budgets   Not allowing public expenditure to exceed income from revenue.

Balfour Declaration (1926)   Stated that the dominions were 'equal in status, in no way subordinate one to another in any aspect of their domestic or external affairs, though united by a common allegiance to the Crown'.

BBC   Began in 1922 as the private British Broadcasting Company; in 1926 it became the British Broadcasting Corporation, funded by a compulsory licence fee paid by those with wireless sets.

Big five   USA, USSR, Britain, France and Nationalist China.

Bill   A legislative proposal that has to go through separate stages in the Commons, before going to the Lords for a similar process. When this is completed the Bill receives royal assent and becomes a binding Act.

'Black and Tans'   An irregular British force specially created to contain the violence in Ireland; it was so-called from the colour of its outfits, which were made up from a job lot of police and military uniforms.

Blitz   Sustained German bombing raids, mainly at night, on London and other selected British cities; it was at its most intense between September 1940 and May 1941.

Board of Trade   A government department concerned with promoting British manufacturing and exports.

Boer   Afrikaans and Dutch word for farmer.

British Communist Party   Set up in 1921, it was always subservient to the Comintern, which provided the bulk of its funds.

British decolonisation   The granting of independence by Britain to the majority of its colonies and dependencies.

Building societies   Finance companies which advanced mortgages (loans) over long periods of time (for example, 25 years), making it possible for those on regular incomes to buy houses knowing that they would be able to pay back the capital and interest.

Central Powers   Principally Germany, Austria-Hungary and Turkey.

Chief whips   The MPs who perform the vital function of organising their party in Parliament.

CND   The Campaign for Nuclear Disarmament, established in 1957, to agitate for Britain's unilateral abandonment of its nuclear weapons.

Cold War   The period of tension between the USSR and its allies and the USA and its allies 1945–91.

Collective security   The concept of all nations of goodwill acting together to stop an aggressor.

Collectivist   The notion that, in times of crisis, individual rights must be subordinated to the greater good of the group.

Comintern   The Communist International, the Soviet agency for fomenting revolution in other countries.

Conciliation Bill   A 1910 cross-party compromise which proposed dropping the idea of votes for working-class women in return for Parliament's granting it to women who owned property. It came to nothing since Asquith's government declined to support it.

Conscientious objectors   Those who opposed war on moral or religious grounds and refused to fight.

Consensus politics   The parties' suspending their differences and working together on agreed policies.

Conservative and Unionist Party   The Conservative Party had added Unionist to its title after 1886 in order to indicate the strength of its opposition to home rule for Ireland.

Constitutional   Issues relating to the conventions and methods by which Britain was governed.

Conurbations   Concentrated urban areas of high population density.

Convoy system   Merchant ships sailing in close groups, protected by a ring of accompanying warships.

Corporate state   Power concentrated at the centre, entitling the government to direct the running of society and the economy without reference to a Parliament.

Cost effective   Manufactured items produced more cheaply than in rival economies.

D-Day landings   A massive Anglo-American invasion of occupied western France.

Deficit budgets   Allowing the government's annual planned expenditure to exceed the amount raised in revenue.

Differentials   Separate rates of pay for different levels of skill.

'Dilution'   The employment of unskilled workers in jobs previously restricted to skilled workers.

'Ditchers'   Those peers who were prepared to defend their power of absolute veto to the 'last ditch'.

Dollar gap   Since sterling was weaker than the dollar, the goods that Britain bought from North America had to be paid for in dollars.

Dunkirk spirit   In June 1940, a volunteer armada of private vessels, helped transport 300,000 stranded British troops to safety from the beaches at Dunkirk. It was common thereafter to refer to this as an example of the spirit that would carry Britain through the war.

East of Suez   A traditional shorthand way of referring to Britain's military and naval bases and commitments in the Middle East and Asia.

Edwardian   Refers to the reign of Edward VII (1901–10), but is often extended to include the early years of George V's reign (1910–14).

Emergency Powers Act   Introduced during the days of the Lloyd George coalition, this measure granted the government wide authority and extraordinary powers in the event of a major disruption of essential services.

Entente   Not a formal or binding alliance, but an expression of mutual goodwill between states.

Entryism   Infiltrating a political party with the aim of subverting its policies.

Establishment   Individuals or groups, whose political connections or intellectual status, gave them the means to influence government policy and shape public opinion and attitudes – sometimes called the 'old boy network'.

Eugenics   The science of improving the quality of the human stock by breeding out inherited weaknesses and deficiencies.

European dictators   Chiefly Adolf Hitler (German leader, 1933–45) and Benito Mussolini (Italian leader, 1922–43).

February Revolution   In February 1917 the Russian tsar, Nicholas II, had abdicated and been replaced by a Provisional Government.

Fire watchers   Members of the public who took up vantage points on high buildings to report outbreaks of fire.

First past the post   The electoral process by which the candidate with more votes than his or her nearest rival wins the seat, irrespective of whether he or she has an overall majority of the votes cast.

Franchise   The right to vote in parliamentary elections.

Free vote   Individual MPs allowed to vote without instructions from their party.

French Algeria   A French colony, the majority of whose indigenous Arab population supported the Algerian independence movement. French forces became involved in a bitter struggle (1954–62) against Algerian nationalists.

Friendly societies   Non-profit-making bodies which pooled contributions from members and paid out when members were in need.

Gallipoli campaign   In April 1915, an attempt was made to knock out Germany's ally, Turkey, by an Allied landing in Gallipoli in southern Turkey. It proved a costly failure.

'Garden Suburb'   So-called because the secretariat was housed in a makeshift building in the gardens of 10 Downing Street, London.

'Geddes Axe'   Named after Sir Eric Campbell-Geddes, chairman of the special government committee which recommended the spending cuts.

General Strike   All the unions affiliated to the TUC calling their members out on strike.

Gestapo   The notorious Nazi secret police which had terrorised Germany under Adolf Hitler between 1933 and 1945.

GNP   Gross national product. The annual total value of goods produced and services provided by Britain at home and in trade with other countries.

Gold standard   The position in which a nation's currency is kept at a high value by tying it to the price of gold.

Heresy   False religious doctrine; all faiths are heretical to each other.

Home Guard   Local defence units largely made up of service veterans and those too old for the call-up; the movement was later lovingly caricatured in the BBC television series *Dad's Army*, which ran from 1968 to 1977.

Home rule   A measure granting a colony or dependent region control over its own affairs.

Hung parliament   A situation in which no single party has an overall majority in the House of Commons.

Imperial preference   An alternative term for tariff reform, a system for protecting home-produced food and manufactured goods by placing restrictive duties on imports unless they came from the British dominions and colonies.

Imperialism   The acquiring of colonies principally for the purposes of prestige and economic exploitation.

Indian Congress Party   The main nationalist party in India, dedicated to ending British rule, which had formally operated since the Government of India Act of 1858.

Industrialisation   The spread of manufacturing, accompanied by the movement of workers from the land into the towns and cities.

Inflation   A decline in the value of money, which leads to rising prices.

Infrastructure   The interlocking systems which enable a nation's industrial economy to operate, for example, transport, power supply, communications.

Interest rates   A mechanism for raising or lowering the cost of borrowing money by adjusting the amount of interest charged on financial loans.

International Brigades   The pro-Republican forces made up of foreign volunteers who fought in the Spanish Civil War.

Internment   The holding in detention of those members of the population whose nationality or political views made them a potential risk to national security.

Invisible earnings   The sale abroad of services (usually in the financial sector) rather than tangible goods.

Invisible exports   The sale of financial and insurance services to foreign buyers, traditionally one of Britain's major sources of income from abroad.

Irish Volunteers   An Irish nationalist volunteer army, formed in 1913 to counter the UVF and fight for Irish independence.

Iron Curtain   An imaginary line that divided Western Europe from Soviet-controlled Eastern Europe.

Italian invasion of Abyssinia   In 1934–5 Mussolini's expansionist Italy had attacked and occupied parts of Abyssinia. Although Britain and France initially disapproved, they declined to take any military action against Italy and in 1936 formally recognised the Italian takeover.

Khaki   British forces adopted this as the colour of their standard uniform during the Boer War.

King's Party   An unofficial grouping of some 60 MPs, including Winston Churchill, who argued that Edward VIII should be allowed to make his own decision free from political pressure.

Landed   Referring to the people whose wealth and status derived from their ownership of substantial areas of land.

League of Nations   The body, to which all nations were entitled to belong, set up in 1919, with the aim of settling all future international disputes by referring them to the collective judgement of the League's members.

League of Nations Union   Formed in October 1918 with the aim of educating the public to the need for supporting the League, as the only guarantor of peace through collective security.

Left-wing intellectuals   Writers and thinkers who believed in radical social and economic change.

Lend-lease   An arrangement that operated from 1941 under which Britain imported war materials from the USA with no obligation to pay for them until the war was over.

Lib–Lab pact   An agreement between the LRC and the Liberal Party that their constituency candidates would not stand against each other in parliamentary elections.

Lock-outs   Preventing workers from attending work by locking the gates to workplaces.

Marconi scandal   There were allegations that Lloyd George used his inside knowledge as chancellor of the exchequer to buy and sell shares in the Marconi Company in 1913 for a large profit.

Means test   In the interwar period, to qualify for dole or relief, individuals or families had to give precise details of all the money they had coming in.

Military Service Act   Imposed compulsory enlistment on single males between the ages of 18 and 41; by 1918, the age limit had been raised to 50 and the scheme extended to include married men.

Ministry of Reconstruction   A body which drew together the various committees that had come into being during the war, its main task being to plan the improvement of social conditions.

Mixed economy   A system in which the private and public sectors of the economy both operate.

Mobilisation of resources   Drawing on and organising the whole of the nation's material and human potential.

Mod cons   Short for modern conveniences, for example household accessories such as vacuum cleaners, refrigerators and wirelesses.

National debt   The total amount owed by the government to its domestic and international creditors.

National grid   A nationwide network of high-voltage lines carrying electricity from generating stations to homes and factories.

NATO   The North Atlantic Treaty Organisation, a defensive alliance formed in 1949 by Britain, France and the Benelux counties (Belgium, the Netherlands and Luxembourg) as a safeguard against Soviet expansion into Western Europe. The USA became a member by invitation.

Nazi–Soviet Pact   A ten-year non-aggression agreement signed between Germany and the USSR in August 1939, which contained a secret protocol allowing the two countries to carve up Poland between them.

Nazism   The National Socialist (Nazi) movement which, under Adolf Hitler, ruled Germany 1933–45.

New Commonwealth   Official immigration statistics distinguished between the Old Commonwealth, referring broadly to the people of the dominions, and the New Commonwealth, referring broadly to the people of the newly independent ex-colonies.

'New Liberalism'   The movement within the Liberal Party that pressed for the adoption of social reform as the principal party policy.

'New' unions   Representing large groups of workers, such as dockers, transport workers and miners.

Niche market   A particular section of society targeted by advertisers and manufacturers.

No-Conscription Fellowship   A body set up in 1914, devoted to resisting any attempt by the State to introduce measures obliging citizens to fight.

Nonconformists   Members of the various Protestant Churches who refused to accept the doctrines and authority of the Anglican Church. Nonconformists had become an influential moral force in Victorian Britain.

'Old' unions   Established organisations representing skilled workers.

Opposition   The official title given to the main party opposing the government. In recognition of its place in the constitutional system, it is referred to as His/Her Majesty's Loyal Opposition.

Osborne Judgment   A 1909 appeal court ruling that it was illegal for a trade union to use its funds to support a political party or to pay candidates or MPs.

Parliamentary Reform Act of 1949   Reduced the delaying power of the House of Lords over a Commons Bill from two years to one.

Pawnbroking   Exchanging items for money in the hope that they can later be reclaimed by paying back the sum borrowed plus interest.

PAYE   Pay As You Earn. A system by which the tax due from workers is extracted from their wages before they have received them.

Phoney war   The period from September 1939 to April 1940 when, although the population was preparing for hostilities, nothing of military significance happened.

Picketing   Strikers stationing themselves at the gates of the factory or workplace so as to deter other workers from entering.

Political levy   The portion of a member's trade union subscription that went to the Labour Party.

Poor Law   As amended in 1834, a scheme for providing relief by taking the destitute into workhouses where the conditions were made deliberately harsh so as to deter all but the most needy from entering them.

'Popular front'   An alliance of all Communist, socialist and progressive parties.

PRC   The People's Republic of China created by Mao Zedong after he had led his Communist forces to power in China in 1949.

Property-owning democracy   A society in which as many people as possible are encouraged to become homeowners, an extension of the principle that the ownership of property is an essential component of democracy.

Proportional representation (PR)   The allocation of seats to parties according to the number of votes they gain overall.

Rapprochement   A French expression for the resumption of working relations.

Rates   Taxes levied on householders to pay for local government services.

Real wages   The purchasing power of earnings when set against prices. When prices are high money will buy less; when prices are low the same amount of money will buy more.

Recession   A slowing down of economic growth, caused by a fall in demand for manufactures, followed by falling profits, lowered wages and job losses.

Renationalised   Brought back into public ownership (in effect, government control).

Reserved occupations   Work done by dockers, farmers, merchant seamen, miners, scientists engaged in war projects, key transport workers (for example, railwaymen) and workers in the vital utilities (water, gas and electricity).

Retail price   The price paid for goods by the purchaser in the shops.

Revisionist historians   Those who challenge the accepted interpretation of historical events.

Revolutionary Russia   In 1917, the Bolshevik (Communist) revolutionaries had taken power under Lenin and then called on workers everywhere to do the same.

Revolutionary socialism   The wish to overthrow the existing state and replace it with a worker-led government.

Salvation Army   Founded in 1878 by William Booth to put Christian values into practical form by directly helping the unfortunates of society, such as the destitute, the homeless and the victims of alcohol abuse.

Samuel Commission   A body of inquiry, 1925–6, under the chairmanship of Herbert Samuel with the remit to examine the problems of the mining industry and put forward solutions.

Satellites   The Eastern European states under Soviet control.

Scramble for Africa   Between the 1870s and 1914, the major European colonial powers, France, Germany, Belgium, Portugal and Britain, separately took over large areas of the African continent.

Self-determination   The right of people to form a nation and government of their own choice.

Seven-year rule   At this time, the law required that a general election be held at least once every seven years.

Shell crisis   Since much of the war on the Western Front took the form of artillery barrages, a constant supply of shells was vital. In 1915 supply was falling short of need.

Sidney Street siege   A police and military action against a group of heavily armed anarchists who had occupied a house in London's Sidney Street.

Sinn Féin   Gaelic for 'Ourselves Alone', the title adopted by the ultra-nationalist party, formed in 1905 and committed to freeing Ireland from its bondage to Britain.

Sino-Japanese War   A struggle fought from 1937 to 1945 in which the Japanese deliberately terrorised Chinese civilians by bombing raids.

'Smack of firm government'   Eden had a habit, when emphasising a point, of smacking the palm of one hand with the back of the other. It was this image the press used to mock his indecision.

Social reconstruction   Shaping society so as to provide protection and opportunity for all its citizens.

Socially cohesive nation   A country whose people broadly agree on fundamental social principles, for example welfare provision.

Somme offensive   On the first day of battle, 1 June 1916, Britain suffered 57,000 casualties; by the time the offensive had petered out four months later the figure had risen to 420,000.

Soviet bloc   The countries of Eastern Europe under the domination of the USSR, for example, Poland, Hungary and Czechoslovakia.

Staple industries   Those enterprises on which Britain's industrial strength had traditionally been based, for example, textiles, coal mining, iron and steel production, and shipbuilding.

Starred workers   From 1914, volunteers who were already doing vital war work had a star put against their name and were exempted from military service.

Suffrage   Essentially the same meaning as franchise, the right to vote.

Suffragette   A militant movement that was prepared to break the law in agitating for the female franchise.

Suffragist   A non-violent movement demanding votes for women.

Supranational   An organisation having power over its individual member states.

Sweated   Unhealthy, overcrowded premises, such as clothing workshops, where unscrupulous employers exploited cheap, often immigrant, labour.

Syndicalism   A revolutionary movement calling on workers to smash the industrial–capitalist system by violent action.

Temperance   Opposition to the taking of alcoholic drink.

The Six   France, Germany, Italy, Belgium, the Netherlands and Luxembourg.

Total war   A struggle which directly and indirectly involves the whole population.

Treaty of Sèvres   The agreement that formally ended the war between the Allies and defeated Turkey.

Truman Doctrine   In 1947 President Truman pledged the USA 'to support free peoples who are resisting attempted subjugation by armed minorities or by outside pressure'. Although he did not mention the Soviet Union by name he clearly had it in mind as the aggressor.

TUC   Trades Union Congress. The body created in 1868 to represent the unions collectively.

Two-chamber structure   The elected House of Commons and the unelected House of Lords, made up of hereditary peers; to become law, a Bill has to be passed by both Houses.

Two nations   The term was first used in the nineteenth century to define the division of Britain between the rich and the poor, between the areas of Britain which were flourishing and those which were in decline.

UN Security Council   The United Nations' body responsible for maintaining international peace, using military force where necessary.

Uniformed auxiliary services   Auxiliary Territorial Service (ATS), Women's Auxiliary Air Force (WAAF), Women Royal Navy Service (WRNS or Wrens).

Union of Democratic Control   A pressure group of Liberal and Labour politicians and journalists set up to protest against the war and urge a negotiated peace.

US dollar   As the world's strongest currency, the dollar was taken as the financial benchmark. All other currencies were measured in terms of their exchange value against the dollar.

USSR   Union of Soviet Socialist Republics (often shortened to Soviet Union), the formal title of revolutionary Russia.

UVF   Ulster Volunteer Force. A volunteer army formed in 1913 to fight to prevent home rule being implemented.

V1   *Vergeltungswaffe* – retaliation flying bomb. A pilotless jet-propelled plane loaded with explosives.

V2   An armed rocket, launched from static or mobile sites.

Versailles Treaty   The post-war peace settlement drawn up by the major Allied victors, Britain, France, Italy and the USA; it redrew the map of Europe and sought to create the conditions for the future settlement of international crises.

Veto   The procedure which allows each individual member of the UN Security Council to cancel the collective decisions of the others.

Victorian   Relating to the years of Queen Victoria's reign (1837–1901).

Vote of no-confidence   A standard parliamentary method for testing the strength of a government. If a government defeats such a vote, its security is confirmed; if the vote goes against it, its resignation invariably follows.

Wage freeze   An undertaking not to press for higher wages.

Wall Street Crash   The collapse of the US stock market in 1929, which destroyed share values and investments.

War indemnities   Reparations paid by the losing side for the cost of the war.

War of attrition   Wearing the enemy down by sheer persistence and willingness to suffer casualties.

Welfare State   A comprehensive State-funded programme to provide the essential social, health and educational needs of all the people, regardless of their income or social status.

White Russian *émigrés*   Anti-Communists who had fled from Russia following their defeat by the Communists in the civil war there (1918–20).

WSPU   Women's Social and Political Union, founded in 1903.

Yalta Conference   Attended by the USSR, Britain and the USA to consider the post-war settlement. The discussions were continued at the Potsdam Conference in July and August 1945.

Young Plan   Named after Owen Young, an American banker who chaired the conference, the plan greatly reduced Germany's reparation payments and advanced it a loan of $300 million.

Zeitgeist   The spirit of the time, the dominant prevailing attitude in society.

Further reading

Books of overall relevance

Robert Blake, *The Conservative Party From Peel to Major* **(Arrow Books, 1997)**
An authoritative survey by the outstanding historian of Conservatism

Brian Brivati and Richard Heffernan, editors, *The Labour Party: A Centenary History* **(Macmillan, 2000)**
A very useful survey of developments within the Labour Party across the period

Francesca Carnevali, editor, *Twentieth-Century Britain: Economic, Cultural and Social Change* **(Routledge, 2007)**
An illuminating collection of scholarly essays covering the themes in the subtitle

Peter Caterall, editor, *Britain 1918–1951* **(Heinemann, 1994)**
A set of short essays on major themes by some of the leading authorities in the field

Peter Clarke, *Hope and Glory Britain 1900–1990* **(Penguin, 1996)**
A lively and often provocative analysis

Nicholas Crafts *et al.,* **editors,** *Work and Pay in 20th Century Britain* **(Oxford University Press, 2007)**
A fascinating study of the change in the conditions of British workers during the twentieth century

Richard Kelly and John Cantrell, editors, *Modern British Statesmen 1867–1945* **(Manchester University Press, 1997)**
Very valuable assessments in separate chapters of all the prime ministers from Salisbury to Churchill

Arthur Marwick, *A History of the Modern British Isles 1914–1999* **(Blackwell, 2000)**
An important and absorbing book by a pioneering social historian

Malcolm Pearce and Geoffrey Stewart, *British Political History 1867–1995* **(Routledge, 1996)**
A very useful survey, illustrated with well-chosen documents

Bernard Porter, *Britannia's Burden: The Political Evolution of Modern Britain 1851–1990* **(Edward Arnold, 1994)**
Particularly strong on the period after 1900

Martin Pugh, *State and Society: A Social and Political History of Britain Since 1870* **(Bloomsbury, 2012)**
An updated edition of a highly authoritative analysis

A.J.P. Taylor, *English History 1914–1945* **(Oxford University Press, 1965)**
Half a century old, this study remains a must read for all those who like their history to be entertaining and controversial as well as informed

Ina Zweiniger-Bargielowska, *Women in Twentieth-Century Britain: Social, Cultural and Political Change* **(Routledge, 2001)**
A detailed account of the experiences of women in the twentieth century

Chapter 1

Paula Bartley, *Emmeline Pankhurst* **(Routledge, 2002)**
Informed study of the suffragette movement

Stephen Bates, *Asquith* **(Haus Publishing, 2006)**
A clear and concise treatment of the Liberal leader in peace and war

Vyvyen Brendon, *The Edwardian Age* **(Hodder & Stoughton, 1996)**
An illuminating documentary approach to the pre-1914 period

Michael Scott-Baumann, *Years of Expansion: British History, 1814–1914* **(Hodder & Stoughton, 2002)**
The later chapters have very helpful studies of the politics and crises of the Edwardian era

Chapter 2

David Brooks, *The Age of Upheaval* **(Manchester University Press, 1995)**
Particularly good on the pre-1914 crises

George Dangerfield, *The Strange Death of Liberal England* **(MacGibbon & Kee, 1966)**
First published in 1935, this book remains a starting point for all subsequent studies of Liberal decline

Michael Lynch, *Lloyd George and the Liberal Dilemma* **(Hodder & Stoughton, 1998)**
Particularly concerned with Lloyd George's impact on the Liberal Party

Ross McKibbin, *The Evolution of the Labour Party 1910–1924* **(Oxford University Press, 1974)**
Analyses the reasons for Labour's rise to being a party of government in 1924

Chapter 3

Joe Finn and Michael Lynch, *Ireland and England 1798–1922* (Hodder & Stoughton, 1995)
A set of documents and linking narrative; later chapters deal with the Troubles and the Treaty

R.F. Foster, *Modern Ireland 1600–1972* (Penguin, 1988)
The outstanding study of the Anglo-Irish question

Keith Laybourn, *The General Strike Day by Day* (Sutton Publishing, 1999)
A dramatic, chronological reconstruction of the Strike

Margaret Morris, *The General Strike* (Penguin, 1976)
Arguably still the best book for students of the General Strike

G.R. Searle, *The Liberal Party: Triumph and Disintegration, 1886–1929* (Macmillan, 1992)
A synthesis of the main arguments on Liberal decline

Chris Wrigley, *Lloyd George* (Haus Publishing, 2006)
An analysis that effectively combines concision and precision

Chapter 4

Derek Aldcroft, *The British Economy Between the Wars* (Philip Allan, 1983)
Offers important insight into the Depression

David Marquand, *Ramsay MacDonald* (Jonathan Cape, 1977)
An absorbing study of the first Labour leader

Kenneth Robbins, *Appeasement* (Blackwell, 1997)
An outstanding short summary of the appeasement debate

A.J.P. Taylor, *The Origins of the Second World War* (Penguin, 1991)
The seminal work on the causes of the war to which all later studies are essentially a reaction

Philip Williamson, *Stanley Baldwin. Conservative Leadership and National Values* (Cambridge University Press, 1999)
An important analysis of the leader and prime minister who aimed for political consensus and co-operation

Chapter 5

Angus Calder, *The People's War: Britain 1939–1945* (Pimlico, 2008)
Long established as the classic account of the impact of war on Britain's Home Front

John Charmley, *Churchill, The End of Glory: A Political Biography* (Hodder & Stoughton, 1993)
Takes a strongly critical view of Churchill by emphasising his shortcomings

Martin Gilbert, *Churchill: A Life* (Minerva, 1992)
The distillation into one book of Gilbert's multi-volume biography of Churchill

Max Hastings, *Finest Years: Churchill as Warlord 1940–45* (HarperPress, 2010)
A detailed and involving study of Churchill's wartime leadership

Boris Johnson, *The Churchill Factor: How One Man Made History* (Hodder & Stoughton, 2014)
An adulatory but highly readable treatment of Churchill as a towering British statesman

Chapter 6

Corelli Barnett, *The Audit of War* (Macmillan, 1986)
An important and controversial book that seeks to explain Britain's post-war decline

Vernon Bogdanor and Robert Skidelsky, *The Age of Affluence 1951–64* (Penguin, 1970)
Highly recommended study of the thirteen years of Conservative government

Kevin Jeffreys, *The Attlee Governments 1945–51* (Longman, 1994)
Short, accessible coverage of the Labour government's policies and achievements

Dennis Kavanagh and Peter Morris, *Consensus Politics from Attlee to Major* (Blackwell, 1994)
The early chapters provide a detailed and authoritative study covering the period 1945–57

David Kynaston, *Austerity Britain 1945–51* and *Family Britain 1951–57* (Bloomsbury, 2007 and 2009)
The first volumes of a series, 'Tales of a New Jerusalem', an absorbing social history based largely on the words of the people themselves

John Ramsden, *The Age of Churchill and Eden, 1940–57* (Longman, 1996)
An illuminating assessment of the first two post-war Conservative prime ministers

D.R. Thorpe, *Supermac: The Life of Harold Macmillan* (Pimlico, 2011)
A spirited treatment of Macmillan and the major issues in which he was involved

Index

Every effort has been made to trace all copyright holders, but if any have been inadvertently overlooked the Publishers will be pleased to make the necessary arrangements at the first opportunity.

Acknowledgements: Arrow Books, *The Conservative Party from Peel to Major* by Robert Blake, 1998. Bloomsbury, *Austerity Britain 1945–51* by David Kynaston, 2008; *Family Britain 1951–57* by David Kynaston, 2009. *British Journal of Sociology* by Martin Francis, September 1962. Cambridge University Press, *R.H. Tawney's Commonplace Book* by J.M. Winter and D.M. Joslin, editors, 2006. Cassell, *The Memoirs of the Rt Hon. the Earl of Woolton* by Frederick James Marquis (Earl of Woolton), 1959. Caxton Publishing, *Life of David Lloyd George* by Herbert du Parq, editor, 1912. Collins, *The Downfall of the Liberal Party 1914–1935* by Trevor Wilson, 1966. *Daily Mail*, 3 May 1926. *Daily Mirror*, 28 May 1940. *Daily Telegraph*, 11 February 2000. Edward Arnold, *The General Strike* by C.L. Mowat, 1969. Fordham University. Granada Publishing, *The Strange Death of Liberal England* by George Dangerfield, 1970. *Hansard*, 3 September 1939, 18 November 1946. Hodder & Stoughton, *Churchill: The End of Glory* by John Charmley, 1993; *Suez 1956* by Barry Turner, 2006; *The First World War 1914–18* by Vyvyen Brendon, 1985. Hutchinson, *Our Times* by A.N. Wilson, 2008. Longman, *Beatrice Webb Diaries* by M. Cole, editor, 1942; *The Conservative Party and British Politics* by Stuart Ball, 1995; *The Rise and Fall of British Liberalism 1776–1988* by Alan Sykes, 1997; *War and Society in Britain* by Rex Pope, 1995. MacGibbon & Kee, *The Suez War* by Paul Johnson, 1957. Macmillan, *Poverty: A Study of Town Life* by Seebohm Rowntree, 1902. Minerva, *Churchill: A Life* by Martin Gilbert, 1992. Muller, *Call Back Yesterday* by Hugh Dalton, 1953. National Federation of Women's Institutes, 1940. Oxford University Press, *Consensus Politics from Attlee to Thatcher* by D. Kavanagh and P. Morris, 1989; *English History 1914–45* by A.J.P. Taylor, 1965. Penguin, *The Pity of War* by Niall Ferguson, 1999; *The Second World War* by W.S. Churchill, 1985. Phoenix, *From Blitz to Blair* by Dilwyn Porter, 1997. Sweet & Maxwell, *Chitty's Statutes 1927*, 1928. *The Times*, 25 August 1931. University of Michigan Library, *Better Times: Speeches by the Right Hon. D. Lloyd George* by David Lloyd George, 1910. Weidenfeld & Nicolson, *Baldwin: A Biography* by Keith Middlemas and John Barnes, 1969. *Western Evening Herald*, 17 November 1914. Yale University Press, *Five Days in London: May 1940* by John Lukacs, 2001.